Married to the Mouse

Married to the Mouse

Walt Disney World and Orlando

RICHARD E. FOGLESONG

Yale University Press   New Haven & London

Published with assistance from the Louis Stern Memorial Fund

Designed by James J. Johnson and set in New Aster type by Achorn Graphic Services, Inc. Printed in the United states of America by R. R. Donnelley & Sons.

Library of Congress Cataloging-in-Publication Data

Foglesong, Richard E., 1948–
Married to the mouse : Walt Disney World and Orlando / Richard E. Foglesong.
    p. cm.
Includes bibliographical references and index.
  ISBN 0-300-08707-1 (cloth : alk. paper)
  ISBN 0-300-09828-6 (pbk. : alk. paper)

  1. Walt Disney World (Fla.)—planning. 2. City Planning—Florida—Orlando. 3. Urban Policy—Florida—Orlando. I. Title.
  GV1853.3.F62 D574 2001
  791'.06'875924—dc21

                               00-012560

A catalogue record for this book is available from the British Library.

10 9 8 7 6 5 4 3

In memory of my father

Contents

Maps

Tables

Abbreviations

CDD	Community Development District
DCA	Department of Community Affairs (State of Florida)
DDC	Disney Development Co.
DRI	development of regional impact
EDC	Economic Development Commission
ERA	Economic Research Associates
FHP	Florida Highway Patrol
FRL	Florida Ranch Lands (real estate broker)
HAP	Housing Assistance Plan (Osceola County)
JNR	Japan National Railways
OSS	Office of Strategic Services
OUC	Orlando Utilities Commission
RCID	Reedy Creek Improvement District
SEIU	Service Employees International Union
SRB	State Road Board
WDP	Walt Disney Productions

Preface

In the Epcot film, Walt Disney's last screen appearance, viewed for the first time in Winter Park, Florida, on February 2, 1967, two months after Walt died, he famously declared: "I don't believe there's a challenge anywhere in the world that is more important to people everywhere than finding solutions to the problems of our cities." I agree. This book views Walt Disney World through the prism of urban politics and urban history. Whether the Disney enterprise makes a virtue of unreality and promotes the values of patriarchy and patriotism, as scholars writing from a cultural perspective have argued, is irrelevant here. Taking seriously Walt Disney's urban vision, yet examining it critically, *Married to the Mouse* assesses the significance of Walt Disney World for city-building and urban governance in the new millennium.

True, the Disney Co. never built the Experimental Prototype Community of Tomorrow that Walt described on screen. What they did build—Walt Disney World—is like a city, though. It has many urban-like qualities, at least—a workforce of 55,000 as of this writing; a nightly residential population exceeding 100,000 ensconced in twenty-five on-site hotels; shopping, dining, and nighttime entertainment facilities; its own "public" officials; an overall land-use plan; and, of course, unparalleled amusements and attractions. And more to the point, Walt Disney World incorporates the free-enterprise vision that Walt had for Epcot.

In planning Epcot, Walt and his "imagineers," as the company's creative people are called, produced more than a physical model. Beneath the glitter and all the futuristic imagery, they offered a governance solution to "the problems of our cities." Their agenda of reform aimed to remove the "impediments to change," among which they included "traditional property rights and elected political officials," as company consultants wrote in 1966. In other words, both capitalism and democracy were problematic; each produced fragmentation of effort. The Disney solution was centralized administration—benign, paternalistic, based on expertise.

Walt Disney World thus raises the interesting question of how cities should be built and governed and their services provided. Is the Disney model of centralized land-ownership and private government best, or is the status quo of democracy and capitalism a better arrangement? *Married to the Mouse* addresses this and other questions by examining the "economic-development marriage" between Disney World and the surrounding governmental community, tracing that relationship from the 1960s to the present. This perspective allows us to compare two methods of urban administration, one based on fusing public and private powers, the other on their separation; one based on centralized control, the other on political and economic fragmentation.

This book is written in the style of history-as-narrative. Believing with the historian C. Van Woodward that the best history is informed by art, I have tried to marry the analytical approach of political science—my discipline—with historians' more discursive approach to explaining, in Bernard Bailyn's words, "how the present got to be the way it is." More than a matter of taste, I use this narrative style to put the people back in the story. Political scientists have constructed sophisticated quantitative studies of the politics of urban development policy, yielding macro-level insights into the determinants of such policies. Though valuable, these studies de-emphasize the role of human agency by taking a policy type rather than "the deal" as their unit of analysis. Instead, this book uses a storytelling motif to emphasize the role of human beings rather than abstract forces in making choices, coping with consequences, and shaping events.

This project spanned two sabbaticals, explaining why the interviews occur in two intervals, 1990–91 and 1998–99. My interviews with most elected officials and with important participant-observers such as Billy Dial were conducted in person. In other cases, I interviewed people over the phone, typing copious notes as we spoke. All quotations from interviews are supported by notes or tape recordings; none of the quotation is imagined. In some cases, the quotations are attributed by persons who were present, as when I rely on Billy Dial's recollections for Martin Andersen's side of their conversations. (Andersen died before my research commenced.) Attributed quotes are apparent in the text or from the notes.

In writing this account, I have tried to be fair. Yet fairness does not mean, as a journalist once told me, going straight down the middle and not offending anyone. It does not mean offering equal measures of praise and criticism to all concerned. Rather, it means being fair to the story, fair to the facts, so that some persons get knocked more than others. For those painted in unflattering tones, I have tried to offer your perspective, too, subject to limits of space and evidence, so readers can judge for themselves. I have also tried to be mindful that while people make history, they do not always do so just as they please.

Acknowledgments

This book was made possible by two grants from the National Endowment for the Humanities. An NEH summer research grant to study high-tech development in central Florida convinced me, ironically, to write a book about Disney World and tourism instead. Much later, an NEH fellowship gave me the luxury of a yearlong sabbatical during which I wrote most of the manuscript. I also received several Critchfield grants from Rollins College to defray my research expenses.

For access to their archives, I am grateful to the Orlando Public Library Disney Depository, the Orange County Historical Museum, the Florida State Archives in Tallahassee, the Rollins College Floridiana Collection, and the *Orlando Sentinel*. In particular, I thank the Walt Disney Co. for granting me access to their corporate archives, something that few other major corporations might do. The State of Florida Archives, the Orange County Historical Society, and *Orlando Weekly* newspaper kindly made photos available for the book.

I am indebted to all those who granted me interviews, some lasting for several hours. My most memorable interviews were with William H. (Billy) Dial and W. A. McCree, Jr., both now gone, who educated me about Orlando's formative period in the 1950s and '60s. As well, I thank Nelson Boice, Chuck Bosserman, and the late Martin Segal for informing me about the Disney land purchase and related events; Robert Howard, Manning Pynn, Emily Bavar Kelly, and especially the late Charles Wadsworth for conversing with me about Martin Andersen and the *Orlando Sentinel;* Henry Land, Robert Elrod, John Ducker, and the late Sarah Howden for recounting how the Reedy

Creek charter was approved; Harlan Hanson, Don Greer, David Johnston, Cliff Guillet, Susan Caswell, Bruce McClendon, David Russ,
Rick Bernhardt, Mike Kloehn, and Carl Gosline for explaining urban
planning issues; Tom Moses, Ray Maxwell, and Tom DeWolf for an-
swering my questions about the Reedy Creek Improvement District;
Vera Carter, Lou Treadway, Harry Stewart, and Lisa Fisher for telling
me about Orange County controversies; Robert Day, Alan Starling,
Gary Lee, and Larry Whaley for talking with me about Osceola
County; Henry Swanson, Jane Hames, Jim Harris, James Robinson,
Bill Frederick, Marshall Vermillion, Bruce Gordy, Martha Haynie,
Jim Moye, Tom Kohler, Ted Edwards, and Jacob Stuart for speaking
freely about Orlando and Orange County politics; Harris Rosen, Bill
Peeper, and Alan Eberly for educating me about the tourist industry;
Peter Rummell and Todd Mansfied for telling me about the Disney
Development Co.; and not least, Linda Chapin, Tom Wilkes, and Mel
Martinez for talking with me about the Orange County–Disney rela-
tionship.

In addition, numerous professional colleagues read and commented on parts of the manuscript. For their encouragement and con-
structive criticism, I thank Paul Kantor, Susan Fainstein, Todd Swanstrom, Robyne Turner, William Buzbee, Brian Taylor, Martin Wachs,
and Leigh Ann Wheeler. As reviewers for the Press, Theodore Lowi
and Amy Bridges provided sage advice, helping me to extend and clar-
ify my analysis of the Disney-local relationship. I benefited as well
from the comments of three anonymous reviewers. This book is un-
mistakably better for the generous peer review it received.

My initial editor at Yale University Press, John S. Covell, offered
encouragement and wise counsel as I prepared the manuscript. Jef-
frey Schier provided skillful editing of the text.

During this long undertaking, I have benefited from the support
and friendship of Judson Starr, Robert Smither, Maurice O'Sullivan,
Bruce Stephenson, Thomas Lairson, Ann Ford, and Mary Wismar,
among others. They, along with my friends from Harpers, kindly listened to the many stories from my research, and in listening, they
helped me to refine the stories and hone the arguments found in these
pages. Cathleen Craft, my cartographer, skillfully made and remade
the maps used here. My research assistants—Lissy Musante, Bridget
Kohn, and Lisa Olen—were invaluable in keeping me organized and

saving me footsteps; Lissy in particular labored earnestly and well. Austa Weaver helped with the details of expense reports, photocopying, and more, always pleasantly.

Finally Carol and my sons, Eric and Christopher, endured my frequent absences from home, not to mention my continual distraction due to this book, while Suzanne provided aid and comfort as the book came to print. Of course, any errors in this work are my own.

Married to the Mouse

ONE

Serendipity

W alt Disney didn't say anything. He merely raised his right eyebrow in response to the offending remark. His staff, seated around him at the dinner party, knew what that meant. There he was—a self-made man, renowned as the world's greatest showman, his corporation pursued by a host of European nations, as well as Egypt, to build a Disneyland in their countries. And he was being insulted by the local business titan, the scion of inherited wealth, a bit tipsy, in the city where the cartoonist-showman proposed building a major tourist attraction. Walt was fuming.

The remark concerned an old issue that the Disney organization had already addressed. In late 1963, the city's mayor had raised the liquor issue again, leading Disney Co. vice president Donn Tatum to restate the company's position: liquor could be sold in "adjacent facilities" but not on Disney premises.[1] Their executives were not teetotalers—cocktails before dinner were part of their corporate culture—and they understood as businessmen how alcohol could lubricate deal making, hence they allowed cocktail parties in areas reserved for industrial exhibitors. But selling alcohol to the public violated the Disney image. Thus the remark had not offended Walt's sense of morality; it was actually worse than that. It had insulted his business acumen.

Until that night the deal was nearly set. The Disney Co. was poised to launch their first major venture since Disneyland's opening in 1954, following a search process stretching back to 1959. In all, thirteen venues were considered, mostly in the eastern United States. The company knew from market surveys that only two percent of Disneyland's visitors in California traveled from east of the Mississippi, where three-fourths of the nation's population resided. Before the fateful remark, the planning for the expansion site was on track: company officials were negotiating the financial arrangements and planned to sign a letter of commitment the next day.

This new Disney facility would crown a larger project intended to resuscitate the city's economy. Walt liked that the project was a private-sector undertaking, planned by private business people rather than government bureaucrats, and he wanted it to succeed as a show-case for free enterprise. He had commissioned a study of the area's history to help his "imagineers" develop authentic themes for the fa-cility. Having flown in with twelve of his executives to finalize the deal, he was busy imagineering himself. "Boy, this is going to be great," he told Adm. Joe Fowler, the vice president for construction who had built Disneyland, as they sat on Walt's hotel balcony, gazing over the site. Bubbling with enthusiasm, he talked of using paddle-wheel steamers like those in their movie "Hannibal" to ferry visitors to their gate.

That night, the Disney entourage attended a big dinner party with the politicians, businessmen, and local bankers involved in the proj-ect. It was there the offending remark was made. *Any man who thinks he can design an attraction that is going to be a success in this city and not serve beer or liquor, ought to have his head examined,"* said the head of the city's leading business. Hearing the remark, the mayor gasped, "Oh, my god." He turned to Adm. Fowler, who sat next to him, and apologized, saying, "I just can't control that guy."

But the damage was done. Walt hated being challenged, especially in public. Upon returning from the dinner party to his hotel suite, he asked Card Walker, another Disney vice president, "What time can we have the plane in the morning?" Surprised, Walker responded, "But you know we've got—" He tried to say they had legal papers to sign the next day, but Walt cut him off. "It's all finished," said Walt. "We're not coming. Forget about it."[2] Afterwards, local bankers made three trips to California trying to change Walt's mind, all unsuc-cessful. August (Gussie) Busch, Jr.'s insulting remark had killed the deal—Disney World would not be in *St. Louis.*

As this incident shows, urban economic development involves an element of serendipity. A city's growth—its increase in population, employment, and tax base—can be planned, but only so much. Local development efforts are subject to chance events and the influence of human conduct, for good and ill. So it was that night in St. Louis in November 1963. Were it not for Gussie Busch's boorish behavior, a Disney "River Front Square" might shoulder the banks of the Mississippi, next to Busch Stadium, its entertainment drawn from the themes of old St. Louis and New Orleans, Lewis and Clark, and the Louisiana Purchase. The events that evening changed the history of two cities. For the beer baron was like the guilty party in a broken engagement: in repulsing the Disney fiancée, he enabled another city to win her. The failure of the first relationship facilitated the second one.

As everyone knows, it was Orlando that "won" Walt Disney World. What Orlando got was the glitz, international name-recognition, and growth bonanza that few corporations besides Disney could offer. In the refrain of a commemorative Disney movie, it was "a dream come true"—not only for the Disney executives who built the Magic Kingdom following Walt's death in 1966, but also for the local civic boosters who sought a "gimmick," said one, to stop tourists from bypassing Orlando en route to Miami.[3] "Show me a mayor in the United States of America who wouldn't just love to have Walt Disney sitting on his doorstep as a neighbor," said Carl Langford, Orlando's mayor when Disney came to town.[4] His comment came on the tenth anniversary of the giant theme park, before Langford retired to the mountains of North Carolina to escape "from all the traffic," as he said in 1990.[5]

Back in 1969, before Disney World opened, a mere 3.5 million tourists visited central Florida. But that soon changed. In 1971, the Magic Kingdom's first year, the tourist count zoomed to 10 million. By the unveiling of Epcot in 1982, Orlando had become the most popular tourist destination in the world. With the launching of Disney–MGM Studios in 1989, the annual visitor count reached 30 million, and when Disney's fourth theme park, Animal Kingdom, opened in 1998, company officials predicted 55 million visitors annually by 2001.[6] Like bees to honey, a swarm of other attractions followed Disney to Orlando, as shown in Table 1. *Amusement Business* magazine finds six of North America's eight largest theme parks in greater Orlando, and *Fodor's Guide* counts more than 80 fun zones in the area.[7] Seldom has the location decision of a single corporation so transformed a city.

Table 1. Major attractions within two hours of Orlando

Adventure Island of Tampa	Kennedy Space Center Visitor
Astronaut Hall of Fame	Complex
Blizzard Beach (D)	The Magic Kingdom (D)
Busch Gardens of Tampa Bay	Malibu Grand Prix
Cirque du Soleil (D)	Mystery Fun House/Lazer Tag
Citrus Tower	Paintball World
Congo River Golf & Exploration Co.	Pirate's Cove Adventure Golf
Cypress Gardens	Richard Petty Driving Experience (D)
Daytona International Speedway	Ripley's Believe It or Not! Or-
Daytona USA	lando Odditorium
Disney's Animal Kingdom (D)	River Country (D)
Disney–MGM Studios Theme Park (D)	SeaWorld Orlando
DisneyQuest (D)	Silver Springs
Epcot (D)	Skull Kingdom
Fantasia Gardens Miniature Golf	Typhoon Lagoon (D)
Finish Line Racing Adventures	Universal Studios Florida
Florida Splendid China	Universal Studios Islands of
Fun Spot of Florida	Adventure
Fun World at Flea World	The Walt Disney World Wide
Gatorland	World of Sports (D)
Green Meadows Petting Farm	Water Mania
Jungle Adventures	Wet 'n Wild
Jungleland Zoo	WonderWorks

(D) = Walt Disney World property

Between Disney's opening in 1971 and 1999, Orange County's population more than doubled, swelling from 344,000 to 846,000 residents. The fast pace of metro Orlando's growth is shown in Table 2. Post–Disney World construction, Orlando has consistently ranked among the nation's ten fastest-growing urban areas. In the mid-1980s, it was the second fastest-growing area in the Sunbelt, and in 1994, it became the nation's fastest growing urban region. With a metropolitan population exceeding 1 million, it received 17 million air passengers a year in the mid-1990s, making its sleek, modern airport the fastest growing and one of the busiest in the nation. And its hotel room count exploded from 8,000 before Disney World to over 100,000 by 2000—more than New York, Chicago, and Los Angeles, and second only to Las Vegas in the United States.

But there is another side to the story, reflecting that urban growth both gives and takes away. It transforms cultural life, the natural environment, and the character of the urban economy while expanding

Table 2. Population growth of metropolitan Orlando

Year	Orange County	City of Orlando	Four-county region*
1950	114,950	52,367	189,579
1960	263,540	88,135	394,899
1970	344,311	99,066	522,575
1980	470,865	128,291	804,774
1990	677,491	164,674	1,224,844
1999	846,328	184,639	1,561,715

* Orlando metropolitan statistical area (Orange, Seminole, Lake, and Osceola counties)
Source: U.S. Department of Commerce, Bureau of the Census; University of Florida, Bureau of Economic & Business Research.
Projections: University of Florida, Bureau of Economic & Business Research, Florida Population Studies #117, February 1997.

employment and economic opportunity. It creates public expenditure needs, but not always matching tax resources; it brings new employment, though not always living wages. It is a process, moreover, in which some gain while others lose. Some say it is Disney that snared Orlando, not the other way around.

On the cost side, Disney World has generated traffic congestion, public facility deficits, affordable housing shortages, and a low-wage economy. These problems frequently accompany urban growth, but there is a complicating factor in the Disney-Orlando case. For the Disney Co. got something special in coming to Florida: their own private government, a sort of Vatican with Mouse ears, with powers and immunities that exceed nearby Orlando's. The entertainment titan was authorized, among other things, to regulate land use, provide police and fire services, build roads, lay sewer lines, license the manufacture and sale of alcoholic beverages, even to build an airport and a nuclear power plant. (In fact, Disney never established the public police force, relying instead on over 800 private security guards; nor did they build an airport or nuclear power plant, though they retain authority in state law to do so.) To the envy of other developers, Disney also won immunity from building, zoning, and land-use regulations. Orange County officials cannot even send a building inspector to Disney property, and sheriff deputies are obliged to check in when they come on property and to avoid conspicuous display of their marked cars on such occasions.

Officially, these powers were granted to permit the construction of a model residential community where "20,000 people would live and work and play," as Disney representatives told Florida lawmakers. The company wanted "flexibility to plan for the future" so their model community would "always be in a state of becoming."[8] In other words, they wanted freedom from government regulation, from local elected officials, and from the reach of democratic government. What they got was a twin-tier government, with two general-purpose local governments on the bottom and a special-purpose district, the Reedy Creek Improvement District, on top. Essentially, the District controls both tiers: the forty-seven residents in the two cities are trusted, supervisory-level Disney employees, and the special-district government is controlled by the landowner, Disney. Of course, these governments are overlain by federal and state government, though the Disney property is exempted from most state land-use and building regulations. Map 1 shows the location of the Reedy Creek government, encompassing the entire Disney property, relative to Orlando.

Yet power, like growth, is two-sided. It is enabling—giving an actor, whether an individual or corporation, the capacity to do what it otherwise could not do. But it is also constraining—preventing other individuals, corporations, or government agencies from achieving their ends. So it has been with Disney's private government. On one hand, it has enabled the Disney Co. to build a giant pleasure palace that is the most popular tourist mecca in the world, not to mention the largest contributor of sales-tax revenue in Florida. Without their freedom from government regulation, without their ability to self-provide government services tailored to their precise needs, that success might not have occurred. On the other hand, the Disney Co. under Michael Eisner has used its powers and immunities to acquire a competitive advantage over other entertainment and hotel companies, building nightclubs and hotels on a scale never contemplated in their original government charter. Their immunities have impeded local government's ability to manage growth, even as Disney competes with surrounding governments for convention business, tourist spending, retail and professional office space, and entertainment venues.

More, the Disney Co. never built and, as detailed here, never planned to build the Epcot residential community that, in their presentation to Florida lawmakers, was the reason for their governmen-

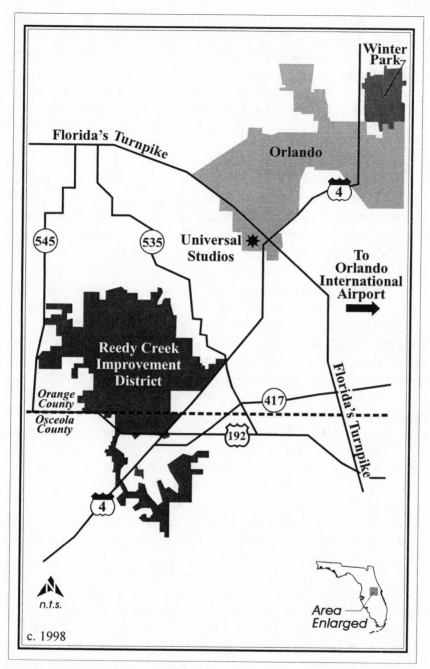

Map 1   Disney World and Orlando

tal powers in the first place. They wanted the powers of government but not real residents who could challenge their managerial prerogatives. Told here for the first time, it is nevertheless an old Florida story—of a big company that makes big promises to get concessions from government, then fails to keep its word. Hence the paradox of Disney World: its powers were ill-gotten, but they spawned amazing growth. In urban politics, is not growth the ultimate justification for power?

This book uses the metaphor of love and marriage to relate this story of growth and power. The underlying perspective, drawn from the academic field of urban political economy, assumes a city's relationship with a big local employer is like a marriage between people, a relationship characterized alternately by conflict and consensus, individuality and mutual dependence. The chapter headings—Serendipity, Seduction, Secrecy, Marriage, Growth, Conflict, Abuse, Negotiation, and Therapy—accord with this analogy.

Consider how the stages of love and marriage correspond with corporate–local relationships. Take the broken engagement: corporate officials reject a location deal and begin searching for a new plant site. Or the chance encounter: a traveling executive fortuitously learns of a business opportunity in a distant city. Or courtship: at chamber of commerce bazaars, like singles bars, local officials lure business executives with promises of tax breaks and land-lease agreements, while business executives dangle new investment, jobs, and tax base. Or the marriage contract: local officials and corporate CEOs stipulate their respective contributions to a corporate location deal. Or the extended honeymoon: the business grows and the city prospers. Or hard times: government regulators and company officials wrangle over the business's impact on air quality. Or divorce: the corporate–local relationship sours and a business relocates.

This analogy derives from the mutual dependence found in both relationships. When business–government partnerships form, as when people marry, reciprocal though sometimes unequal needs exist. The city needs investment, jobs, economic opportunity, philanthropic contributions to support cultural institutions, and, above all, tax resources. For its part, business needs a government that listens, favorably zoned land, a pro-business tax and regulatory climate, an appropriately trained and educated workforce, an efficient surface transportation system, and more.

There is no harm *per se* in government servicing businesses' needs; no more than when consenting adults do the same. The government that fails to compete with other governments for new business investment risks losing tax base and employment. Of course, the players in this competition are seldom evenly matched. Some cities are more attractive as places to live and do business; they can offer fewer overt incentives and still prosper. Some cities need a new employer more than the employer needs them; hence they offer the employer blandishments of all sorts. This mismatch of needs creates unequal bargaining strength, enabling one side to leverage the other.

For local government the challenge is this: not to concede so much that the benefits of a new employer are traded off. If the city grants too much tax or regulatory relief, or spends too liberally on sewer and highway extensions, the deal may cost more than it is worth. Neither does a business wish to concede too much. It wants assurance that the benefits of a locale exceed its tax and regulatory costs. Governments and businesses thus pose a threat to each other besides offering a potential helping hand. Each can make their relationship untenable. That old chestnut "Can't live with them, can't live without them" applies to business and government too. Complicating urban economic development, this aphorism also applies: "Whom you marry affects what you may become."

Another complication is that divorce is sometimes too costly. Governments and corporations may not be able to extricate themselves from one another, or the cost of dissolving their relationship may be too high. The corporation may be dug in; the local government may extract too many benefits from the corporation to risk a major blowup. It is like the situation of many nineteenth-century women for whom divorce was a practical impossibility. Here the categories used by economist Albert Hirschman are helpful.[9] He recognizes three methods of recuperation in political and economic affairs: exit, voice, and loyalty. Voice (complaining) is less effective, he writes, without the threat of exit behind it, creating a tendency toward loyalty or accommodation. Thus the impracticality of divorce (exit) makes loyalty more likely, however grudgingly accepted. This insight applies to corporate–local relationships as well as to married couples.

The Disney World–Orlando story is not only about growth and power, however. It is also interesting for what it reveals about the metamorphosis of Orlando, from citrus town to world-class tourist destination, and for what it relates about Walt Disney's urban vision, the Disney Co.'s pursuit of that vision after Walt's early death, the transformation of the company under Chairman Michael Eisner, and the company's use and abuse of their governmental powers. It is a story of CIA operatives, dummy corporations, private police powers, secrecy, and chicanery—but also of creative genius and commitment to a dream.

Beyond Disney lore and the metamorphosis of Orlando, the Disney–Orlando story relates to three sets of questions confronting modern postindustrial cities. The first concerns the power of global corporations over local governments and, realistically, whether local leaders can resist corporate demands. The trend toward corporate bigness is well known. Home-grown firms—like the business Walt and his brother Roy started in their garage in Kansas City in 1920— go international, marketing their products abroad and creating a global scale of operation. These firms establish multiple locations in places where they can find the cheapest production costs, the most compliant governments, and the best market access.[10] Reflecting this trend, the Disney Co. became multilocational in building their East Coast Disneyland in Orlando in the late 1960s. The company then went multinational in adding Tokyo Disneyland in 1983, followed by Euro Disneyland (now Disneyland Paris) in 1992.

This corporate trend bodes ill for local government, it is said. Global corporations are essentially stateless, having little local or national loyalty. Global in their operations, footloose in their loyalties, they play one political jurisdiction against another in bargaining for lower taxes, less regulation, subsidized infrastructure, and more. The result: local governments become interchangeable parts in a global game of corporate survival.

So it is said. But are local governments always mismatched in bargaining with global corporations? Must the competition among cities for new businesses cause a loss of political autonomy as governments comply with business demands? These questions relate to an important debate in urban political science. On one side, political scientist Paul Peterson argues that cities have a "development interest" driving local leaders to press for growth.[11] On the other, political scientists known as "regime theorists" say that cities have choices about how to grow, and that how these choices are made depends on the local "regime"—the informal network of groups and individuals that dominates local governance.[12] At issue is whether external economic factors (says Peterson) or internal political factors (say regime theorists) exercise more influence on local growth strategies. Peterson's perspective suggests that local governments are largely at the mercy of global corporations, while regime theorists think local leaders can resist corporate demands. This is a key issue in interpreting whether Orlando might have avoided, and can now better manage, the problems spawned by Disney's growth.

A second set of questions concerns the division of labor between public and private, government and market, in city building and municipal service provision. How should buildings, land-use, and transportation be controlled—by private corporations responding to market incentives, or by elected governments catering to voter preferences? How should municipal services be provided—by private corporations or by popularly elected governments? And what values should be incorporated into local governance institutions—private or public ones? As political scientist Nancy Burns relates, the later question is especially important where special-purpose governments are concerned, since most are havens to private values.[13]

These questions are well asked about Walt Disney World because it is not only an amusement park. As noted in the Preface, it is like a city—with its own public officials, a workforce of 55,000 as of 2000, a nightly population exceeding 100,000, a comprehensive city plan, and more. It is no ordinary city, moreover, but a proprietary city— a "showcase for free enterprise," in Walt's phrase—founded upon two private-sector strategies: privatization and deregulation. As an experiment in privatization, municipal services at Disney World are provided by the Reedy Creek Improvement District, the governmental arm of the Disney Co. As an experiment in deregulation, the Florida legislature agreed in 1967 to roll back state and local regulation of building construction, land use, and so forth, in return for Disney's promised $600-million investment.

In the U.S. debate, privatization has meant "enlisting private energies to improve the performance of tasks that would remain in some sense public," writes political economist John Donahue.[14] Within this frame of reference, economists have debated whether refuse collection, street maintenance, and other discrete municipal functions should be provided by private corporations working for government or directly by government. The Disney World experience pushes this debate to another level, however. Here the question is not whether this or that municipal function should be privatized but, rather, whether the whole business of city building and municipal service provision should be entrusted to a private corporation instead of elected political officials.

A third set of questions concerns the possibilities for transcending Orlando's tourist economy, and whether past decisions lock Orlando into a determinate path of development. Consider that the economic role of cities is changing as new types of cities emerge. Cities are evolving from places for manufacturing to places for shopping, office work, and entertainment. As tourism becomes a large-scale industry linked to the world economy, and as urban culture itself becomes a commodity, some cities have developed tourism-based economies. These tourist cities differ in the appearance and extensiveness of their tourist spaces; in the degree to which those spaces are integrated into the urban fabric; and in the objectives of their visitors, ranging from sin (Bangkok) to spiritual redemption (Jerusalem) to personal fortune (Las Vegas) to family fun (Orlando).[15] Yet tourist economies share a reliance on low-wage work, often with limited job benefits. In the Orlando area, over half the metro workforce is engaged in the service and retail sectors, and despite a booming economy and record low unemployment in the late 1990s, average real wages have been stagnant for a decade.[16]

These developments pose what some historians term the "path dependence" question. As cities and their economies evolve, are the weak and inefficient examples eliminated so that evolution always moves in a positive direction? Will Orlando follow a path from agriculture to tourism to high-tech, as local leaders hope? Or will Orlando remain stuck with a predominately service-sector tourist economy? Path dependence theory, while not a proven theory, helps to explain why some destinations are unreachable in economic development. "Where you can get to," the theory postulates, "depends on where you are coming from; and some destinations you simply cannot get to from here."[17] Orlando's economic development origins in tourism and passive government may eliminate destinations like Silicon Valley. The "networks" that support existing economic arrangements may make the "switching costs" too great. The mere possibility of this path dependence makes the history of Disney World and Orlando, of the formation and evolution of this economic development marriage, important to understand.

The Disney World–Orlando story is thus richly complex. It is interesting for what it reveals about how Disney World and Orlando, individually and together, got to be what they are. And more, it provides fertile ground for addressing important questions about the choices available to local governments confronted by global corporations, the viability of privatization and deregulation, and the path dependence of a tourist economy founded upon passive government. Yet these questions are not addressed all in one place, so that one chapter focuses on the first question, another on the second, and so on. Rather, they are addressed in the context of a chronological narrative with tangents, noted in the text, to the above agenda. The final chapter— Therapy—weaves these questions and answers together in assessing the options and switching costs confronting greater Orlando.

The story begins with roads, for it was through roadbuilding that visionary local elites worked to put Orlando on the map, to link it commercially with the rest of Florida, the Southeast, and the nation if not the world. Their efforts laid the groundwork for Disney's coming to Orlando. In this pre-figurative stage of economic development, we see the formation of a new regime of power based on commitment to growth, as private sector leaders dress up Orlando with high-speed roads to seduce investment and employment for the area.

TWO

Seduction

O n November 22, 1963, Walt Disney and an entourage of his top executives flew in a borrowed plane from Tampa, Florida, to Orlando, fifty miles to the east. The night before they had checked into a Tampa hotel under assumed names to avoid alerting the press and stirring up land speculation. They were going to Orlando so Walt could see it from the air once more before making a tentative commitment to the area. The many consultant reports that Walt had read on "Project X," as the stealth project was known to a handful of company officials, could take him only so far; ever the artist, he needed to visualize the possibilities for himself.

They were close to selecting an expansion site. After the debacle in St. Louis, they flew to other potential sites—Niagara Falls, on both sides of the U.S.–Canadian border; the Baltimore–Washington area; and now Florida. An early favorite, Niagara Falls was rejected because its winter cold would prevent the park's year-round operation. Walt wanted to avoid a seasonal workforce, fearing that carnival-type workers like those in existing amusement parks would corrupt the family atmosphere he sought to achieve. So the search turned to Florida with its natural advantages of sunshine and water. Walt wanted to avoid the coasts, however, both to dissociate his theme park from an older genre of boardwalk amusement parks, and to facilitate 360-degree expansion. Ocala, located fifty miles northwest of Orlando amidst white-fenced horse farms, was an early favorite. It appealed to Disney consultants because it was near the state's epicenter, and it had emotional appeal to Walt because, as a child, he had visited his aunt in the nearby hamlet of Paisley. Yet it lacked a good road network.

Unlike Orlando. As their plane reached Orlando and circled south of the city, Walt looked down and saw the nexus of two major highways, shown in Map 2. One was Interstate 4, then under construction, spanning Florida from Tampa on the Gulf Coast to Daytona Beach on the Atlantic. The other was Florida's Turnpike, running northwest from Miami to Orlando and terminating at I-75, east of Tampa. Nearby was a vast stretch of virgin land, much of it swampy and alligator-infested, enough land to buffer their theme park from adjacent properties. To the east was McCoy Jet Airport, a hybrid military–civilian base that would later metamorphose into Orlando International Airport, adding to Orlando's stock of federally financed transportation facilities.

"That's it," said Walt as he looked down from the plane.[1] Later, when asked what attracted him to Orlando, he said: "The freeway routes, they bisect here."[2] Roads were so important to Disney planners because they needed to import tourists from afar to make their business plan work. There were fewer people in all of Florida than in the Los Angeles metropolitan area surrounding Disneyland, yet they originally wanted to build a park ten times the size of Disneyland. It would not be a Florida theme park so much as a tourist spa for the East Coast, located in Florida. This "total destination resort," as Disney planners called it, needed enough hotels, restaurants, and amenities to serve the many tourists traveling down from the Northeast, or across the Gulf states, to visit. Above all, that meant good road linkages, an advantage for Orlando since I-4 connects with I-95, which runs up the Atlantic coast from Key West to Maine, and since Florida's Turnpike links via I-75 with I-10, which spans the country from the Florida panhandle to California. Whether tourists were driving south from New Jersey or east across Mississippi and Alabama, Orlando was well located—just what Disney consultants wanted.

From Orlando, the Disney entourage flew west along the Gulf coast to New Orleans, where they disembarked for the night. In the cab ride to their hotel, they saw people crying in the streets and turned on the radio to learn that President Kennedy had been assassinated. It was a fateful day for the nation. It was also a fateful day for central Florida for entirely different reasons, though area residents were un-

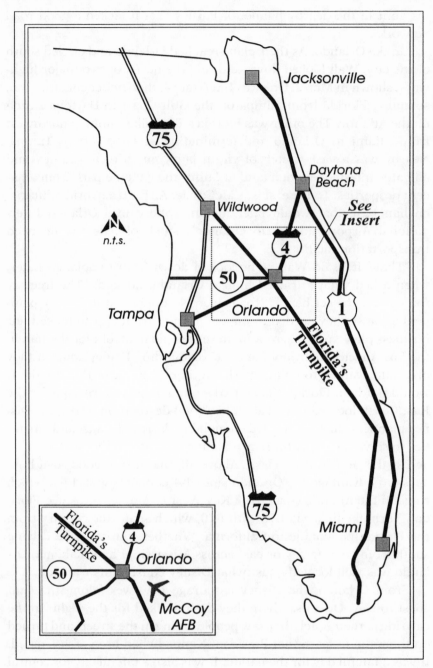

Map 2   Orlando road network

aware for eighteen months that Orlando would become Disneyland East. While the land remained to be purchased, Walt had made a tentative commitment to Orlando. His gut decision that day, made high in the sky in a plane borrowed from TV host Arthur Godfrey, led to the transformation of Orlando from a sleepy agricultural community, more dependent on citrus than tourism, into the world's most popular tourist destination.

To understand this transformation, one must appreciate the sources of what Walt saw as he gazed down from the plane. The land and sunshine were the gratuitous gifts of nature, but the transportation network was man-made, the fruit of leadership and political savvy. Serendipity killed the St. Louis option, while seduction brought Walt Disney to Orlando. The seducers were Orlando's pro-growth regime of private businessmen, known to themselves as the "movers and shakers," an informal group that existed independent, for the most part, from the area's elected officials. The latter had a caretaker orientation toward government, focusing on delivering municipal services and keeping government small and taxes low. In contrast, the pro-growth regime of the 1950s and early '60s had a more activist concept of government. These private businessmen, centered on the newspaper and largest bank, saw how spending on public facilities could generate future growth, and they used their connections and political skill to procure major facilities for the area, from navy bases to defense plants to roads.

What they sought was not tourism. The area's pro-growth regime wanted to attract manufacturing with its high wages, provided it was clean industry. Their tool of seduction was transportation; they saw roadbuilding as the key to progress. As federal and state highway programs expanded in the 1950s, they saw how nonlocal public funding could make Orlando not merely an in-state transportation hub, but a regional and national hub as well. Importantly, they were also committed to private decision making through politically insulated government institutions. They wanted to keep the decision making private, even when public resources and large public impacts were involved, a preference that would shape the institutions supporting Orlando's growth.

"We used to have a group," said Billy Dial, Orlando's power broker in the 1950s and '60s and a man who could have been governor, said his newspaper publisher friend, Martin Andersen. Dial never ran for elective office, however, serving in appointive roles instead, and as advisor and confidant to governors, mayors, and corporate heads.[3] A person of modest upbringing, he was born in Lake City, 150 miles north of Orlando, and arrived in Orlando in 1932 fresh from the University of Florida Law School. Earning a reputation as a competent attorney who could render a neatly written legal opinion in a day's time, and aided by a folksy manner that meshed with Orlando's business culture, he rose quickly in business and social circles, becoming attorney for the city, the newspaper, the largest bank (First National), the largest employer (then Glenn Martin Co., later Martin Marietta), the CSX railroad, and the Florida Bankers Association, among other important clients. As friend and advisor to the most important actors in the city and much of the state, it seemed only natural that Dial became Orlando's principal dealmaker. His stock in trade, other than his many connections, was his personal honesty. As a contemporary said, "Billy always put his family and community ahead of personal wealth."[4] He became wealthy but did not live ostentatiously. A visitor to his home in the 1960s said that it looked like it was furnished out of Sears and Roebuck.[5]

"Our group didn't have a name," said Dial, "although some of them called us the movers and shakers." There were about ten of them, he said, naming Clarence Yates, Joe Crosson (head of First Federal Savings & Loan), former Orlando mayor Billy Beardall, Clarence Gay (president of Citizens Bank), and Henry Leu (owner of the leading hardware store in town), among others.[6] At the apex of the group with Dial was Martin Andersen, owner and publisher of the *Orlando Sentinel* and *Orlando Evening Star*, the area's morning and evening newspapers. Billy and Andy, as the two were known, were linked by social as well as business ties. As Dial put it, "Andy was about my best buddy." For his part, Andersen called him "kingfish," suggesting a relationship in which Dial hatched the ideas and Andersen promoted them.[7]

Andersen, then 34, came to Orlando in 1931 as the emissary of Charles Marsh, a Texan who also mentored young Lyndon Baines Johnson and who had just purchased the *Orlando Morning Sentinel* and the *Evening Reporter-Star*. The two newspapers were nearly bankrupt. Andersen put them back on their feet, eventually buying them in 1945 from Marsh in installments paid over twenty years.[8] Under Andersen's leadership, the combined papers became highly profitable and achieved a readership exceeding the city's population, rare for a local newspaper. An early fan of color, he ran front-page editorial cartoons that blasted his foes and promoted his favored politicians and projects. Like Lyndon Johnson, whom he knew through Marsh, Andersen was often profane—a "rough and tumble Texan," one *Sentinel* executive termed him[9]—and sometimes wrote editorials at home while "in his cups."[10] One such editorial described Florida Senator Spessard Holland as a "nadir," defined for the reader as "the lowest form of animal life." Said one of his managing editors: "He had a monopoly operation and was very outspoken. A lot of times he was wrong. He abused people who didn't deserve it."[11] His rough treatment of others may explain why he feared for himself. He was obsessed with the Kennedy assassination and, while riding in the motorcade opening I-4, asked the copy boy who doubled as his driver, "Do you think they will try to get me too?"[12]

Andersen feared flying but never met a road project he did not like. The combined and renamed *Sentinel* and *Evening Star* was one of four major papers in the state. Andersen ran the paper without the encumbrance of an editorial board, and governors and would-be governors all sought his endorsement, giving him a powerful tool to promote area road projects. The Charley Johns–LeRoy Collins race for governor in 1954 attests to the publisher's influence as well as his priorities.

Charley Johns was president of the Florida Senate when he became acting governor after Governor Dan McCarty suffered an incapacitating heart attack soon after taking office in 1952. A plumber by trade, Johns was ill-prepared to be governor. He was supported by Andersen, however, who instructed the acting governor on the need for the "Bithlo cutoff," a proposed road branching off from S.R. 50 that would create a more direct route between Orlando and Cocoa on Florida's east coast. The new road (S.R. 520) would not only benefit beach goers; it would make it easier for workers at the U.S. Missile Test Center in Cape Canaveral to live in Orlando and commute to the Cape. When Johns sought election in his own right in 1954, Andersen supported him, while the state's other major papers endorsed LeRoy

Collins, an attorney and well-known state senator. Collins won, but Orlando got the Bithlo cutoff.[13]

Roads were key to the movers and shakers' growth strategy, explained Dial. "That was before Orlando had spread out into shopping centers. We recognized that Orlando needed roads. Martin Andersen was one of the group; he used his newspaper, he used his influence to promote the highways. He was a great supporter of Governor Collins [after the 1954 election]. In those days they allocated state road money by districts. We used the district funds to build the roads wherever they were needed. But we were concentrating on improving our primary highway system, such as [the north-south] 441, which was four lanes all the way to Gainesville and the Bithlo cutoff, which goes to Cocoa. We did everything we could to promote the city like that."[14]

When LeRoy Collins was elected governor in 1954, Dial went to him at the behest of his friend Campbell Thornall, who preceded Dial as city attorney. Thornall, who was serving on the State Road Board (SRB), sought nomination to fill a State Supreme Court vacancy. Dial asked Collins if he would name Thornall to the Court and Collins agreed, provided Dial took Thornall's place on the road board. It was a good arrangement for Orlando, since it preserved Orlando's voice on this powerful body. Dial consented to serve but said he could not fill the full four-year term. "I was up to my eyeballs in my law practice," he explained. "Besides I knew I was going over to the bank (First National, now Sun Trust) in '58."[15]

Orlando leaders made good use of the road board system. Politically, their task was to ensure that the board member from District 5, which stretched from Orlando to the east coast and included Daytona Beach, was from Orlando. Through the mid-1960s, Orlando placed three consecutive representatives on the board. It was a "string of luck," said Andersen in a speech honoring Dial, though he knew it was more than luck. Orlando had helped elect five governors in a row and was "riding high, wide, and handsome in Tallahassee and Washington," said the publisher. In the same speech, he praised Dial as the area's "number-one road builder."[16] Less modestly, his newspaper claimed in 1966 in an editorial titled "Roads the Key to Progress," that it had "led the fight for every new highway development in the area."[17]

The movers and shakers' roadbuilding strategy was hardly unique. Local leaders who want their cities to grow need good road linkages. It may seem that a city's size determines the roads it gets so that big cities would get big roads, but the process often works in reverse: cities grow because they get big roads. As Jane Jacobs has written, the task of economic development is to export goods and services and import wages and profits.[18] In practical terms, that requires a good transportation system and hence the political clout to secure transportation funding. What distinguished Orlando's movers and shakers was not simply their grasp of the connection between roadbuilding and growth but, rather, their ability to act on that strategy by securing road funding and withstanding opposition to controversial road projects.

In the immediate postwar period, Orlando and Orange County leaders "got the jump" on neighboring counties through an ambitious program of road building, wrote local agricultural extension agent Henry Swanson.[19] Their efforts opened up previously rural areas of the county for urban development. One early project was the routing of S.R. 50 east-west through Orlando. Completed in 1949, this "super highway" led to the six-laning and resurfacing of Colonial Avenue across Orlando's midsection. It put the city at the center of the state's only bicoastal east-west highway. Orlando was likewise on the state's major north-south highway, U.S. 441, which local leaders had convinced the State Road Department, working in conjunction with the federal Bureau of Public Roads, to widen through Orlando in the 1950s.

But these road projects took their toll, changing the character of the community and imposing losses as well as gains. In slicing S.R. 50 through the middle of Orlando, magnificent trees were uprooted to howls of protest, parts of two lakes were filled, and once-attractive Colonial Avenue was transformed into a major commercial strip.[20] Likewise, the widening of U.S. 441 converted the Orange Blossom Trail, the city's major north-south arterial, into a commercial thoroughfare, producing a tacky strip of car lots, vacant lots, hamburger stands, and endless traffic—everything it seemed but orange blossoms.[21]

In retrospect, these activities were nothing new. Controversy and road building, like growth generation and federal works investments, go hand in hand. When the first session of the Florida Legislative Council, held in Pensacola in 1822, was delayed more than a month because of poor road conditions, early Floridians started a now time-honored tradition: they asked for federal help. The Congress complied, authorizing the expenditure of $20,000 and the use of federal troops to build a public road from Pensacola to St. Augustine, a road to be twenty-five feet wide and clearly marked. Completed in 1826, the highway sparked controversy from the start. Settlers complained that it was only sixteen feet wide, that tree stumps were left high above the ground, and that causeways and bridges were inadequate. One man wrote the Secretary of War to grumble that rain would make the road absolutely impassable and that it would not last twelve months. Captain Daniel E. Burch, in charge of building the western section of the road, complained in his letter of resignation about needing to mollify so many conflicting interests in constructing the road. "People of the country near such construction deem it a matter exclusively their own and no military officer can expect either to give satisfaction or be free from open censure," he declaimed.[22]

Like Captain Burch, Orlando's movers and shakers recognized that growth yielded winners and losers. Someone had to suffer a disrupted neighborhood, a failed business, or inconvenient road access. "There is no progress," an Orlando merchant group said amidst a road controversy in the 1960s, "without inconvenience to some."[23] Accordingly, the movers and shakers favored centralized, politically insulated institutions for making decisions on growth projects and the like, institutions that played a key part in Orlando's transformation. To cope with the conflict over road building, the state had created two similar institutions, the Turnpike Authority and the State Road Board. These were mini-governments for road building; they gave pro-growthers the power of government without the accountability of elected officials. It was Orlando's ability to dominate these agencies—thanks to the business consensus forged by Dial and the political clout of Andersen's newspaper—that brought the confluence of I-4 and Florida's Turnpike to Orlando, catching Walt Disney's eye.

Florida's Turnpike was authorized in the state's Turnpike Act of 1953 and modeled after the New Jersey turnpike system. The idea was to use private enterprise to construct roads and draw tourists to

the state. Tourists would help finance the road with their tolls, salesmen would be hired to market the road, a corporate-style board would
make route decisions (to minimize political squabbles), and bond
holders would take a gamble, since the state did not pledge its credit
behind the turnpike bonds.

This state agency was controlled by what amounted to a private
board of directors. The ten-person board had one member from each
of the five congressional districts as they existed in 1937, four members appointed by the governor and confirmed by the senate, and one
member from the State Road Department who was designated to
serve as chair. The state authorized the sale of revenue bonds to finance a turnpike running the length of Florida, from Miami's Dade
County to Duval County surrounding Jacksonville. The first segment
would extend 110 miles from Dade County to Fort Pierce, midway
up the state's Atlantic coast. For the northern segment, the Turnpike
Authority would study an east coast and a central Florida route. The
Authority could "determine the exact route and exact termini of turnpike projects," but the legislature would ratify the choice between an
inland and coastal route.[24]

As work began on the southern leg, there emerged "tremendous
opposition from land owners, citizens and State's Attorneys," wrote
Turnpike Authority Chairman Tom Manuel. "We are going to have
organized resistance from motel owners, the gasoline industry, and
other interests who feel they would be injured by any turnpike," he
advised Authority members.[25] True to prediction, opposition arose
from the American Automobile Association, which then opposed all
toll roads; from Jacksonville business interests, which objected to the
through-city route; and from tourist-oriented businesses in Daytona
Beach and along nearby U.S. 1, which feared the turnpike would
whisk motorists past their tourist courts, restaurants, and shops. The
latter group found an influential voice in Saxton Lloyd, who was
prominent in political circles in Daytona Beach and who had been
appointed chairman of the newly created Florida Development Commission by Governor Collins.[26]

Seeing this conflict, Dial and Andersen went to Tom Manuel, telling him, according to Dial, "If Daytona Beach doesn't want the turnpike, Orlando will take it." They then went to Governor Collins and
repeated this message, offering him their assistance in getting the in-

land route approved by lawmakers. To make the route more attractive to cost-minded road engineers, Dial, who had worked with First National Bank president Linton Allen to bring the Glenn Martin Co. to Orlando, persuaded the military supplier to donate land for the turnpike. As a result, the turnpike runs past their plant gate. In making these deals, Dial and Andersen worked as a team: "I suggested the idea to Andy and the two of us worked together," said Dial.[27]

Before Dial and Andersen's deal could be ratified, the inland route needed to be certified as "financially feasible." For this, the Turnpike Authority hired two respected engineering consulting firms—Colverdale and Colpitts to compare revenue projections for the two routes, and Howard, Needles, Tammen, and Bergendoff to estimate construction and capital costs. These alternative routes are shown on Map 3. The inland route, which was 75 miles longer, would cost $59 million more to build but would yield slightly higher gross earnings. Equally important, the inland alternative would cover maximum annual debt service 1.47 times, compared with 1.8 times for the coastal route.[28] Debt service was critical because the bond covenants required that debt payments be covered a minimum of 1.4 times. In other words, the inland route would cost more and make less money, but it was profitable enough to be considered financially feasible, said the consultants.

The person responsible for the Howard, Needles cost study was C. H. ("Pete") Peterson, known to Florida road engineers as "Mr. Turnpike." He had served as project manager in charge of all engineering design work for the New Jersey and West Virginia turnpikes before taking a like job in Florida. When he directed the study, Peterson had just come to Florida to establish a Howard, Needles office. "The study was very exploratory," cautioned Peterson. He had completed it in less than three months, spending much of that time driving around the state to familiarize himself with the alternative routes. "There is no question that the coastal route was the most viable route from a traffic engineering viewpoint," said the road engineer. "Otherwise you have to argue that southbound traffic from Georgia wanted to bend out to Orlando to get to Miami."[29] But politics had triumphed over economics; he clearly knew what conclusion politicians wanted.

Next the inland route needed legislative approval. To do this "we offered something for everyone," explained Henry Land, a member

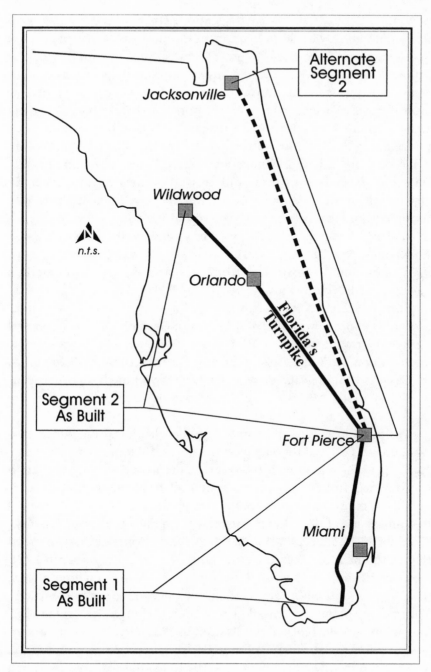

Map 3   Florida's Turnpike alternative routes

of Orange County's legislative delegation. The bill, as drafted by Collins aide Alan Boyd, whom Lyndon Johnson would later name as the first secretary of the Department of Transportation, authorized the full-length inland route. It would have a crescent shape, running from Miami northwest to Orlando and then back to Jacksonville. There was even a provision for an extension to Tampa—to get support from west coast legislators. In lobbying for the route change, Dial was aided by the relationships he formed during the previous legislative session, when he worked with lawmakers as general counsel for the Florida Bankers Association in overhauling the Florida Banking Code. He also had the powerful support of Senator William Shands, a fraternity brother from his days at the University of Florida.

Dial and Andersen worked together in making these deals, though Andersen got more credit because his role was more visible. Accordingly, some political insiders from this period call the Turnpike's curve toward Orlando at Fort Pierce the "Martin Andersen bend." Regardless of who was responsible, it was a great victory for Orlando. Motorists could now drive from Miami to Orlando, or, once I-75 and I-10 were completed, from Atlanta and the lower Gulf states to Orlando, all on limited-access highways. Without these highway links, the case for building Disney World in Orlando would have been weakened and another Florida city might have been chosen.

The other key piece of Orlando's road network was I-4, which connected with I-95 and thereby with the bountiful tourist market of the Northeast. The planning of I-4 occurred in the mid-1950s, as Orlando transformed from a downtown-centered urban area into a multi-nucleated metropolis. In 1956, the twenty-acre Colonial Mall opened two miles east of downtown, the largest expansion of retail business since the city's incorporation in 1875. While Colonial Mall sounded the death knell for downtown, the larger city was booming. In 1954, local voters approved a $3-million bond program to build fire stations, widen streets, and add sewer lift stations needed to support growth. The opening of the U.S. Missile Test Center at Cape Canaveral in 1955 had an impact like Florida's land boom of 1925, as workers there were soon making Orlando and Winter Park their bedroom community. The Glenn Martin Company arrived the following year, purchasing a twelve-square-mile reservation and producing its first La Crosse artillery missile a year later. Fueled by Martin's arrival, a record $18.6 million in building permits was granted in 1958, ten new industries arrived, and eleven new subdivisions were added to the city. The Census Bureau in 1960 listed Orlando's metropolitan growth as the nation's largest.[30]

Amidst this expansion, a newly formed Orlando Planning Board appointed by Mayor J. Rolfe Davis sponsored an area-wide traffic survey to identify future road needs. Orlando, together with Orange County and Winter Park, contracted with the State Road Department in 1954 to conduct an origin–destination study, for which the Department was paid $11,000. Following the survey, the Department recommended an elevated, limited-access highway running through Orlando and Winter Park. It would be part of a proposed interstate highway linking Daytona Beach, Orlando, and Tampa. Within the Orlando area, the eight and one-half mile expressway would enter from the south and then turn northeast, running along the east side of S.R. 17–92 through the city of Winter Park across the site where a shopping mall (the Winter Park Mall) was later built. This route conformed to the "desire lines" identified in the Orlando–Winter Park traffic survey.

Although Dial and Andersen are sometimes credited—or blamed—for bringing I-4 through Orlando, they did not influence the proposed route. The through-Orlando expressway became part of the interstate system because it was in state road plans when the federal Interstate Highway Act was adopted in 1956. Credit Mayor Davis, the Orlando Planning Board, and state road planners for that. When state planners first proposed the expressway, based on their earlier Orlando traffic survey, Mayor Davis was alarmed at the $30-million price tag. But state road planners were a step ahead: they saw how the expressway could become part of the interstate highway program then under debate in Congress, making it eligible for 90 percent federal funding. Though it was intended for interstate roads, Florida officials wanted to use the Act for urban traffic relief. "We wanted to get ahead of the game with our expressway program," explained Wilbur Jones, SRB head from 1955 to 1958. The critical traffic needs were in the cities and, by building early, they could save money on land costs.[31]

Rather, Dial and Andersen's crucial role was in defeating opposition to the through-Orlando route. As a new road board member in 1956, Dial foresaw the tremendous conflict that would occur—between downtown property owners who would benefit from better access to their stores and office buildings, or so they thought, and those in the expressway's path whose homes, neighborhoods, and businesses would be destroyed. Before the route was made public, the attorney went to Andersen and said, "Andy, this thing is going to create a real donnybrook, and if the paper isn't going to support it, I don't want to move. Even with newspaper support, it's going to be difficult." After he explained the plan to Andersen, the publisher said, "Hell, I'll go all the way." So Andersen's newspapers began supporting the expressway project "with cartoons on the front page and everything else," said Dial, who meanwhile began pressing for local approval.[32]

True to Dial's prediction, the I-4 project was soon mired in controversy. As proposed it would bisect the city of Winter Park, an independent city rather than a suburb bordering Orlando. Winter Park was largely a residential city, though it had an attractive commercial strip, Park Avenue, described in travel brochures as a European-style walking street, and a secondary business district to the west on U.S. 17–92. It was a city driven by what Paul Peterson would term "status interests" (acquiring and maintaining status) rather than "economic interests" (achieving economic expansion).[33] Many of Winter Park's citizens had made their wealth elsewhere and did not depend on the local economy. As snowbirds and transplants, moreover, they had seen the destructive effects of growth elsewhere. "They knew how much land its takes to build a highway interchange," said one longtime resident. "They also knew that growth could be resisted. They had seen how places like Shaker Heights had avoided being run over by the growth of Cleveland."[34] This attitude about growth, captured in the city's motto, "Winter Park, a city of homes," shaped local reaction to the expressway controversy.

Winter Park leaders protested that I-4 would bisect their city and disrupt nascent plans for a shopping mall along U.S. 17–92. The mall project was saved, however, when Winter Park mayor Ray Greene got the Florida Cabinet to approve the construction of a state office building next to the mall, in the expressway's path. Winter Park also hired an internationally known city planner, Maurice Rotival, who proposed running the expressway across Lake Killarney at the city's western edge. But homeowners around the lake opposed the plan, and after eight years of wrangling, the State Road Department finally pushed the highway completely outside Winter Park, to the west of Lake Killarney, as shown in Map 4.

Winter Park had won an important victory, providing a model for other communities to follow when confronted by growth projects that are presented as necessary and inevitable. Yet it was also a mixed victory. As long-time Winter Park City Attorney Webber Haines said of the ordeal, "We would have preferred having I-4 closer in. We took one thing (the bypass route) in order to avoid another (being bisected). You're never sure where you're going to end up in something like this."[35] It was a statement that both sides in the routing controversy might have made.

In Orlando, a Citizens Expressway Association was formed to oppose the through-town route. This group, which had a downtown office with a neon sign and a paid staff, agitated for a westerly bypass route. They also questioned the expressway concept itself, opining in one leaflet that housewives and tourists "drive too leisurely for a high-speed highway."[36] Other expressway critics attacked the *Sentinel* for its steady barrage of front-page, pro-expressway editorials with titles like "Expressways Increase Property Values and Improve the Beauty of Cities" and "Expressways Save Lives and Property."[37] The publisher of the *Coffee Cup*, a small weekly newspaper, claimed that an interchange was placed at Colonial Drive, close to the *Sentinel* building, for Martin Andersen's convenience in distributing his newspaper.[38] Other critics resorted to scare tactics. At a meeting of expressway opponents from suburban Maitland and Altamonte Springs, just north of Orlando, one speaker warned: "The expressway will create slums on either side of it. If you own property in the route you had better get rid of it now, if you can find a sucker."[39]

The conflict peaked at a public hearing in Orlando, required by state law and attended by over 2,000 persons. It was the city's largest town meeting ever. Exhibits were displayed in the municipal auditorium before the 7:30 p.m. meeting, including a twenty-eight-foot aerial photo of the route and six "before" and "after" pictures of the expressway. Dial presided, backed up by Rueben Bergendoff, senior partner in the Howard, Needles firm, who had flown down from Kan-

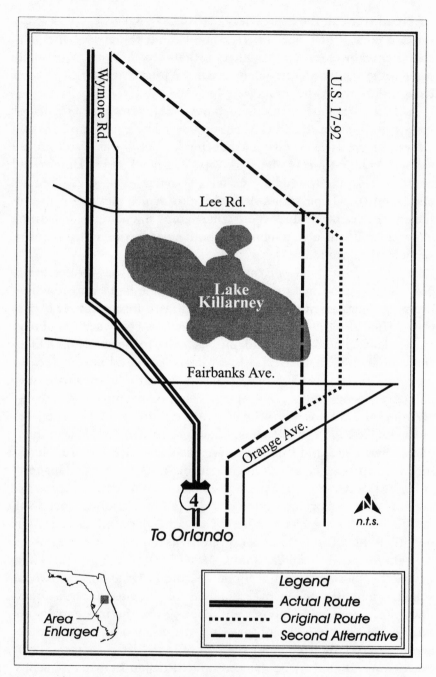

Map 4   Alternative I-4 routes in Winter Park

sas City for the occasion. Bergendoff, an imposing figure in his perpet-
ual three-piece suit, led off with a ninety-minute presentation; but his
stiff, formal style proved ineffective with the angry crowd, and he was
interrupted by frequent boos and catcalls. The Citizens Expressway
Association was clearly spoiling for a fight. Their leader, LaMonte
Graw, complained in his comments from the floor about the project's
uncertain cost, eliciting from Bergendoff that the cost had risen by
$9 million since the expressway was first proposed.

The unflappable Dial stopped the opponents from taking control
of the meeting, however. In his words, "the meeting got a little raun-
chy. We had to turn the lights off several times in order to regain
order."[40] Said Bill McCree, an Orlando planning board member and
expressway supporter, "I've never seen a meeting handled better. Billy
really knew how to do it."[41] To critics, though, the meeting was a farce.
"You already have your minds made up," one woman said to Dial.
Unperturbed, he responded that the Howard, Needles plan was only
a proposal; he had not recommended it to the state yet. "We are not
trying to cram this down anyone's throat," he told the audience.[42]

A week later, however, Dial endorsed the through-city route to the
State Road Department. In his letter, he said the opposition did not
represent the best interest of the community. He had received some
calls from critics, but "not as many as he expected," considering the
opponents' claim of widespread objections. The opposition was "en-
gendered in the main by affected property owners, one or more of
whom stated to me that they were prepared to spend a lot of money
to kill this project," he wrote to the State Road Department head.[43]

Unquestionably, self-interest drove both sides of the controversy.
While affected property owners led the opposition, Dial and Andersen
had property interests at stake, too. "Both of them ran monopoly or
near-monopoly operations," said John Tiedtke, a Winter Park investor and contemporary of theirs.[44] As owner of Orlando's only daily
newspaper, Andersen would benefit from the added advertising and
subscriptions that growth would bring, and he was defending his
downtown advertisers as well. Dial represented both First National
Bank, which he joined as executive vice president in 1958, and his
former law clients. First National lacked the *Sentinel*'s monopoly
power but was the largest bank in the area and would benefit dispro-
portionately from Orlando's growth. It also had its headquarters and

investments downtown. Yet there is no evidence that either man used his position for direct financial gain.

What motivated Dial and Andersen to promote Orlando's growth were their big stakes in the region's future. What was good for the region was largely good for them, and vice versa. Their pro-growth regime also had the advantages of propinquity and familiarity, helping them to mold an elite business consensus. "There used to be a time," said Dial, "when you could go down Orange Avenue (Orlando's main street), talk to ten people and put over almost anything." That was before Orlando's economy diversified away from citrus; before businesses moved away from downtown; before the area's largest firms became externally owned; and before local corporate leaders grew diverse in their background and schooling. If Dial and Andersen's leadership group had a bias, it was in believing that growth was good for everyone, and that the interests of downtown equated with the broader interests of the community.

The movers and shakers did not get everything they wanted, however, reflecting that urban economic development is an uncertain process. In prospect, the expressway's beneficiaries were the downtown Orlando businesses that were already losing customers to outlying shopping plazas and that needed fast and convenient access to their stores and offices. The losers were the many property owners with homes or businesses in the path of the roadway. Yet the results were decidedly mixed. On one hand, the expressway initially did more to foster suburbia than to support downtown. Among other suburban developments, I-4 was a direct stimulus to Altamonte Mall, a 900,000 square-foot shopping mall eight miles north of downtown Orlando, and Maitland Center, a 268-acre office park five miles to the north. On the other hand, the movers and shakers did succeed in bringing a giant new employer to town. It was not the high-wage industry they sought but, nonetheless, a growth engine that would change the region forever. Their efforts showed that private investment can be seduced through public spending, though with uncertain results. At the same time, their efforts helped to create a path dependence favoring tourism rather than manufacturing.

The legacy of Andersen and Dial and the pro-growth regime they led was more than a regional road network and Disney World, however. It was also a preference for private decision making and politically insulated institutions like the SRB and the Turnpike Authority. That, too, was part of the path dependence they created, a dependence that put growth decisions beyond the reach of voters and elected officials. To their defenders, these independent authorities wisely put the right people in charge. They permitted decision making by "businessmen who were accustomed to making decisions," said one road engineer.[45] They ensured that proven leaders of the community, people with communication skills and public relations sensitivity, were explaining road plans, instead of faceless traffic engineers, said a former road board chairman.[46] The flip side was that the SRB was unaccountable to the public and, in that sense, undemocratic.

Dial saw this arrangement as a virtue. He wrote an open letter to Winter Park mayor J. Lynn Pflug, in 1958, following a referendum in which local voters decisively rejected the original expressway route. In his letter, he stated that interstate highways should be built "not on the basis of popular vote or referenda, but on traffic and engineering standards by qualified persons with consideration for the needs of the traveling public, the effect the location might have on existing businesses and residents, and by the accessibility of the facility to those who, in their daily lives, require its use."[47]

Here Dial was making a classic argument for the kind of centralized, closed decision-making process typically used to make what political scientists call "developmental policy."[48] These are policies, like road projects, that support an area's growth. The question that urban scholars have posed is why developmental policies are typically formulated in this way. Is it, as Dial argued, because the issues are so complex that only "qualified persons" can decide them? Or is it because centralized, closed decision-making processes allow elite interests to prevail? This is a key question in understanding the politics of urban growth. As shown, the answer is mixed in Dial and Andersen's case: closed decision-making benefited them, but their interests largely coincided with Orlando's. In the land-purchase story that follows, we see a more extreme example of closed decision-making, raising questions about who benefits from secrecy.

THREE Secrecy

I t was November 27, 1963, and Walt Disney was presiding at a roundtable discussion in the conference room of the company headquarters in Burbank, soon after the project team returned from their Florida flyover. Seated around the long conference table, in addition to Walt and his brother Roy, the company's financial genius, were the other members of the team—vice presidents Donn Tatum, Mel Melton, Card Walker, and Dick Morrow, and general counsel Robert Foster. Within the company, only this select group knew about the stealth project, also known as "Project Winter."

They were listening to a presentation that would have historic consequences for Orlando, putting in motion the land search that would bring Disney World to central Florida. The presenter was Harrison ("Buzz") Price, head of Economics Research Associates, site consultant for the Disney firm.[1] Price had previously worked at Stanford Research Institute, the real estate consultant for Disneyland, before Walt urged him to start his own business. With Price at the meeting was Bill Lund, a real estate consultant and financial analyst for ERA, who would later marry Walt's adopted daughter, Sharon. As part of Project Winter, Price was proposing a "Central Florida Study" that would add some analysis to the gut reaction formed on the flyover.

While Walt liked to see things, to judge firsthand, his brother Roy, who always managed to find money for his brother's projects, believed more in analysis. Said Jack Lindquist, who became vice president of Disney World, "Roy had a different way [than Walt] of how he judged things to make a decision," adding, "You had to prove to

Roy what the rationale was for something to be done that way."[2]
Much discussion had followed the Buzz Price presentation, during
which Walt and Roy mostly just asked questions. In the end, a decision was made that would culminate in their Orlando land purchase.
Lund would go to Florida and comparatively study Orlando and
Ocala. His assignment was to assess their general economic environment; research topographical, highway, and climate data; and inquire
about the availability of property, its location, size, general prices,
and terms—all in sixty days.[3]

Lund was to proceed in secrecy, concealing the names of both ERA
and the client. Such covert activity was common for Lund. For example, two months earlier he had used false identification at a "people-
mover" conference in Tampa, lest someone figure out that his association with Disney meant a new theme park was in the works. To
conceal Lund's Orlando–Ocala mission, Dick Morrow contacted the
company's New York counsel, William Donovan, of the firm Donovan,
Leisure, Newton, and Irvine at One Wall Street. He was the same William ("Wild Bill") Donovan who, during World War II, had directed
the Office of Strategic Services (OSS), forerunner of the CIA. An expert
in clandestine operations, Donovan procured a business card, letter-
head stationery, and phone number for Lund from the law firm of
Burke & Burke, located one floor beneath Donovan and Leisure at
One Wall Street.

Such secrecy is common in economic-development marriages.
Like the closed decision-making discussed in the last chapter, it had
a dual quality. On one hand, secrecy was clearly necessary to assemble the company's 27,500-acre parcel. As a consequence, private land
brokers did the sales work that helped bring Disney to Orlando. Because of their fiduciary responsibility to their client, real estate sales-
people could be trusted to be more discrete than elected officials. On
the other hand, secrecy provided cover for questionable behavior, as
shown below. Secrecy enabled the Disney Co. to display their sometimes arrogant behavior because they could easily take advantage of
the land brokers who worked with them to assemble their vast
property.

Looking back, the Disney Co. had moved cautiously in getting to
this stage. Their motivation for a second theme park was financial;
they wanted to diversify their business away from motion pictures.

As Walt told Dick Nunis, the future president of Disney World, he wanted to escape "the damn fickle motion picture industry." It was the same motivation that drove Martin Andersen and Billy Dial to seek new industry for Orlando: just as Orlando leaders wanted to counter the economic effects of crop freezes and defense-spending cutbacks, Walt wanted to counter the unpredictability of the movie business.[4] Unlike Disney Co. movies, Disneyland reliably made money. The business question was how to access the East Coast tourist market, since only two percent of Disneyland's visitors came from the East. So many local boosters wanted a Disneyland for their city; it seemed to make sense—but where?

They used the New York World's Fair of 1964–65 to test the East Coast market, following the suggestion of Robert Moses, president of the Fair and a friend and admirer of Walt's. Moses had visited Disneyland and saw a mock-up of the moving and talking Abe Lincoln, created for the Hall of Presidents. Disney people called it "audio-animatronics"—making things move and talk at the same time—and Moses wanted it for the Fair. With his encouragement, Disney approached Walt's birth state, Illinois, as well as Ford Motor and General Electric, proposing to build audio-animatronic displays for their Fair exhibits. Later, Pepsi-Cola asked Disney to build their "It's a Small World" attraction. The response was overwhelming—Disney was the hit of the Fair, attracting more than ninety percent of the attendees to their shows.[5] They clearly had East Coast appeal.

This experience also led Walt to hire away General William E. (Joe) Potter, the Fair's executive vice president. Potter officially joined the company in September 1965, though he became an informal adviser to Walt months earlier. Potter was an MIT engineering graduate, an Army Corps of Engineers road-builder, and the former governor of the Panama Canal Zone. In hiring Potter, Walt took away Moses's right-hand man, yet the famed power broker was more flattered than angry. Walt feared that hiring Potter would signal the company's expansion plans and asked Moses to delay his announcement about the move. Moses, always publicity conscious, agreed and then boldly proclaimed, two days later, that Potter was leaving the Fair for a job with Disney.[6]

Demonstrating their penchant for painstaking analysis, the Disney organization had commissioned dozens of studies of potential expansion sites. These began in 1958, only three years after Disneyland opened. They ranged from a broad report on "The Market for an Eastern Disneyland" in 1959, to a focused study of "Recreation Potentials in Florida" in 1961, to a site analysis of "Development Opportunities in Aspen, Colorado" in 1962, to a design-stage "Planning Parameters for Disney Circarama in Niagara Falls" in 1963. Sometimes the plans led to exploratory conversations about purchasing land. In 1959, for example, Walt commissioned Buzz Price to explore the potential for a City of Tomorrow in Palm Beach, but that plan was shelved for lack of suitable land. In most cases, the studies just piled up without Walt or Roy making a final decision. Finally, in October 1963, company executive Jack Sayers sent Walt a memo urging closure on thirteen outstanding projects.[7] The locations included St. Louis, Niagara Falls, and New Orleans, as well as multiple sites in New Jersey, Florida, California, and Colorado.

After buying their Gulfstream plane in the early 1960s, Walt could fly about and observe the possibilities firsthand, sometimes taking the plane's controls himself. For example, he took Donn Tatum, Card Walker, Buzz Price, and Jack Sayers with him on the November 1963 trip. They flew first to St. Louis, where the incident with Gussie Busch occurred; from there to Niagara Falls, which felt too cold; then to the Baltimore-Washington area, which continued to captivate Card Walker; and finally to the Sunshine State, arriving in Orlando on Thursday, November 21. On a later trip, Potter was intrigued that they visited new towns like Columbia, Maryland, and Reston, Virginia, as well as shopping centers in New York, Pennsylvania, and Texas. These visits indicated Walt's urban planning interest. In Potter's words, Walt was interested "in what attracted people, held their attention, and moved them in and out."[8]

Orlando proved an easier real estate proposition. Following the November 27, 1963, meeting at Disney headquarters, Bill Lund flew to Florida, arriving in Tampa on December 9. From there the thirty-three-year-old Lund rented a car and drove to Orlando, checking into the Robert Meyer Hotel. He visited two banks, First National and Florida National Bank, to inquire about reliable real estate brokers and was given two names, Florida Ranch Lands and Brass & Haynie.[9] Calling on FRL, he was introduced to salesman David Nusbickel, to whom he presented the Burke & Burke identification supplied by William Donovan. He told Nusbickel in strictest confidence that he represented a large investment trust and that he was looking for large tracts of land near the crossing of I-4 and Florida's Turnpike.

As Nusbickel recalled, the two men tried to feel one another out at this first meeting. The FRL salesman was impressed that Lund, like he, was a Stanford graduate and that he knew a lot about real estate. The Stanford Research Institute, where Lund said he had worked, also rang a bell with Nusbickel. He gave Lund a *Sentinel* article based on Nusbickel's own research, showing how Orlando's road network had influenced its growth and predicting the area's future path of development. For their meeting Nusbickel had his secretary prepare a brochure on a 12,440-acre property owned by Bill and Jack Demetree and their partner Bill Jenkins, a parcel also known as the Expressway Tract since it paralleled I-4. Besides this parcel, they discussed property known as the Bay Lake Tract, owned by ten investors, and land east of the Demetree Tract owned by Wilson and Carroll Hamrick. These three tracts were contiguous, lying southwest of Orlando in unincorporated Orange County.

Important for later events, Nusbickel says he told Lund at the time that FRL expected a ten percent commission on the sale of any land they showed. After Lund left his office, Nusbickel called FRL's law firm and asked them to check out the Burke & Burke firm. They reported back that it was a reputable firm, though they did not check on Lund in the Martindale-Hubbell national listing of attorneys, which would have exposed his cover.

On the following day Lund met with a Mr. McElwee at Brass & Haynie, who showed him properties to the north and east of Orlando. That afternoon Nusbickel and another FRL salesman, Jim Morgan, took Lund to the Demetree and Bay Lake tracts, driving close to Bay Lake on a little clay road, since they knew Lund was interested in water features. They explained the topography of the area—the sloughs, fields, flatwoods, and citrus lands. Consistent with FRL's philosophy of selling the town to sell the area, they also took a general tour of the Orlando area to familiarize Lund with its geography and economic environment. Dinner with Nusbickel and his wife in their home capped the day.

Since Lund was supposed to investigate Ocala as well, he went there on the third day and spent several hours making phone calls to inquire about the availability of large tracts of land. Upon returning to Orlando, he lunched with Nusbickel and his boss, FRL president Nelson Boice, at the University Club. Preserving his cover, Lund joked with the two men about staying in Orlando instead of returning north for Christmas. He then returned to California, where his mail and calls were forwarded from Burke & Burke in New York. On January 13, Nusbickel wrote to him at Burke & Burke, advising him that the Demetree tract was coming off contract. On January 21, Lund wrote back on Burke & Burke stationery and expressed his continuing interest in the property. "I am pleased to see that the Expressway Tract may be available again. As soon as any definite commitment or decision can be made, I will be in contact with you either by mail or telephone," he stated. Responding to a call from Nusbickel, Lund wrote to FRL for the last time on March 24, thereafter failing to respond to their repeated calls and letters.[10]

By January 1964, the Disney Co. was cautiously moving ahead on Project Winter. A decisive meeting occurred January 16, in the big conference room at the Burbank studios, with Walt and Roy Disney and their top executives all present. On the walls were 30 × 40-inch visuals created from charts that Lund had picked up in Orlando. One was a map, prepared by Dave Nusbickel and reproduced in the *Sentinel*, showing the topography of the area and the anticipated direction of future growth. It was the map that Nusbickel had given Lund at their first meeting. Another map showed the convergence of major highways in Orlando. That map, and a third one indicating drive times between Orlando and major Florida cities, imparted a visual message that Orlando was blessed with good road linkages. In addition, Lund distributed a map that he reproduced without covering the FRL designation.

Supported by these visuals, Lund made the case for an Orlando location, his report confirming Walt's "that's it" reaction on the Orlando flyover. The area had the state's best tourist bypass traffic, he said. In 1961, ERA had given that designation to Ocala, but that was before Florida's Turnpike and I-4 made Orlando a road transportation hub. The area would soon have a good commercial airport, he reported, explaining that negotiations were under way to convert McCoy Air Force Base to full civilian use. Likewise, economic and population factors favored Orlando. It was larger and faster growing than Ocala and had a more diverse employment base, Lund conveyed. Not least, it had several large properties available—land like the Bay Lake Tract that was relatively cheap with interesting water features and convenient access. The area's only drawback was its heavy summer rainfall, but the rain fell in short bursts and "did not disrupt business to any significant extent," Lund declared.[11]

Following much discussion, the Project Winter team accepted ERA's recommendation. Bob Foster, general counsel for Disney, was dispatched to Florida to acquire options on 7,000–12,000 acres of land. After five years of site visits and consultant reports, they were a giant step closer to choosing Orlando officially. Of course, Walt had already made a gut decision in favor of Orlando, but that decision had to be confirmed by the company's highly involved process of study and investigation. It was true, too, that Foster was authorized only to purchase options, which guarantee a price for a period of time without binding the buyer to carry through with the purchase, so the commitment to Florida was still revocable. But once they started, Disney would not turn back.

Because of the secrecy that shrouded Disney's land search, local boosters were not involved directly in courting Disney. For the most part, the company chose Orlando, not the reverse. The only direct sales work was FRL's. Dial's movers and shakers were involved indirectly, however, since their road projects helped attract the Disney Co. to the area. In all, it was private sector–led economic development— private on the part of Disney, the FRL land brokers, and the movers and shakers who championed local roadbuilding. The only public involvement was the public dollars used to fund the road projects.

The Disney Co. needed secrecy even more now. They were assembling land, and the slightest leak that a large company like Disney was acquiring property would quickly escalate land prices. Accordingly, they went back to their spymaster in New York, William Donovan, who put them in touch with an oss buddy of his, Paul Helliwell, a Miami lawyer who had reportedly laundered money for the Bay of Pigs invasion and other covert CIA operations in Latin America.[12] Besides being a brilliant attorney, Helliwell could keep a secret. Bob Foster met him in Miami on April 20, 1964, and explained their mission: to acquire land for an East Coast Disneyland somewhere between Palm Beach and Daytona, but not on the ocean. They needed roughly 7,000–12,000 acres, and it all had to be kept confidential. Helliwell, knowing he had limited real estate expertise, asked to involve Roy Hawkins, an experienced Miami real estate hand. Hawkins, 63, had managed properties for the Phipps family for a number of years, developing much of Miami's Biscayne Boulevard for the Phippses before going into business for himself. Foster agreed to bring in Hawkins, provided they did not disclose the client's name or the intended use of the property. Because Foster's name had appeared in a Disney annual report, he decided to adopt a pseudonym, combining his first and middle names to become "Bob Price."

Helliwell invited Hawkins to his office and introduced him to "Mr. Price." "This is my client," said Helliwell. "He represents a substantial company and that is it." Hawkins, who had recently put together a 76,000-acre deal for Aerojet in south Florida, was unfazed. "Listen," he said, "this is the rub of the green and I work this way all the time. If I accomplish something, fine. If not, I have enough money to take care of my expenses."[13] Foster, who knew Florida in a limited way from taking Navy frogman training in Stuart, proceeded to follow Hawkins all across the state, surveying large properties. Their search ranged afar even though the ERA's Lund had recommended at the important January 16 meeting that they focus on the area southwest of Orlando. Hawkins and "Price" (Foster) were particularly interested in the Tomoka Ranch near Daytona Beach, the Tosohatchee property on the St. Johns River east of Orlando, and the Deltona property north of Orlando on Lake Monroe. Keeping Hawkins in the dark became a problem, though. He was "splashing around looking at all kinds of property," said Helliwell, who finally got permission from Foster to reveal the client's identity to Hawkins.[14]

With the search re-centered on Orlando, Foster and Hawkins secured an option on the Demetree property. The six-month option, later extended another six months, cost $25,000 and guaranteed a discounted price of $145 per acre. The Demetrees, who bought the property in 1960 as an investment, had a $90,000 payment coming due and were anxious to sell.[15] They could not interest anyone in the land because Tufts University in Massachusetts owned the mineral rights. At one time, Tufts owned a 25,000-acre spread in central Florida. In the 1940s, the university had sold the surface land without mineral rights to Irlo Bronson, a state senator and the patriarch of a large ranch-owning family in Osceola County south of Orlando. Bronson sold 12,440 acres of the land, in 1960, to cousins Bill and Jack Demetree and their partner Bill Jenkins, who were builders and veteran land speculators. "Nobody wanted to buy the land when [Tufts] could come in and tear down houses to get to the minerals," said Jack Demetree. "I had truthfully given up any chance of ever talking to that bunch of Yankees up there."[16]

Enter Helliwell. The veteran dealmaker took "Price" (Foster) and Bill and Jack Demetree to Boston to negotiate with a committee of Tufts trustees. After cordially receiving them, one of the three trustees asked, "Why should we relinquish anything? It's not costing us anything." It was true, Tufts did not even pay taxes on the land. Then Helliwell left the room with the trustees, leaving the Demetrees behind. Possibly, this was to tell the trustees what the cousins did not know: that an East Coast Disneyland hung in the balance. When Helliwell returned with the trustees, he said, referring to one of them, "Well, I have known this man for a long time, and they have agreed to sell."[17] The Tufts trustees accepted a mere $15,000 for the mineral rights.[18]

The other problem was the "outs"—the many small parcels within the perimeter of the former Tufts property that were separately owned. In 1912, the property had been subdivided by the Munger Land Co. and sold through catalogues. It was a classic old-Florida story: scrubland without roads or other improvements, much of it underwater and alligator-infested, sold by mail. Jack Demetree was supposed to work on buying the outs but was not making much progress. So Hawkins, who knew Boice as a young man in Miami, asked Helliwell for permission to recruit the services of Boice's firm, Florida Ranch Lands (FRL). The outs were critical for Hawkins. "I knew if I didn't get the outs, I would have no deal."[19] It was one of many chips that had to fall for Orlando—the debacle in St. Louis, the Orlando flyover, the confirming Project Winter report, the land search that ranged afar before refocusing on Orlando, getting the mineral rights. And now the outs.

Boice, a Yale graduate from an old Miami family, received a call from Hawkins in early July 1964. Hawkins asked to come see him, leading to a meeting that figured into a lawsuit that Boice would file later. Hawkins brought Foster with him to the meeting, introducing him as "Bob Price." "Nelson," he said, "I'm so glad to see you, and I'm sorry about your father's death. I have a client I'm doing some work for, and I have need of someone in the greater Orlando area, so I immediately thought of you. Can you help us out?"[20] Boice said that he would. Then, Hawkins explained that his client already had an option on the Demetree property but needed help getting the outs. It seemed strange at the time, Boice recalled in an interview, that Hawkins appeared to have FRL brochures under his arm. FRL brochures were easy to recognize by a yellow band on the bottom. He later said that the brochures should have tipped him off that FRL's services had been used in optioning the Demetree property. But at the time Boice had no reason to connect Bill Lund to either Hawkins or his client. Besides, Hawkins was a well-respected real estate broker who had known his father, and he was offering business to FRL.

After they agreed to do business, Boice took Hawkins and "Price" (Foster) to the University Club for lunch. Boice recalled that he was suspicious about "Price" from the beginning. At one point in their conversation, he remarked that "Price" talked like an attorney. Was he? Boice asked. "Price" stammered, which Boice thought confirmed his suspicion; he knew "something was up," as he said in an interview, but did not know what.[21]

Hawkins and Boice agreed to split the brokerage commissions 50–50, with Hawkins representing the buyer and Boice and FRL, the seller. Hawkins and his client would decide on the commission amounts, though the customary figure was ten percent. In real estate, there are two types of property listings: exclusive listings that only one broker can show, and open listings that anyone can show. The Demetree property, for example, had an open listing when it was optioned on June 23. Normally the seller paid the commission and sales prices included brokerage fees, though that was negotiable. Real estate brokers use the language of "net" and "gross" prices, the net price being the price after paying the brokerage fee. Thus Jack Demetree first offered his land at a gross price of $165 per acre (meaning he paid the brokerage fee), then agreed to sell at $145 "net to him." The total sales price was $1,804,200, and the commission was paid by the buyer and split between broker Jack Davin for Demetree, and Hawkins for the anonymous buyer.[22]

Besides getting the Demetree outs, Hawkins asked Boice to pur-
chase options on the 1,300-acre Bay Lake Tract and the 2,700-acre
Hamrick Tract. They did, splitting the commission with Hawkins.
With these parcels, they controlled most of the perimeter of Bay Lake.
Next Hawkins negotiated with Irlo Bronson, who was unaware that
Disney was the buyer, for the remaining 9,000 acres that the cattle-
man and state senator had bought from Tufts in the 1940s.

Over the following eighteen months, Chuck Bosserman, Dave Nusbickel, and Jim Morgan at FRL worked on getting the remaining outs.
First they searched Orange County land records to identify the owners
of the many parcels. This was no small feat for land that had been
purchased from a catalog, or won in a poker game, or passed on to
heirs. They then started calling the landowners systematically, beginning each day at 6 p.m. eastern time and moving through the time
zones from east to west. They swore their secretaries to secrecy and
kept the materials for this project, which they dubbed "Wet Over-
shoe," locked in one room of their office.[23] The average price for the
outs was $350 per acre, compared with $200 per acre for the larger
parcels. Keeping track of FRL's and Hawkins' work, the Project Winter
team took over the conference room at Disney's Burbank studios,
plotting each day's acquisitions on a large map. Walt visited the room
daily.[24]

A special phone relay system was another way in which the Disney
Co. went to great lengths to ensure secrecy. Tom DeWolf, a law partner of Helliwell's in Miami, explained in an interview that Donovan's
law firm in New York set up this system. "If we wanted to talk to
anybody at Disney, we could not call Disney. Instead we had to call
this special number in New York, and they would call Disney and
then connect us," said DeWolf. "The other rule was that nobody at
Disney could talk to anybody in Orlando, period." Helliwell's firm was
selected, in part, because of their background in undercover work,
said DeWolf. Helliwell was a former oss officer, and DeWolf had
worked for the Justice Department in Washington during the Eisenhower administration.[25]

Still, so much real estate activity was bound to attract attention. Helliwell had set up five dummy corporations to purchase the
options—Bay Lake Properties, AyeFour Corporation, Reedy Creek

Ranch, Tomahawk Properties, and Latin American Development and Management Corporation. Either Helliwell or an FRL salesman was listed as the buyer's trustee on land documents. By the summer of 1965, speculation about the mystery land buyer was rampant in Orlando. It was rumored to be McDonald Aircraft, Hercules Powder, Ford Motor, Hughes Tool, and even Walt Disney Co., among other large corporations. The attention focused on manufacturing firms because of Bay Lake; people thought that a big industry wanted the lake for its coolant capacity.

One local TV station issued a news bulletin stating that it had received a telegram from Detroit identifying the Ford Motor Co. as the mystery buyer. The bulletin noted that further details would follow on the 11 p.m. news. The next day, the station profusely apologized after admitting they were the victim of a hoax: a second telegram had arrived saying that Ford wanted the land to grow hay for the auto manufacturer's popular Mustang model. This story and other rumors were vetted through Charley Wadsworth's *Hush Puppies* column on the *Sentinel*'s front page. When Foster came to Orlando, he scrupulously avoided Wadsworth. Besides using his pseudonym, he would list Kansas City as his return destination, and he sometimes planted false rumors to throw Wadsworth and others off the trail. He would later learn that one investigator had called Disney headquarters in Burbank asking for Bob Price, unsuccessfully. The same investigator reached a real Bob Price at General Dynamics in California but, after talking with him, realized it was the wrong person.[26]

Boice and his staff eventually identified their client. It happened after Hawkins asked them to take several client representatives on a boat tour of Bay Lake. Jim Morgan, who led the tour, was intrigued by a man in the party whom the others called "Skipper." He noticed the monogram "J. F." on the man's shirt and thought he had seen him in a magazine photo. When the salesman returned home, he rummaged through some old *National Geographic* magazines and found a picture of the man. The caption identified him as Adm. Joe Fowler, chief engineer for Walt Disney Productions.

According to Boice, "we knew, and they knew we knew, but we didn't talk about it."[27] He had a fiduciary responsibility to his client, after all. Divulging his client's identity might also kill the land deal, costing Boice his brokerage commission. A leak did occur within the

Disney organization, though. At one point, a California man came to FRL saying he had just flown from Tampa to Orlando on a private plane and had noticed the nice citrus groves along the way. He wanted to buy some citrus land—"about here," he said, pointing on a map to a location near the Disney site. "I'm sorry, I can't help you," Boice told the man. A recent freeze had destroyed most of the area's citrus, so Boice knew the story was phony. Afterwards, he reported the incident to Hawkins, prompting Disney officials to discover the source of the leak within the company.

By June 1965, the Project Winter group had bought or optioned 27,258 acres, far exceeding their original goal. Several factors propelled them on. Once into the process, they decided to enclose Bay Lake and gain control of road intersections touching the property. They also wanted enough land to buffer their development from adjacent land uses. At one point, Roy balked at buying another 5,000 acres for $200 per acre. "Why do we need more?" Roy asked, "we already have 12,000 acres." Walt tactfully responded: "Yes, but wouldn't you love to own another 5,000 acres around Disneyland now?"[28] The California theme park, comparatively small at 230 acres, was surrounded by a neon jungle of souvenir shops and fast-food joints. According to Foster, there was also a political explanation for buying so much land. Walt told him they should always deal with two jurisdictions at once. That was why they wanted land in both Orange and Osceola counties; it gave them more bargaining power. They would use Osceola, said Foster, as their alternate site.[29]

Some members of the Project Winter team disagreed on the Orlando-area site, though. Foster himself favored the Tomoka Ranch near Daytona Beach. That was until Walt exploded at a meeting, saying, "Bob, what the hell are you doing way up there."[30] As with Disneyland in Anaheim, Walt wanted the ability to expand in 360 degrees while not competing with the ocean for attention. And Card Walker remained uncommitted to Florida as late as June 1965. Hawkins attended a June meeting at Disney headquarters where Walker was promoting a Washington-Baltimore site. At Foster's urging, Hawkins stood up and gave an impromptu "chamber of commerce speech" for Florida, adding that they could always sell their land there and make a profit if they changed their minds.[31]

The work of getting the outs snagged when the owner of a thirty-seven-acre property, strategically located on Bay Lake, refused to sell. Boice turned to Billy Dial, taking Hawkins and "Price" (Foster) to meet with the local power broker. They told him that they represented a big industry that would mean a lot of jobs for Orlando. They absolutely needed the property, or the project would go elsewhere, they said. As Dial recalled of the meeting, "They wanted me to wave the flag and get him to sell." After listening to their predicament he said, "Let's go talk to Martin Andersen." Hawkins responded incredulously, "Isn't he the guy who runs the paper? He's the last guy we want to talk to." Dial said not to worry, "Andy can keep a secret."[32]

Andersen was normally cautious about supporting land deals, but he was impressed with Hawkins and "Price" (Foster) and sensed that their project was bona fide. When the two men offered to reveal their client to Dial and Andersen, the Orlando leaders said no—or claimed to. They feared being blamed if the secret got out and the project was killed, said Dial. After hearing about the holdout landowner, a man named Willie Goldstein, Andersen said they should get Martin Segal to help. Segal was a local lawyer and dealmaker who might know Goldstein, Andersen reasoned. "Segal owes me one," he added.

Andersen invited Segal to his office and, with Dial present, explained the problem. "Billy says this is something that will revolutionize Florida, but it won't happen unless they get that property," said Andersen. He said Segal should help as a "civic endeavor" and not try to make a profit from any real estate information he acquired. Segal did not know Goldstein, but he figured that Sam Behr, a local shoe-store owner with Alabama roots, probably did. Indeed, Behr knew Goldstein but advised Segal that the landowner was unlikely to sell his "little piece of heaven." He has plenty of money and "loves his house and loves his groves," said Behr.[33] As described by Mrs. Goldstein, the property was indeed heavenly. It had a one-hundred-year-old log cabin; the lake produced ten–twelve-pound bass; the citrus was sweet; and the wildlife was abundant, including two flocks of turkeys, as well as deer, bobcat, and "the biggest rattlesnakes you ever saw." It was "just like the Lord made it," she said.[34] In Segal's mind, though, everyone "has something that moves him," and he learned from Behr that, for Goldstein, University of Alabama football was that special something. "He thought (legendary Alabama football coach) Bear Bryant hung the moon," said Segal.

So a plot was hatched, only here the stories diverge. Segal recommended to Andersen that he use someone from the newspaper's sports department to get Bryant to intercede with Goldstein. He assumed this happened because, a few days later, Andersen called and said "the dirty deed is done."[35] Andersen and Dial told the story differently, saying that Segal visited Goldstein and presented himself as Bryant's close personal friend to get him to sell.[36] According to Mrs. Goldstein, neither story is true. "We kept saying no, no, no. But finally we sold because they offered so much money, and it meant so much to Orlando." Having paid $45,000 for the land in 1954, and having earned $40,000 from a bumper citrus crop in 1958 alone, they agreed to sell for $194,000. The Goldsteins then retired to the rural area of Maggie Valley, North Carolina.

As rumors of the land sales flew, many of them fueled by Charley Wadsworth's reporting in the *Sentinel,* the paper took a lofty stance in a May 28, 1965, editorial. The quest for secrecy was understandable, said the paper, and the community should be patient and wait for a scheduled December announcement. Based on information from FRL, an article in the same issue gave a detailed breakdown of the land purchases. In all, there were 47 transactions totaling 27,258 acres at a cost of $5,018,779. The land deals included 17 major transactions at an average price of $200 per acre, and 30 minor transactions involving parcels filling only 1,000 acres that averaged $350 per acre. Boice was quoted saying that the public should be patient because much was at stake. "The land buyer would not hesitate to pull out and leave a $5-million real estate investment," he warned.[37]

Finally the story broke in mid-October 1965. Disney PR people, probably unaware of Project Winter, invited the *Sentinel* to join a press junket to Disneyland. The trip involved flying to California on the Disney plane, touring Disneyland, and then interviewing Walt. Martin Andersen decided to send Emily Bavar, editor of *Florida Magazine,* the paper's Sunday magazine. After touring the park, the reporters from six newspapers were ushered into Walt's plush office at the Burbank studio. When it was Bavar's turn to ask a question, she asked, almost on a lark, "Mr. Disney, are you buying all that land in Orlando?"[38] Taken aback, he sputtered a nondenial denial and offered

climate and population reasons why Florida would be inappropri-
ate—but then explained how those factors could be overcome.

Thinking Walt protested too much, Bavar wired a story from Disneyland opining that Disney was the one. The October 16 story was
treated like other speculation and buried on page 23. When she returned to Orlando, she met right away with Andersen and elaborated
on her conversation with Walt and her reasons for thinking it was
him. Finally, the publisher nodded and said, "It's got to be Disney."
A page-one story headlined "Girl Reporter Convinced by Walt Disney"
followed on Thursday, October 20. (Bavar, then 45, says Andersen
was "spoofing her" with the headline.) In an unusual postscript, the
editors apologized for "underplaying" her original story.

Bob Foster and Joe Potter had flown to Orlando that weekend,
checking into a hotel under assumed names before taking a helicopter
tour of the property. On Sunday they awoke to the *Sentinel* headline,
"We Say It's Disney." Potter hurriedly called Card Walker, using a pay
phone to ensure secrecy, and, after discussions with Project Winter
team members, Walt made the decision to break secrecy. They then
had to scramble. Foster and Potter flew to Miami to meet with Florida
Governor Haydon Burns, who was preparing to address the Florida
League of Municipalities the next day. They wisely let the governor
make the announcement himself. To wild applause, he told his audience of local officials the next morning that Disney was poised to
build "the greatest attraction yet known in the history of Florida."[39]
The *Evening Star* responded with a banner headline, "It's Official: This
is Disneyland."[40]

Improbably, the Project Winter team had maintained secrecy for
eighteen months—from Hawkins' purchase of the Demetree option
in June 1964 until Governor Burns's announcement on October 25,
1965. It was a huge feat—assembling a forty-three-square mile parcel,
an area twice the size of Manhattan and about the same size as San
Francisco. They stayed on schedule, too, since the story broke one
month ahead of their scheduled announcement. The downside was
that 300 acres remained unpurchased, and asking prices shot to
$1,000 per acre. Years later, they still could not come to terms on
four parcels totaling 30 acres. Their secret out, the Disney company
scheduled an Orlando press conference for November 15.

There has been much discussion in Orlando about whether Dial and Andersen, in fact, knew the mystery land buyer's identity. Charley Wadsworth, who sleuthed the story in his *Hush Puppies* column, thought Andersen probably knew. "He kept coming by my desk and asking how I was coming on the story," said Wadsworth.[41] Another theory is that the publisher disingenuously used Emily Bavar to break the story, though Bavar herself rejected this speculation. She thought that the Disney Co.'s cover was exposed by mistakenly inviting a *Sentinel* reporter to Disneyland. Disney executive Joe Potter remarked in a taped interview for the tenth anniversary of Disney World that both men knew, though he did not say when or how they knew. Dial said that he learned only three weeks before the announcement. "No one told, but I was convinced by things that came through the bank."[42] He shared this information with Andersen, who claimed to have been dubious that it was Disney. "He's just too big," the publisher thought. "He wouldn't be checking out Orlando, Florida."[43]

On the day before the November 15 announcement, Walt and Roy Disney, along with the Project Winter team members and their wives, were invited to the governor's mansion in Tallahassee for a big dinner and reception. There, they posed for obligatory pictures with the governor, members of his cabinet, and other political dignitaries. The next day they flew to Orlando and toured the property before proceeding by motorcade to their 2 p.m. press conference, held in the Egyptian Room of Orlando's Cherry Plaza Hotel. Governor Burns was in charge of invitations, and the standing room only crowd was made up of 400–500 leading citizens of the city and state.

Present at the press conference but not recognized from the podium were Nelson Boice, Chuck Bosserman, Jim Morgan, and David Nusbickel, the FRL land brokers who had labored for eighteen months to assemble the land. Their role in this affair involved more than getting the outs—though they did not realize it then. They had known for a year that Disney was their client, and they had a good working relationship with Hawkins and "Price" (Foster). But they did not connect either of them with the mysterious Bill Lund. They did not realize that their sales work and the information that they provided to Lund had aided him in selling the Project Winter team on coming to Orlando. Nor did they realize that Disney's purchase of the Demetree option, using Hawkins as their land broker, had come from their sales work. That brokerage fee had gone to Hawkins. Instead, they would later argue, it should have gone at least partly to them.

The November 15 press conference itself was a slight letdown. "Whereas the press was expecting more fantasy," one observer wrote, "[Walt] Disney shocked them into the reality of what was possible— that which is financially feasible."[44] After introducing his brother Roy as the company's financial manager, Walt spoke in vague terms about building something bigger and better than Disneyland that would cost $100 million and employ 4,000 people. He refused to be specific, saying they were still in the planning stage. "All this takes time," he said. Their timetable depended on "how fast the state will work with us."[45]

Though a model city theme pervaded the advance publicity, Walt talked only very generally about this idea. "I would like to be part of building a model city, a City of Tomorrow, you might say, because I don't believe in going out to this blue-sky stuff that some architects do. I believe that people still want to live like human beings." He mentioned "putting people back as pedestrians" and even building a "school of tomorrow."[46] The reporters pressed but got no more from him about the City of Tomorrow. Whatever they built, it would be self-contained—that was the implicit message. They had acquired enough land to control the periphery of the park. A greenbelt would entirely surround it, said Walt. Speculators who were buying land at inflated prices outside the property would be disappointed, warned the *Sentinel*.[47]

Following the Disney announcement, eighteen officials from four central Florida counties that would be impacted by the theme park flew to Anaheim. The trip would have unanticipated consequences. Walt had invited the delegation to view firsthand the impact of Disneyland, and Chuck Bosserman, one of the FRL salesmen, had accompanied them on the trip. By coincidence, the pilot of the plane, Sim Speer, was an avid real estate investor who knew Bosserman. He had been flying the Los Angeles to Florida route for several years and had invested in Anaheim-area real estate. Speer invited several members of the Orange County delegation to sit in the front row, behind the cockpit, so he could talk with them and show them research reports he had collected on Anaheim. One of those reports was prepared by

Economic Research Associates under the direction of William S. Lund, listed as a company vice president. The name rang a bell with Bosserman, who wondered if he was the same Bill Lund who had visited FRL two years ago. He told the delegation that he might know the ERA executive and that his expertise might be helpful to them. He would contact the man when they arrived in L.A., Bosserman said.

He arranged the meeting, and the delegation met with Lund at ERA's offices on their first day in California. Bosserman and Lund recognized each other right away but did not discuss their prior relationship until the meeting ended. When they talked, Lund said to give his regards to Dave Nusbickel and that he was sorry about not getting back to him. "He said he thought we probably knew the reasons why," said Bosserman. He also told Bosserman that he had helped FRL by recommending them to the Disney Co. Surprised, Bosserman said he had always given that credit to Roy Hawkins because of his relationship with Nelson Boice's family.

It was the first indication of Lund's link to Hawkins and Disney. Before Lund and Bosserman's chance encounter, the FRL group had often talked about what happened to Lund. Boice could not believe that they had misjudged him. After hearing Bosserman's story, he remembered the three brochures that Hawkins had under his arm when he first came to FRL's office. Then the whole story dawned on him— he realized that they had been circumvented on the Demetree property and denied their commission. When they presented a property to someone, that client was obligated to work through them. Instead, Disney had gone around FRL, approaching the seller through Hawkins. At least that was Boice's view of the matter.

So Boice called Hawkins and said he wanted to come see Helliwell and him in Miami to discuss commissions on the Demetree, Bay Lake, and Hamrick properties. Boice took his local attorney with him and they met in Helliwell's office. "We went in and everyone was smiles. We said good morning and what a lovely day it was, and then Paul (Helliwell) says 'Gentlemen, I have been directed not to talk with you.' We said, 'Paul, we just want to discuss the subject and clear something up.' Paul says, 'Gentlemen, I'm very sorry, but I cannot talk with you.' So it was just a complete stonewall. We chatted about the weather for a few minutes and then we left."[48] Boice said he was never so insulted—"not to even be heard." His response was to hire the best trial lawyer he could find, Harris Dittmar in Jacksonville.

FRL sued both Walt Disney Productions and ERA. They alleged that FRL was denied their 10 percent commission on the Demetree property, as well as their full 10 percent commission on the Bay Lake and Hamrick properties. At issue legally was whether FRL was the "procuring cause" of Disney's purchase of the three properties. FRL was due the full commission on the Demetree property, they thought, since they showed the property to Lund, who was acting as the Disney Co.'s agent. Instead, the commission had been split between Roy Hawkins and Jack Davin. On the Bay Lake and Hamrick properties, they had accepted a co-brokerage with Hawkins based on misinformation, not knowing Lund's connection to Disney. Since FRL showed the property to Lund before Hawkins was in the picture, they wanted their full commission.

In his deposition for the lawsuit, Lund said he would have ended their relationship had he known FRL expected a commission. Moreover, he said that he was unaware that Disney had decided to move ahead until only a few days before the announcement. Bosserman maintained that Lund had said during their conversation at ERA that he had written to the Disney Co. recommending that they hire FRL in return for their services to him. If true, that would shift the responsibility for circumventing FRL to Disney. Lund could not recall making this statement, however. His correspondence with the Disney Co. regarding FRL was lost, he said, when he moved his office two years earlier.[49]

FRL sued for $242,142, plus interest and costs. The $242,142 amount represented the brokerage commissions they thought were due them. On the day before the trial, the Disney Co. settled for a "significant amount," says Nelson Boice. The settlement stipulated that neither side could reveal the exact figure. However, the figure was presumably close to what FRL sought. Boice saw Disney's action as more opportunistic than conspiratorial. "Walt and Roy Disney did not go through all of this secrecy to cheat Florida Ranchlands out of a commission," he said. Secrecy to facilitate a land deal was okay, but in his view they took advantage of the situation. "They knew, no question about it, that they had an obligation to pay a commission, but since there was all this secrecy, they just did not bother to come up and say, 'Hey fellows, we appreciate the work you did and here's your commission.'"[50] Their actions displayed an arrogant side of the Disney Co. that would be apparent, in the future, in their dealings with Orange County officials, among others.

In a larger sense, this story of Disney's land purchase is a cautionary tale of secrecy in economic deals. Secrecy might be necessary for business reasons, but it provides no guarantee against chicanery. It worked as long as everyone behaved honorably, but that was not assured. Unless decisions were made in the light of day, there was no public accountability, no surety that a private corporation would perform in a public-regarding way. This issue of guarantees—of how to assure public-regarding behavior on the part of a private corporation—would arise more explicitly when the Disney Co. asked the Florida legislature for public powers in 1967.

Building I-4 through Orlando in the early 1960s. A process of creative destruction, the through-city route required the demolition of hundreds of homes and businesses, yet it also helped attract Walt Disney World to Orlando.

Reception for Walt Disney at the Florida governor's mansion in Tallahassee on November 14, 1965. After eighteen months of secrecy, Walt and his entourage came to Florida to announce plans for an East Coast Disneyland. Left to right: Roy Disney, Governor Haydon Burns, Mrs. Burns, and Walt Disney.

Walt and Roy Disney at the November 15 Orlando press conference. To Walt's left is William (Joe) Potter, the former Army Corps of Engineers general who headed Disney's private government, the Reedy Creek Improvement District, which was responsible for building Disney World's utilities and public works. Left to right: Walt Disney, General Potter, Governor Burns, and Roy Disney. (Florida State Archives)

Press conference in the Egyptian Room of the Cherry Plaza Hotel in Orlando on November 15, 1965. Before a standing-room only crowd, Walt spoke in vague terms about building something bigger and better than Disneyland that would cost $100 million and employ 4,000 people. This was Walt's only public appearance in Orlando; he died of cancer thirteen months later. Left to right: Walt Disney, Governor Haydon Burns, and Roy Disney. (Florida State Archives)

Walt Disney talking with *Orlando Sentinel* publisher Martin Andersen during the November 15 press conference as Governor Burns looks on. Andersen and his close friend Billy Dial, a lawyer and banker, promoted the road projects that attracted Walt Disney to Orlando. (Florida State Archives)

Disney executives studying a map of their Florida property during a site visit in February 1967, following Walt's death. The visit coincided with their February 2 press conference in Orlando. Left to right: E. Cardon Walker, Roy Disney, Jack Sayers, Donn B. Tatum, and Joe Potter. (Florida State Archives)

Disney executives touring their Florida property by boat during their February 1967 site visit. Much of the property was wetland, which accounted for the $200 per acre purchase price. To transform this wilderness into a controlled environment, the company built over forty miles of canals, eighteen miles of levees, and thirteen water-control structures. (Florida State Archives)

Bay Lake viewed from the north before Disney World was built. The Disney Co. worked hard to buy enough land to encircle the lake. They then drained it to remove decaying organic sludge that made the water brown and also dug a 200-acre lagoon to create a water entrance to the park. They used the excavated dirt to raise the theme park twelve feet above its surroundings. (Florida State Archives)

The Disney property and I-4 as Walt would have viewed them from the air before development. Flying over the Orlando area on November 22, 1963—the same day that President Kennedy was assassinated—he made a tentative commitment to building Walt Disney World there. The company liked the area because of its climate, its inland location, its highway network, and, not least, the availability of large tracts of undeveloped land with interesting water features. (Florida State Archives)

Roy Disney and Florida's new Republican governor Claude Kirk at the Park West theater in Winter Park. The Disney Co. presented their legislative demands here on February 2, 1967. Walt had died two months earlier; this was Roy's first appearance as company front man. (Florida State Archives)

Governor Kirk and Roy Disney at the signing of the Disney legislation on May 12, 1967. Members of the Florida legislature are in the background. The complex legislation granting Disney governmental powers and immunities moved through the legislature in twelve days, passing unanimously in the Senate and with only one dissenting vote in the House. At the governor's right is his daughter Claudia. (Florida State Archives)

Magic Kingdom with Bay Lake in the background just before opening. Disney's monorail runs through the Contemporary Hotel at the top right. At far right is Seven Seas Lagoon, scooped from the earth and lined with white sand to make its water an ersatz blue. (Florida State Archives)

Secretary of State Henry Kissinger arriving at the Epcot preview, in conjunction with the Southern Governors Association meeting in Orlando, September 1975. Kissinger's praise for the project obscured the fact that Epcot would be another amusement park, not the residential community described to the state legislature in 1967. Left to right: Donn B. Tatum, E. Cardon Walker, and Secretary Kissinger. (Florida State Archives)

Orange Avenue at the heart of downtown Orlando in 1980. Though Orlando became the world's most popular tourist destination, its downtown, slightly shabby, betokened a mid-size city. Few Disney tourists set foot in Orlando except when arriving at the airport. (Orange County Historical Society)

The confluence of I-4 (from top-left to bottom-right) and the East-West Expressway in downtown Orlando. Pro-growth leaders in the 1950s and 1960s wanted
to save downtown by running expressways through it. As happened elsewhere,
these expressways ultimately fostered suburbia more than they supported downtown. (Orange County Historical Society)

Orange County Chairman Linda Chapin (1992). She was the county's first elected chairman, serving two terms, from 1990 to 1998. By her own admission, Chapin was favorably disposed toward Disney. With her in charge, the county adopted a more congenial attitude toward the company. (Doug Dukane)

Orange County Chairman Mel Martinez (2000). After Chapin stepped down because of term limits, he won office in 1998 promising to cut taxes and reduce government. He talked about taking on Disney but left office in 2001 to become President George W. Bush's Secretary of Housing and Urban Development. (Orange County government)

FOUR Marriage

W hat kind of marriage would it be? What would be the terms and conditions of the Disney World–Orlando relationship? In prospect, Disney seemed like a partner too fantastic to be true. The local business community was "transported into a dreamland from whence they could see nothing but unparalleled economic returns," gushed the *Sentinel*.[1] Orlando was "on the verge of the greatest period of growth this community has ever felt," said Billy Dial. It will be "phenomenal what it will do for real estate," predicted the board of realtors president. "The greatest plum that would ever come here," remarked the director of the Downtown Orlando Council, a business group. Dick Pope, owner of Cypress Gardens, then the area's largest tourist attraction, was equally enthused. "Anyone who is going to spend $100 million near me is good, and a good thing," he said.[2]

Governor Burns promised the state's "100 percent cooperation," saying he had "pledged Mr. Disney to provide roads to move traffic in and out."[3] Other politicians echoed his commitment, though more conditionally. Burns had announced prior to the November press conference that Disney would seek charters for two new cities and "certain assurances in planning and zoning."[4] In response, Orange County state Rep. Henry Land pledged support but wanted "safeguards" on Disney's powers. What would happen, he asked, if they sold their land to someone who was less responsible? And Walt's vague discussion of the City of Tomorrow sparked concern among some county officials. They felt slighted at the VIP-heavy press conference, which Burns organized, and wondered if they had heard everything. "He's (Walt's) going to have to tell us a little more," said the chairman of the Osceola County Commission.[5] Still, local politicians responded favorably overall, with most pledging their cooperation.

Voters, on the other hand, sent a cautionary message. Between the October announcement and the November press conference, they defeated a $300-million state road bond issue that Burns had promoted as essential for tourism. The bond referendum, which failed 60–40 statewide yet won in Orange County, was the brainchild of Burns, who wanted the state to expand its highway system quickly before land prices drove up road costs. He had led the charge to build the Jacksonville Expressway, the state's first urban expressway, during his fourteen years as that city's mayor.[6] Spearheading opposition to the bond program was a young state senator named Lawton Chiles, then 35, who called it a payoff to Burns's cronies in the bond business.[7] Whatever the truth of the charge, the referendum's defeat politically wounded Burns, known to his critics as "slicky Burns," a reference to his slicked-back hair as well as his business associates. The following year, he lost in a Democratic primary bid for re-election.

But more was at stake than Burns's reputation. The bond referendum was a warning bell for Disney. Though not a referendum on their coming to Florida, it would have funded major road projects in the area, and Burns and the *Sentinel* touted it as necessary for the entertainment company. Opponents had argued that it would divert money from education and saddle Florida taxpayers with too much debt. Burns countered that tourists also paid gasoline taxes, helping to retire the bond debt. But voters seemed unconvinced that a tourist economy was self-financing; if they favored Disney and other growth projects, they resisted paying for them. After the referendum, a solemn-faced Burns expressed concern about the vote's effect on Disney interests, noting as he had during the campaign that the tourist industry was "100 percent dependent on roads." "The voters quite properly oppose any new taxes," he conceded. Saying he would explore other road funding options, he flew off to California for secret meetings with Disney officials.[8]

Disney's view of the matter was offered by Paul Helliwell, who had become the representative of Compass East, the company formed to assume ownership of Disney's Florida properties. The day after the referendum, he met with the Osceola County tax assessor, Wade Lanier, an appointment arranged by Burns. Emerging from the meeting, he told reporters from the courthouse steps: "We're still pleased with the cooperation we're getting from government officials." The statement implied that they were displeased with Florida voters. As he spoke, he distributed a typed statement that made Disney's position clear: they had selected central Florida not because its road system was sufficient, but because the state had a sound basis for building an adequate road system in the future. "In all discussions during the past 18 months, it has been made quite clear that satisfactory assurance that such a system would be developed is an essential element in any decision to go forward. This position remains unchanged," the statement declared.[9]

At the November 15 press conference, twelve days later, Governor Burns credited Disney for announcing their intentions before they requested anything from government. That, however, may have been because Emily Bavar's revelation in the *Sentinel* hastened their announcement. In any case, the Disney people began scurrying after the October announcement—meeting with Burns and his Cabinet, inviting the governor and other leaders to California, and contacting local officials. Their government needs, requiring the support of both county and state government, centered on taxes, roads, and—of particular interest—an autonomous political district.

On taxes, they wisely sought administrative interpretations rather than legislative action. State revenue director J. Ed Straughn agreed that 40 percent of the cost of Disney's attractions consisted of nontaxable research, engineering, and design expenses, meaning that Disney would pay sales tax on only 60 percent of the attractions' value.[10] The decision followed a trip Disney officials made to Tallahassee, where they met with comptroller Fred Dickinson, Jr., and other state officials. Meanwhile, Helliwell called upon the tax assessors of Orange and Osceola counties, looking for assurances that their undeveloped land would be classified as agricultural and hence taxed at the lowest rate possible. The assessors agreed to the classification as long as cows grazed on the property, and the Disney Co. quickly entered the cattle business.[11]

Their road needs and the autonomous political district required state approval, which seemed assured considering Burns's and other state officials' pledges of support. County government, on the other hand, posed a potential challenge. It was not because county officials were uncooperative—the opposite was true—but because county government's powers and responsibilities could be threatening down the road. County government provided services, imposed property taxes, and regulated buildings and land use, all vital to Disney interests. As a company official said at the time: "We are not asking for a blank check. But many of our problems get down to a *county* level. When we put on the show here November 15, both counties will see the revenues we will bring in. But it is darned important to us that no one adopts the attitude 'We've got the Golden Goose, let's wring its neck'"[12] [italics mine]. In its autonomous political district, Disney sought state protection from county government—from county regulations such as building and land-use controls, and from inadequate county services such as police, fire, water, and waste treatment.

The approval of Disney's private government, rather than their obtaining tax concessions and road funding, is the remarkable part of this story. More than anything else, it set the stage for the economic-development marriage that followed. It is therefore important to know where this idea came from, what factors shaped it, how it was sold to Florida, and what it meant for the Disney–Orlando marriage. Beyond the particulars of this case, the story of Disney's government charter is emblematic of the contested politics of urban development in general—how agreement on growth breaks down over issues of financing and managing growth, and how new institutions are forged to cope with this conflict, institutions that reflect political choices while appearing to remove the politics from governing. We see here, too, the emergence of an alternative urban vision—evolved from consultant reports, legal advice, and Walt's own thinking—about how cities should be built and governed and their services provided.

The private government idea arose from the urban crisis of the 1960s, the Disney Co.'s experience at Disneyland, and Walt's urban planning interest. As the Burbank-based Disney Co. was purchasing land for its greenfield experiment in Florida, the Watts neighborhood in nearby Los Angeles was erupting in flames. The Watts riots occurred only three months before Walt's Orlando press conference, followed in the next two years by similar outbursts of rioting, looting, and police retaliation in Chicago, Cleveland, Cincinnati, Newark, and Detroit, among other cities. It made this a heady time for thinking about model cities, as members of the Johnson administration would do in pushing the Model Cities Act through a reluctant Congress in 1966.

The frustrating problem confronted by Disney was the uncontrolled growth and ticky-tacky development surrounding Disneyland in California. Walt hated this neon jungle of motels, hamburger joints, and souvenir shops. "We didn't create it, but we get blamed for it," he pronounced at his November 1965 press conference.[13] He could not fix the problem in Anaheim, since he neither owned the land surrounding the park nor controlled the government that should regulate it. His greenfield solution was, first, to buy enough land to encircle his amusement park with a greenbelt that hid adjoining land uses from view, while also providing space for expansion. Second, Walt wanted his own private government. During early discussions of the Florida property, one company executive said that he seemed to want "an experimental absolute monarchy." "Can I have one?" Walt responded.[14] The answer was supposedly "no," yet his corporate successors got something close to a kingdom all their own.

Walt's model city ideas were not entirely the result of his Anaheim experience. He also possessed a genuine intellectual interest in urban planning—in what attracts people, holds their attention, and moves them in and out. This interest was apparent, as Gen. Potter noted, in their plane trip to visit shopping centers and new towns like Reston, Virginia, and Columbia, Maryland. It was also evident in their design of Disneyland, described by the renowned urban planner James Rouse as "the greatest piece of urban design in the United States." Rouse, the designer of Fanueil Hall Marketplace in Boston and Baltimore's Harborplace, said Disney "took an amusement park and lifted it to a standard so high in its performance, in its functioning for people, that it became a brand new thing. It fulfills all the functions it set out to, fully and profitably."[15]

One early influence may have been Walt's father, Elias, who worked as a carpenter on the famous White City at the 1893 Chicago World's Fair. The White City, designed by Daniel Burnham and Frederick Olmsted, provided the originating ideal for American urban planning.[16] Its hallmark was coordination—of building heights, colors, design, layout, and circulation. Cast in plaster-of-Paris, it was not a real-world city but an ideological model, much like the fiberglass-swathed Disneyland. Yet, this ideological model launched the City Beautiful movement as reflected in Daniel Burnham's graceful planning of Chicago's lakefront. The message was clear: a model community could have real-world consequences without real residents.

Another influence was an ERA report on new communities, commissioned by the Disney organization, spanning the American experience with planned communities from Radburn and Garden City to Reston and Columbia.[17] The ERA consultants said that the founders of most planned communities mistakenly looked backwards for inspiration. They were influenced by architectural designs rather than social and economic plans, and were guided by altruism more than sound market thinking. Few contemporary new communities, they wrote, "experimented with new socio-economic, political, fiscal, and technological arrangements and ideas." Most were bedroom suburbs that lacked an indigenous employment base. The lessons of this experience, ERA concluded, were to assess market demand carefully and to craft governmental arrangements "responsive to the community builder's needs." Their consultant report devoted particular attention to the governance issue.

The company received corresponding advice from their engineering consultant, Gee & Jensen of Palm Beach. Much of their land in Florida was swampy or at least periodically wet. Engineers had told Jack Demetree, in 1963, that large capital outlays would be needed for drainage and water control on his 12,440-acre tract, now at the center of the Disney property. He had sought to have the Army Corps of Engineers drain the property, leading to promises but no action.[18] When Adm. Fowler saw the property, with its Amazonian black swamps and vast wetlands, he hired Gee & Jensen to prepare an action plan for it. The firm's lead partner, Col. Herb Gee, stood at Walt Disney's side when he first saw the property. "No, no, this won't do," Walt said of the water, which was black due to tannic acid from cypress trees along the shore and the eutrophication of decaying matter, both common in Florida. He wanted the water blue, Walt told Gee, the way he imagined Florida water should be. "Can you change it?" he asked Gee. "I can if you have the money," Gee responded. "Do it," said Walt.[19]

Gee & Jensen recommended more than recontouring rivers and draining alligator-infested swamps, however. Completed in December 1965, their report offered valuable political advice, informing their client about Chapter 298 in the *Florida Code*, which enabled landowners to form drainage districts that could issue bonds, practice eminent domain, and avoid certain taxes. The Chap. 298 district was made-to-order for Disney. It could encompass properties "other than those applying to create [it]" and be "controlled on the basis of acreage rather than residents." Thus holdout landowners could not stop Disney from creating the district. Nor could the minority landowners impede their operation of the district—the company owned 98 percent of the land and could outvote them. Alternately, Disney could rely on county government for land reclamation, a wrong tack in Gee & Jensen's view. Their reasoning was interesting: relying on county government, they said, would subject them to "control by a political board serving countywide and subject to the influences of surrounding land owners."[20] Just like everybody else.

Disney acted on their consultant's advice, creating the Reedy Creek Drainage District in May 1966. The district required approval by the circuit court rather than a legislative body, as Gee & Jensen approvingly noted. Moreover, the court had no discretion: it was required to create the district provided certain requirements were met. At the court hearing, one minority landowner objected to being included. Roy Disney, who was present at the hearing, told their attorney to "let him win," and the man's property was excluded.[21] The drainage district only partially solved Disney's governance problem, however. It created a proprietary government to move dirt and water but left open how the community would be governed once people lived there. How could the company protect their investment, how could they insure the integrity of their design, when they had residents who could vote?

A subsequent ERA report responded precisely to these questions. The report was prepared to support Disney's application for a federal Department of Housing and Urban Development planning grant.[22] In suggesting the company's approach to HUD, the consultants offered a compromise solution to their governance problem—to the problem of reconciling democracy and capitalist land development. The challenge of city building, they said, was to keep the city "always in a state of becoming." It was an appealing statement, reminiscent of Hegel's discourse in *Philosophy of Mind* on "being and becoming," a statement Disney publicists would make into a catchphrase. Twenty pages into the report, they explained the challenge of "becoming" in more revealing terms. It came down to a question of control: how, they asked, could the community builder ensure that "the full development program [would] be carried out as projected" and that "nothing happens that will emasculate the plan"?[23]

The answer from ERA was to limit the scope of democracy. "New community developers should be exempted from processing their plans and development requests through local governing bodies," they said. To keep their community "in a state of becoming," they should be "freed from the impediments to change, *such as rigid building codes, traditional property rights, and elected political officials*" [italics mine]. They proposed a compromise rather than abandoning democracy altogether. The compromise, on one hand, was a bifurcated government with planning and development under landowner control, and the remaining functions of government entrusted to citizens and elected officials. Democracy would still apply to health, safety, welfare, education, and civil rights, as well as the housekeeping affairs of government. On the other hand, this arrangement would be temporary—the developer's proprietary authority would be relinquished "after a reasonable period of years, after the property is almost fully developed, or when the developer retains ownership of less than 20 percent of the land."[24] Once it was safe, full democratic control was okay.

In more lawyerly terms, the same issue was addressed in a May 23, 1966, memo that attorney Paul Helliwell wrote to Walt Disney and other top company executives.[25] The memo summarized their earlier conversations regarding the threat of county government. Helliwell noted, for example, that Orange County had adopted a comprehensive zoning ordinance in 1964 that might limit the company's "freedom of action." In response, he proposed a Disney-controlled government with powers "superseding to the fullest extent possible under law state and county regulatory authorities." Like the drainage district, the governing body would be elected on the principle of acreage: one acre equaled one vote. But how could this governing body be established democratically, in a way that observed constitutional niceties, and for how long could landowner control continue?

Helliwell's answer was to found a two-tier government, with the landowner-controlled government embracing the whole property and, beneath it, one or more municipalities exercising carefully circumscribed powers. Creating the municipalities would solve two problems. First, it would prevent residents from incorporating "independent of WDP [Walt Disney Productions] and its program." Second, it would empower the Disney Co. to exercise planning and zoning authority, while shielding itself from external regulation. Florida law appeared to say that only a popularly elected government could regulate buildings and land use, explained Helliwell. This was a potential stumbling block for their proprietary government, since they wanted to avoid external regulation. But Helliwell had an ingenious solution: to create their own municipalities, give them popularly elected governments, and secure regulatory powers for them. Then they would subordinate the municipalities to their proprietary government.

Helliwell's scheme was not foolproof. There was still the problem of who would govern the municipalities, of how the Disney landowner could permit popular government and not be bound by it. The law was constraining, explained the attorney. They could name the initial members of the municipal governing boards, possibly for as long as four years, but after that residents would elect the board. He cautioned against a property qualification for voting, an idea that Disney executives had discussed, saying it was unconstitutional.

Walt's response to the memo clearly indicates his thinking on these issues. He wrote comments directly on the memo, which was found in his desk when he died. Every place where Helliwell referred to the problem of "permanent residents," Walt crossed it out and wrote "temporary residents/tourists." Despite his fanciful mind, he clearly grasped the political reality—if people lived there, they could vote there, undermining the company's political control. And where the memo explained that, legally, their private government could not exercise planning and zoning powers unless it was popularly elected, Walt switched from lead pencil to red grease pencil, writing "NO" in inch-high letters at the margin. The message, extremely important for later events, seems clear: Walt wanted no permanent residents in his model community.

On the back of the memo, he sketched an organization chart for governing the community. They would have an elected board of control composed of two–three members each from industry, merchants,

and residents, as well as three–six members from the "corporation."
In addition, they would have a three–five-person executive committee, a city manager, and resident and business advisory committees.
Beneath the chart, he listed the community's constituencies as follows: corporation, industry, merchants, residents, professional, and
at-large. Residents (presumably temporary ones) would have a voice,
but only one voice in a larger choir conducted by the corporation.

Interpreting Walt's political thinking is difficult, because he died
of complications from lung cancer on December 15, 1966, only ten
days after turning 65. A veteran smoker of little cigars, he had part
of a lung removed after a lesion was found on November 2. At the
time, few people knew the gravity of his situation; a press release had
falsely attributed the surgery to an old polo injury. A few weeks earlier, Billy Dial had traveled to California at Walt's invitation to view
Disneyland's impact on Anaheim. Over lunch he had asked Walt, in
front of Roy and other company executives, "What would happen to
this project if you walked out and got hit by a truck?" It was a blunt
question but an important one for Dial and others in Florida who
had stuck their necks out for the project. Walt responded: "Absolutely
nothing. My brother Roy runs this company, I just piddle around."[26]

Dial was unpersuaded by Walt's answer. It was true that Roy managed the company, yet Walt presided over its creative element, WED
Enterprises. This enterprise was loosely organized since Walt hated
organization charts, but it was clearly Walt's: the "WED" stood for
Walter Elias Disney. Three weeks after Dial's Anaheim trip, he was
at Bankers Trust Co. in New York when he received an emergency
phone call from Donn Tatum, who worked under Roy. Tatum informed him that Walt had died and asked, "Do you remember that
conversation you had with Walt in California? You're probably going
to be questioned when you get back to Orlando. I just want to be sure
you remember."[27] He wanted Dial to spread the word back home that
the project would continue.

Despite Tatum's reassurances to Dial, Walt's sudden passing left
the company in the lurch. It was unclear who would lead Disney since
Roy, 73, had announced his plans to retire, rumors circulated of a
takeover by Litton Industries, and speculation was growing in Florida
that the project would be dropped. In the end, Roy agreed to stay. He

polled the company's top executives and discovered that, to a person, they favored continuing with the Florida project. He therefore gave the project his blessing, insisting that it be called *Walt* Disney World in tribute to his brother. A week after Walt's death, Paul Helliwell appeared before the Orange County legislative delegation, telling them, "I talked with Roy Disney by telephone two and one half hours ago—this project goes forward on schedule."[28]

The question was what to build in Orlando. They knew how to build a Disneyland-style Magic Kingdom. According to Bob Allen, chairman of the Walt Disney World operating committee, they never worried about how to do that.[29] But what about the City of Tomorrow idea? On one hand, they were ill prepared to proceed without Walt. He had kept the plans mostly in his head; all they had were the storyboards and Walt talking on camera about a prototype city, in a film never shown. On the other, they needed the model city for political reasons. As the Helliwell memo explained, it offered an escape from county services and regulation. The nagging questions, still unanswered, were how they could have resident voters and not be bound by them, and for how long they could control any government they created. Regarding the latter, Helliwell and ERA thought only temporary control was possible—yet local and state government proved more pliable than they imagined.

Four days after Walt's death, Helliwell told the Orange County legislative delegation that Disney wanted to charter two municipalities. He refused to be specific, saying legislation was still being drafted. His announcement corresponded with ideas circulating in the press, dating from an interview that Walt gave in November to *Chicago Tribune* columnist Norma Lee Browning. There would be two model cities, Walt said. One would be named Epcot (for Experimental Prototype Community of Tomorrow), a planned and controlled community that would showcase American industry and research, schools, and cultural and educational opportunities. The other, yet to be named, would be an experimental laboratory for administering municipal governments. In Epcot, "there'll be no landowners, and therefore no voter control," said Walt; in the second community, however, individual property ownership would be permitted.[30]

It was radically antidemocratic—to deny residents the vote, as if American political history could be repealed. Yet the *Orlando Senti-*

nel, which the *Chicago Tribune* had purchased a year earlier while permitting Andersen to remain as publisher until December 1966, lauded the concept. They ran the Browning article on the front page with an accompanying editorial. Restricting Epcot residents from owning, they said, would give Disney "the kind of control it feels essential." Somehow this would make the city more responsive to residents. "Imagine a city whose sole function is to serve the people who serve it," the editors wrote. "This in itself is a revolutionary new concept. So often the citizens, who make our communities what they are, are the last to get any consideration from the heads of their local government."[31] Not democracy, but freedom from democracy, would make the Disney city responsive to its residents. Such thinking revealed the mesmerizing power of Disney: whatever they wanted must be good.

On February 2, 1967, Disney finally presented their legislative package. Their gala press conference was held in Winter Park's Park West theater, an ironic location. Winter Park, which had resisted the incursion of I-4, was chosen because it had a 900-seat movie theater that Disney needed to show their Epcot film. Conversely, Orlando's graying downtown, which I-4 was intended to rejuvenate, had no movie theater.

Into the Park West poured an impressive crowd—Roy Disney, now 74, with six of his vice presidents; Florida's new Republican governor, Claude Kirk, in his second month in office, along with four Cabinet members and nearly half the state legislature; a contingent of ninety-three press, industrial, and financial people who had flown down from New York; representatives of forty-three national media organizations, as well as state and local media; all the community notables who could wangle a ticket; and reportedly enough police to guard two U.S. presidents. It was Orlando's coming out party, heralding its transformation into a world-class travel destination.

Roy was seated at center stage next to Governor Kirk, Roy's trusted aide Donn Tatum at his side. After brief opening comments by Gen. Potter, the lights dimmed and the film reel whirled on the projector. Suddenly, Walt's persona appeared on screen, like so many times before, looking "as if he had just slipped out for a cup of coffee," said one of those present.[32] Walt described to a chorus of "ooohs" and "aaahs" what they planned to create in Florida. There would be a Magic Kingdom amusement park like the one in California, except five times larger (not ten times larger, as they first imagined). It would be linked by a rapid transit system with a 1,000-acre industrial park and a jetport. "But the most exciting and by far the most important part of our Florida project—in fact, the heart of everything we'll be doing in Disney World—will be our Experimental Prototype Community of Tomorrow. We'll call it Epcot," Walt intoned.[33]

This model city would "take its cue from the new ideas and new technologies that are now emerging from the creative centers of American industry. It will be a community of tomorrow that will never be completed, but will always be introducing and testing and demonstrating new materials and systems. And Epcot will always be a showcase to the world for the ingenuity and imagination of American free enterprise," Walt explained on screen.

It was not merely a futuristic city intended to provoke wonderment. There was a reform impulse behind Epcot, Walt continued. "I don't believe there's a challenge anywhere in the world that's more important to people everywhere than finding solutions to the problems of our cities," he said. "But where do we begin—how do we start answering this great challenge? Well, we're convinced we must start with the public need. And the need is not just for curing the old ills of old cities. We think the need is for starting from scratch on virgin land and building a special kind of new community."

It would be a working community where real people would live and work and play. "It will never cease to be a living blueprint of the future, where people actually live a life they can't find anywhere else in the world," said Walt. "Everything in Epcot will be dedicated to the happiness of the people who will live, work, and play here." A voice-over described the company's plans for a functioning community. Built on a radial design, it would have high-density apartments surrounding a business center, beyond that a greenbelt and recreation area, and an outer ring of low-density residential streets—in all, a place where "about 20,000 people will live." It would have "playgrounds, churches and schools . . . distinctive neighborhoods . . . and footpaths for children going to school," all suggesting a residential community. By implication, transportation impacts would be self-contained. A multimodal transportation system would ferry residents to their jobs in the city center, the theme park, and the adjacent industrial park. They would travel by surface trains, a monorail, and a "webway people mover" involving cars moving on a nonstop conveyer belt.

"You can see this is not a land development promotion in any way," Walt declared, leading to the pitch. "To accomplish our goals for Disney World, we must retain control and develop all the land ourselves." For this, they needed cooperation. "You people here in Florida have one of the key roles to play in making Epcot come to life. In fact, it's really up to you whether this project gets off the ground at all."

The film ended and, as the lights came up, Roy walked softly to the microphone. "Wasn't that a dream? Doesn't that stagger you," he said to applause. Stammering, looking uncomfortable in Walt's frontman role, the loyal brother reviewed their business plan. They would build the amusement park first, and the remaining construction would occur in phases. They were prepared to spend $100 million on the amusement park, which would open in 1970. They had $75 million for the Epcot city; thereafter, they would spend $10 million to $15 million per year. In all, they expected to pump $600 million into the project.[34] But before they started, they needed a "solid legal foundation," he said. Referring to their legislation, Roy called it "something that we would ask (for) in fairness for coming to Florida." Altogether, they were asking for municipal bonding authority, three highway interchanges, the widening of I-4 at the park entrance, bolstered trademark protection, and the creation of two municipalities together with an autonomous political district controlled by the company and empowered to issue tax-exempt bonds. At one point, Roy referred to these as "demands," an apparent slip of the tongue. He smiled and then looked at Governor Kirk. "In the presence of Governor Kirk, I use the word 'demand' softly," he corrected himself.

Tatum, vice president and administrative assistant to Roy, followed his boss to the microphone. He explained that local legislation consisting of three acts had been presented to the Orange and Osceola County legislative delegations. The first two, nearly identical, created two municipalities, one covering the northern portion of the Disney property, including Bay Lake, to be known as the City of Bay Lake; the other encompassing the Disney property for a distance of about two miles on both sides of S.R. 530. The third act created the Reedy Creek Improvement District, which would span the entire Disney property and assume the functions of the Reedy Creek Drainage District, formed in May 1966. "This Act," said Tatum, "is, in essence, a composite of special assessment, improvement, and taxing districts already provided for under existing Florida laws, each of which now provides for a separate and independent district under separate governing bodies."[35] In addition, three other bills were being sponsored for them at their request: a uniform deceptive practices act, an omnibus licensing statute that would permit organizations like Disney to have a single occupational license, and a trademark and tradename statute.

Tatum's rationale for Disney's government charter centered on Epcot as a residential community. "In serving the needs of those residing there, our Experimental Prototype Community of Tomorrow must utilize the technological advances of American industry as they continually develop."[36] They needed "flexibility"—autonomous control—to keep it in "a state of becoming." In return, they were not requesting tax breaks or public spending inside the property, he told the audience. Their tax concerns, he might have added, were addressed previously through administrative interpretations; their bonding authority provided an indirect federal tax subsidy; and their road needs outside the property required large public subsidies.

Next to speak was Governor Kirk. In a showy display of power, he had arrived at the Park West surrounded by a phalanx of highway patrolmen, one of whom stood surveying the crowd as the new governor spoke. Drawing from a report prepared by Disney's ERA consultants, Kirk told the audience that Disney would generate $6.6 billion in economic benefits during the construction phase and the park's first ten years of operation. Of that amount, $3.9 billion would come from tourist spending, $2.2 billion from new jobs, and $414 million from construction purchases and equipment. In addition, the project would create 50,000 new service-sector jobs, half of them outside the park, said Kirk.[37]

Harlan Hanson, director of the area's tri-county planning agency, said of the presentation: "It was as though they'd put a gun to our head. They were offering to invest $600 million, and there was the glamour of Disney. You could hardly be against that. We were all just spellbound."[38] Recalled a senator's aide who was there: "We all thought they were going to build Epcot, a model community. That's what they talked about."[39] One state senator, L. K. Edwards from Ocala, part of the rural "pork-chop gang" that controlled the state legislature, was quick to grasp what Disney proposed. He had heard about company towns from his friends up north, he said during the question period. If the Disney people wanted to build a company town down here, he guessed that was okay.[40]

Following their Winter Park presentation, the California company began a media blitz to sell the legislation. Governor Kirk and Roy Disney flew to Jacksonville, where they taped a half-hour presentation that was televised statewide that evening. Described as a "Report to the People of Florida," it included the Epcot film shown in Winter Park. Floridians thus saw Walt on screen describing Epcot as the centerpiece of the project; as a functioning residential community with 20,000 residents; as a mass-transit mecca with people-movers and monorails replacing private automobiles; and as a showplace for innovations in technology and urban design. To achieve all this, they needed the "flexibility" of an autonomous political district, road interchanges, municipal bonding authority, and the rest. In return, Floridians would get more tourists, more sales and gasoline taxes, more jobs in construction and services, and more construction spending. That was the basis for the proposed economic development marriage.

A public hearing on the Disney legislation occurred two days later, also at the Park West theater. It was hosted by the Orange and Osceola county legislative delegations and drew less than 100 persons, including 11 legislators, Disney aides, public officials, and reporters. The three bills—containing 161, 163, and 157 pages respectively—contained "no gimmicks, no tax concessions, no demands for concessions and no curves," attorney Helliwell told the audience.[41] Yet some Orange County officials expressed concern about giving up normal county control over the Disney tract. Several questioned whether Disney could put ownership of things like swimming pools and convention halls in the district and remove them from the tax rolls. In response, Helliwell said they had no intention of using the district to avoid taxes.

At a second local hearing in March, legislators raised concerns about the police powers being created. It was an unusual arrangement, since Bay Lake in Orange County would police its companion city, Reedy Creek (now Lake Buena Vista), as well as unincorporated Disney property in Osceola County. Phil Smith, an attorney representing Disney at the hearing, responded haphazardly: "You want to give one of these cities police powers throughout the district, because the district has no police force. It isn't critical which city has the power." Extending Bay Lake's police powers to another county was not important, he felt. "It is mostly a water storage area, with no development planned," he said of the Osceola County property, where Disney would build their Celebration planned community in the 1990s.

Questions also arose about taxing and bonding authority. Several legislators worried that the Disney property would be excised from county tax rolls and regulations. "Not so," said Disney attorney Robert Foster, "The immunities only apply to property owned by the district and the cities themselves. Most of the property will be privately owned and *subject to all county and state regulations*" [italics mine]. More, they should be trusted to use tax-exempt bonds appropriately. "The use of governmental bonds for building any function that could be built privately is repugnant to us," Foster added.[42]

Why Foster said the property would be "subject to all county and state regulations" is mystifying. The legislation clearly gave the district immunity from state and county regulation of buildings, land use, airport and nuclear power plant construction, and even the distribution and sale of alcoholic beverages, among other things. Moreover, these powers were protected in the future. A clever perpetuity clause said that if the provisions of future law should conflict with the charter, the charter would "prevail," unless the new law repealed the relevant section of the charter. Noting the district's superior power, Orlando City Attorney John Baker remarked, "We'll take their city charter—either one of them."[43] By all accounts, though, the Disney attorneys were friendly and cooperative, willing to concede on minor issues to gain agreement.

James Robinson, the Orange County attorney who negotiated with Disney, said the county was "kind of shaken by the degree of control" they desired. The county commission wanted some auxiliary control in case the development "didn't work out" or fell into the hands of someone less responsible. It was only natural for county officials to resist having an autonomous entity within their border, he said. "The fear was that Disney was so large, [and had] so much land, that the county might have a competing government exercising government powers that [would] impair the county's ability to control its affairs."[44] It was a problem philosophically, said Robinson, "because we were giving government powers to a business." Some commissioners, particularly Paul Pickett, "just did not want that to happen," he said. Yet none of the commissioners wanted to "negotiate to the point that we stopped them from coming," he added.[45]

On opening day of the biennial legislative session, April 17, 1967, the three Disney bills, along with companion legislation pertaining to trademark protection, deceptive practices, and occupational licensing, were introduced. Senator Robert Elrod and Rep. Henry Land, both from the Orlando area, filed the legislation, though neither participated in drafting it. Although classified as local bills, they were crafted entirely by Disney's team—Robert Foster in California; Paul Helliwell and members of his firm, Helliwell, Melrose, and DeWolf in Miami; and Helmut Furth of Donovan, Leisure, Newton, and Irvine in New York. Elrod arranged for Helliwell and other Disney representatives to appear before a House–Senate joint meeting to explain the legislation. There, Helliwell spoke of "residents" in the two Disney towns, and he and the other Disney representatives talked about including public school sites and other public needs in their two cities—as if a working community would be built.[46] Also, Helliwell said they were not asking for anything "that had not been done before," which was only half-true since the three kinds of special districts had not been combined before.[47]

Disney also plied the old-boy network. One of their lobbyists was J. J. Griffin, a former state representative from Osceola County. A wise choice for his role, Griffin said in an interview, "I knew practically everyone in the legislature." He made the rounds in the House and Senate, meeting with individual legislators to educate them on Disney's legislative needs. One meeting was with Verle Pope, the powerful president of the Florida Senate. Griffin told of going to Pope's office with several attorneys in tow to help explain the complex legislation. They had just launched their presentation, when the senate leader abruptly stopped them. "J. J.," he said, "I just have one question. Is this good for Florida?" Griffin answered, "Yes sir, I believe it is." Pope responded, "Well that's good enough for me."[48]

As hearings on the Disney legislation began, the Orange County Commission filed five objections, embarrassing Elrod, who previously told legislators the bills had commission backing.[49] The commission wanted the Disney district to be inferior to the jurisdiction of the Central and Southern Florida Flood Control District; to be prohibited from constructing, maintaining, or operating hotels and motels; to pay the Orange County tax assessor for collecting taxes in the district; to pay for any use of the county jail; and to be denied authority to condemn public property in the district.[50] Only the last change proved controversial. Helliwell answered that every other municipality and special district had this power under general law.[51] In the end, though, Disney accepted the amendments.

Governor Kirk had promised at the Park West theater that the legislature would act swiftly. It did, moving the complicated and far-reaching legislation through committee and onto the floor of both chambers, where it passed unanimously and without debate in the Senate, and with only one dissenting vote in the House—all in twelve days. Elrod explained that a "friendly environment" existed for Disney's legislation.[52] A few senators complained about creating a company town and giving Disney control over zoning, but "to be against it was to vote against motherhood and apple pie," said Elrod. Besides, he and the Disney lobbyists had recruited sixteen of the twenty-five senators to cosponsor the legislation. In the House, the legislation was unstoppable, said Henry Land, who chaired the House Appropriations Committee. "If I didn't support it, I would have been lynched."[53] At the time, he saw no danger in the legislation, though he had not read it thoroughly, he admitted in an interview. Later, Land called the Reedy Creek charter "one of the worst things that ever happened (in Florida), because it gave them too many powers." Orange County Attorney James Robinson said the negotiations were "sometimes heated" because the legislation was on a fast-track and "our objections caused some annoyance because they (Disney) thought this was going straight through." He added, "whatever came out was the best we could get."[54]

Less than an hour after the vote, the State Road Board approved emergency funding for Disney's road requests. They had asked for three interchanges—at I-4 and S.R. 530, at 530 and their property, and at I-4 and their service entrance—and the widening of 530 from I-4 west to their entrance interchange.[55] (For those familiar with Orlando roads, S.R. 530 is also U.S. 192.) Governor Burns had promised to meet their road needs and, following the defeat of his road bond package, the only recourse was to fund their projects "off the top" before allocating road money among the districts. "It was embarrassing," said Willard Peebles, who was the board's representative for District 5, including Orlando. Board members had just established an objective formula (based on auto registration, gasoline sales, and miles of primary roads) for allocating road money among the districts, which was always controversial. At the same meeting they turned around and took $1 million out each year for the next five years for Disney. "Other road board members weren't happy about it," he said, "but Burns and Kirk had made a promise to Disney." Though not bound by the governors' pledge, board members felt obliged to honor it.[56]

Disney had also requested an interchange connecting Florida's Turnpike and I-4. Incredibly, the two roads crossed but did not join. When their legislation passed, the interchange was already under construction, thanks to the intervention of Orlando attorney Charley Gray. He had become chairman of the Turnpike Authority after serving as Haydon Burns's central Florida campaign chairman in 1965. As one of the few people in Orlando who knew that Disney was the mystery land buyer, Gray had helped Paul Helliwell and Roy Hawkins "on a few issues," he said in an interview. In return, they visited him before the announcement to say they had purchased only three corners of the intersection at I-4 and S.R. 530, which would become the entrance to Disney World. Perhaps he wanted to buy the remaining corner, they suggested.[57] After visiting Disneyland in Anaheim, Gray declined the opportunity. He says he could not imagine building anything on the outside of Disney World that they would not build on the inside. Later, the company did him another favor by moving their initial Florida headquarters into the Metcalf Building, a nearly empty office building in downtown Orlando that he and a partner had recently purchased. After Disney took over one floor, the Metcalf quickly filled with tenants, many of them land developers looking for tips.

Gray says he got the interchange built for Orlando's sake, not Disney's. Whatever the motivation, it was an impressive power play on his part. The Turnpike Authority's consulting engineers had concluded that the interchange was not economically feasible. Refusing to take no for an answer, Gray visited the engineers in New York, where he reminded them that their contract with the Authority expired in thirty days. Would they revisit the interchange issue? he asked. They did and discovered that the project was indeed feasible. With this finding, the Turnpike Authority could release money for the interchange, linking the roads that first caught Walt Disney's eye.

Completing the approval process, the Florida Supreme Court ruled in 1968 that the Reedy Creek Improvement District was legally entitled to issue tax-free municipal bonds. At issue was whether the bonding power permitted public funds to be used for private purposes. In a unanimous ruling, the Court conceded that the District "no doubt will greatly aid the Disney interest and its contemplated Disneyworld project." They continued: "However, it is obvious that to a lesser degree the contemplated benefits of the District will inure to *numerous inhabitants of the District* in addition to persons in the Disney complex" [italics mine].[58] The District was thus free to issue $12 million in improvement bonds for reclamation, drainage, and roadwork on the Disney property.

As the legislature had done, the state Supreme Court approved Disney's autonomous political district on a false premise. They assumed the California company was building a model city, a functioning community where 20,000 would live and work and play. Again and again, that is what Disney representatives said—at the Park West press conference, in the televised "Report to the People of Florida," at the local delegation hearings, and before the legislature in Tallahassee. But it was untrue. As Walt's scribbled comments on the Helliwell memo reveal, he envisioned a fantasy community stocked with "tourists/temporary residents," not permanent residents. Yet the company—and Walt himself in the Epcot film—persisted in creating a different impression. As best explained in the Helliwell memo, they needed to say they were building a residential community; however deceptive, this claim enabled them to escape from county regulation.

In retrospect, the legislature and Supreme Court appear naïve in taking Disney at their word. Realistically, they could hardly have said no, however. "You have no idea what kind of fervor there was in favor of Disney," said Orlando-area state Sen. John Ducker.[59] Their money and mystique, together with the state's pro-business culture and lack of economic development, all created a "friendly environment" for the Disney legislation, added Sen. Elrod. At best, critics looking back can argue that the legislature should have curtailed Disney's vast powers. For example, legislators might have written performance requirements into the legislation to ensure that Disney built what they said they would. Likewise, they might have added a sunset clause, as the legislature routinely does when establishing regulatory authority, requiring a reconsideration of Disney's exemptions at a later time.

What Disney got instead was a prenuptial agreement with their economic-development partners, the county and state. The Disney charter, with its perpetuity clause protecting their powers in the future, froze in time the unequal bargaining relationship that existed in 1967. Then, Disney could have gone elsewhere; at least it could have credibly threatened to build its theme park in another location. Florida, on the other hand, had not yet acquired significant location advantages as a place to live and do business. The Disney charter preserved this unequal bargaining relationship, making it difficult in the future for the two parties to bargain as equals over the terms and conditions of their relationship. James Robinson, who bargained with Disney on behalf of Orange County, said, "No one wanted to kill the golden goose back then. I think Disney realized that [the county] might not be as favorably inclined in the future, so they put everything in the charter they thought they might need later on."[60]

For central Florida residents, there was no guarantee that Disney would perform—no guarantee that they would build the Epcot city, nor exercise their powers responsibly, nor offer economic benefits commensurate with their public service costs. If the roads around the theme park were clogged, if there was a shortage of affordable housing to serve their workforce, if law enforcement was overburdened with the influx of tourists—that was the community's problem. All the public had were vague promises, an implicit social contract perhaps, but no legal guarantee. Such was the deal struck in 1967, a testament to the power of pixie dust and Disney mystique.

That is part of the story. But what about Disney's inventiveness, their creative problem solving, their urban vision? They invented a system of control, a method of urban administration, and skillfully guided it through the Florida legislature. They engaged in creative problem solving to avoid the ticky-tacky surrounding Disneyland and to escape the fate of the model communities surveyed by ERA. Walt, company executives like Foster and Tatum, Disney consultants at ERA and Gee & Jensen, and their outside legal counsel in Miami and New York, all created a vision for how cities should be built and governed and their services provided. In larger historical terms, they fashioned a system of administration for overcoming two forms of fragmentation that have complicated city building in the U.S.: fragmentation of land ownership and fragmentation of political interest. The Disney solution was to replace both with centralized administration. Leaving aside the misrepresentations, leaving aside their aversion to real residents, what if it worked?

FIVE

Growth

I t was February 1972 and NBC anchorperson David Brinkley was telling his viewers about the wonders of the newly opened Walt Disney World. Never mind the exciting amusement park, laid out in radial fashion around Main Street USA, with spokes pointing here to Tomorrowland, there to Fantasyland, over there to Frontierland, and beyond it to Adventureland. What impressed Brinkley was the Disney "new town" that existed outside the park, consisting of roads, transportation systems, lakes, golf courses, campgrounds, riding stables, stores, and motels. "They all fit together in a setting of land, air, and water better than any other urban environment in America," intoned Brinkley. Maybe real-world cities like New York should concede their planning to the Disney organization, he mused. "They seem to be the only people in America who are able to get things done."[1]

What made the Disney new town so impressive to behold? To Adm. Joe Fowler, who supervised construction, their efforts only proved what "planning and dollars can do."[2] But more than fistfuls of money and creative planning were involved. The Disney Co. had powers unmatched by other private developers, or even city governments. Disregarding how those powers were acquired, was this as Brinkley suggested a model for other cities to follow? For city building entails more than designing a system of land use and transportation, more than massing people and buildings and public infrastructure in space. Underlying all that, it involves deciding upon the "division of labor between politics and markets," in the words of economist Charles Lindblom.[3] Here we return to questions posed in Chap-

ter One. How should buildings, land use, and transportation be controlled—by private corporations responding to market incentives, or
by elected governments catering to voter preferences? How should
municipal services be provided—by private corporations or by popularly elected governments? And what values should be incorporated
into government institutions—private or public ones?

The late 1960s and 1970s were a period of growth—an extended
honeymoon—in the Disney–Orlando marriage. In tracing this
growth, we can see not only how Disney World and Orlando got to
be what they are. Building upon Brinkley's observation, we have an
opportunity to compare two approaches to city building: one based
on privatization and deregulation, the other on public services and
weak government regulation; one based on fusing public and private
powers, the other on their separation; one based on centralized control, the other on political and economic fragmentation. As well, we
can see how Disney's powers and immunities together with their deep
pockets gave them advantages over other private developers.

The construction of Disney World was carried out by the company's two arms: the private development arm headed by Adm. Joe
Fowler, the one-time head of the San Francisco Naval Shipyards, who
had supervised the construction of Disneyland; and the governmental
arm led by Gen. Joe Potter, president of the Reedy Creek Improvement District and a Disney employee as well. Fowler was responsible
for building the theme park, Potter for the utilities and public works,
including the power plant, sewage treatment works, and extensive
drainage network. In addition, Potter's governmental arm supervised
building design. Appropriately, both men came from military back-
grounds: "Fowler was the Eisenhower, Potter the Patton," said a
person who worked with them both.[4] When Walt hired Potter, Roy
Disney had said, "We already have an admiral, why do we need a
general?" The answer was that, as military men, they were accustomed to hierarchy and centralized administration, in addition to
possessing design and construction expertise. That was Disney's response to the ordinary process of city building, a process characterized by conflict and chaos. In its place, the Disney organization substi-
tuted top-down decision making by can-do military men, armed with
expertise and an appreciation for hierarchy.

Building the theme park involved first clearing and draining the land, and then constructing the rides and attractions. As Gen. Potter explained, the Chapter 298 drainage district was essential to their work. "We took our master plan and made a proposal to form a 298 district, and we took it down to the court and the judge said okay, and it was permitted. We then had a legal entity to do what we needed to do on the property."[5] Next they had to master the water, transforming a swamp into a controlled environment. The job entailed draining Bay Lake to remove decaying organic sludge that made the water brown, digging a 200-acre lagoon, and using the excavated dirt to raise the theme park twelve feet above its surroundings.

By December 1968, after sixteen months of excavation work—using 200 pieces of heavy equipment, employed around the clock under powerful portable spotlights—the drainage system was essentially complete. This engineering feat required more than forty miles of canals, eighteen miles of levees, and thirteen water-control structures. In all, more than eight million cubic yards of earth were moved to make way for the Magic Kingdom.[6] For this, the Disney Co. and their contractors captured almost every piece of earth-moving equipment in the Southeast.

Gen. Potter was especially proud of the project's gracefully curved canals. "They don't look like canals," he said. "They look more like rivers."[7] Here, Potter took a lesson in creative engineering from the genius of make-believe, Walt himself. Adm. Fowler remembered the scene. "The first canal Joe Potter laid out ran straight as an arrow from Bay Lake to the south part of the property," said the Admiral, recalling one of his last memories of Walt. "I was with Walt when he first saw it. Walt never raised his voice. The only way you could tell he was angry was when he raised his right eyebrow. He raised it now and said, 'Look, Joe, I don't want any more of those Corps of Engineers canals.'"[8] From then on, the canals were plotted in a meandering pattern to resemble rivers. Potter also innovated in creating the "utilidors" or utility tunnels that ran beneath the park. Because so much of the property was wet, the park was built on a raised slab that was crisscrossed with tunnels that carried power and water lines and other utilities. The utilidors also let costumed characters like Goofy and Mickey Mouse access their work locations without being seen with their "heads off," a Disney no-no.

In building the amusement park, they could use the powers of the Reedy Creek Improvement District, which Potter headed. As described by him in 1984, "it gave us all the powers of the two counties in which we sit to the exclusion of their exercising any powers, and of course it let us issue bonds. We could do anything the city or county could do. The only powers that still reside on us from outside are the taxing power of Orange County, the sales tax of the state, and the inspection of elevators."[9] Without those powers, they would be forced to submit to building inspections and planning and zoning controls by Orange and Osceola counties.

"We had to have the power of our own building codes," Potter added. "We adopted the [Southeast's strongest] building codes, which still exist for the Reedy Creek Improvement District. We had to do our own zoning. The zoning of property is a very political thing. If someone wants to sell lots for a gas station the whole neighborhood will get aroused. If we wanted to do something on this property, our neighbors could require that we have public hearings and all this sort of thing, [which] does not lend itself to rapid development, [or] rapid progress. We had to have those two things, and we had to have the financial ability, and we issued bonds in two cases. We had to have the two cities that exist on our property to give us the police power in case we ever needed it."[10]

Integrating the company's government and development arms made possible an efficient system of building regulation. Under Potter, the Reedy Creek government developed a floor building code with its own department to supervise the code. The department was small, never more than eleven persons, but that was only possible because they had a separate office at WED Enterprises in California, where the structures were designed. The arrangement allowed building officials to work directly with the theme park designers. They also collaborated with the designers of the hotels, which were separately owned and not designed by Disney people. Commenting on this arrangement, Potter said, "It saved us from an awful lot of problems because when a design came here we knew that it was a competent design."[11] The standards were stringent, such as requiring a fire sprinkler in every room, an uncommon safety feature in the 1960s. Yet, the performance standards were also flexible; for example, Potter's governmental arm allowed hotel builders to use epoxy in place of traditional brick mortar after they discovered that epoxy held better and was easier to use than mortar.

The person most responsible for Disney's building codes was Tom Moses, who became district manager in charge of the Reedy Creek government in 1982. When Potter hired him in 1969, Moses was a nationally recognized building code expert, then working as technical director of the Southern Building Codes Congress. At first he balked when Potter offered him the job, thinking Disney was building only an amusement park, but when he saw the scale of their plans and realized they were building something like a city, he jumped at the chance to be involved.[12] Under Moses, they innovated not only in setting performance standards and fire sprinkler requirements. They also developed tough standards for new types of structures, such as those made of fiberglass; for rides, where no uniform code existed; and for darkened buildings, in which finding exits would be difficult.[13] To supervise Disney design work, Moses hired a structural engineer in California who worked for Moses and the Reedy Creek government in Florida but who sat in the offices of Disney's design engineers in Glendale, reviewing their plans as they developed. To supervise third-party hotel construction, Moses himself reviewed these plans weekly from his Florida office.

In a business in which time is money, "we saved them money, and we saved ourselves a whale of a lot of time," says Moses, adding that a building inspector might otherwise ask a designer to redo a plan for a single mistake.[14] The fire-sprinkler and smoke-monitoring systems likewise saved money not only for the "property owner," as Reedy Creek officials refer to the Disney Co., but also for their government. Says Moses: "Long before a sprinkler head goes off, we're going to have equipment moving toward this building . . . because of the sophistication of the monitoring system." The District saves money by putting fewer people on fire trucks, knowing less hose will be needed, and building owners, including the third-party hotel owners, save on fire insurance as well.

Disney wanted flexibility in the code to help showcase innovations in industry and technology. Long before construction commenced, Walt had dispatched Gen. Potter to visit a host of major technology companies—Westinghouse, Bell Labs, IBM, Bell Telephone, Allied Chemical, RCA, Rockwell, and Union Carbide—looking for new ideas. "Tell them not to worry, I want you to see it. We're not going to steal ideas," he told Potter.[15] As a result, several revolutionary methods were incorporated into what the Disney organization billed as the largest private construction project in the world. RCA installed a total communication system for guests, residents, and management. Their network provided park-related news for guests, as well as a closed-circuit system for training new employees and monitoring shows and attractions. Aerojet General installed an underground system of pneumatic tubes to transport all garbage and trash, dirty hotel linen, and the like to a central point for handling. And U.S. Steel built two hotels, the Polynesian and Contemporary, containing a total of 1,450 rooms. The steel rooms were built off-site, assembled and even furnished on the ground, and then hauled by truck, connected by an ingenious interlock system and their utilities plugged in, before being hoisted into place by crane.

Nothing was left to chance in Disney's foray into the hotel business. Harris Rosen, administrator of hotel planning for the Disney Co. in the late 1960s, would later become the Orlando-area's largest hotel owner after Disney. Back then, he worked for Disney in a giant warehouse in California, mocking up critical hotel operations as designs came off the drawing board. For example, he mocked up the proposed front desk of the Contemporary and Polynesian hotels, discovering that a clerk of normal height could not pass a key across such a wide counter. His group also tested check-in kiosks, never used, that would allow hotel guests to register from their cars. In all, it was "an extraordinarily innovative approach to hotel planning," says Rosen.[16]

Meanwhile, Tom Moses's group was assessing the fire-worthiness of the Polynesian and Contemporary's modular design. They hired Underwriters Laboratories and took the first unit off the assembly line for a full-scale burn test. To simulate a one-hour burn, they laid carpet on the floor, installed the plumbing and light fixtures, stacked ten pounds of wood carvings on the floor, and set up half rooms on either side. Then they ignited the room and filmed the result. According to Moses, they made one little change around a connecting door where heat penetrated more than the performance standard permitted.[17]

For Walt, the East Coast park was an opportunity to correct minor mistakes at Disneyland, and to test rides and innovations for the California park. He never worried about the new theme park's layout, only about its location relative to Epcot. Hence the designers reapplied Walt's insight that the structures along Main Street USA should be built to five-eighths scale. Actually, the first floor was 90 percent full-size, the second floor about 80, and the third 60 to 70. The result gave visitors a sense of perspective as they gazed down the street, imparting a storybook character to the scene. The designers also reapplied the idea of a single entrance, like a circus midway, through Main Street and Cinderella's Castle. This was coupled with Walt's "weenie" concept: the idea that something—a weenie—should hold people's attention as they looked down a vista. Radiating from Main Street were the different "lands," each with a terminal vista to hold visitors' attention and provide a transition to another theme area. These design principles reflected Walt's "instinctive intuitiveness, of knowing what felt right and what was wrong," said Dick Irvine, who helped design both theme parks.[18]

It was nevertheless the Disney "city" that enthralled visitors, as David Brinkley's comments indicate. Writing in *New York* magazine soon after the park opened, architectural critic Peter Blake said that Disney World and Disneyland were the only new towns of any significance built in the United States since World War II. What the designers had created was an entire city with fire stations, environmental protection, a phone company, its own landscape department, and dozens of other urban services. On stage were exciting attractions, themed shops, restaurants, resort hotels, campgrounds, and recreation facilities. Backstage was a network of utilities, supply and maintenance facilities, and crisscrossing service tunnels that connected the vast underground hidden from public view. "The only way to have Fun City, urban-design wise, is to take it away from the do-gooders and lease it to Walt Disney Productions," Blake concluded.[19]

One Disney designer, quoted in a company press release, attributed their success to their ability to coordinate the theme park with its support facilities. "We were very careful to avoid any contradictions in architecture and design," he said. "The challenge was not just in the theme park this time but outside the park because for this project we had total control . . . we owned all the immediate surrounding land."[20] Disney World's first two resort hotels, the Contemporary and Polynesian, were built as architectural extensions of Tomorrowland

and Adventureland, respectively. What Disney planners had been shut out from designing at Disneyland was opened up for planning at Disney World, because the "outside world" of hotels, restaurants, shops, and the like was still Disney; it could still be incorporated into the "themed experience."

Florida's deregulation strategy worked famously for Disney. Freed from land-use and building controls, the whole 2,500-acre complex—ten times the size of Disneyland—was built in just four years from the time earth-moving equipment first lumbered onto the property. Meeting Walt's original deadline, the Magic Kingdom opened on October 1, 1971. By that time, the company had poured $320 million into the project, and 9,000 workers had labored on it. Among other tasks, the Disney workforce transplanted into man-made jungles and lagoons more than 60,000 trees and shrubs, collected from around the world. They scooped out a mile-wide lake, Seven Seas Lagoon, the water entranceway to the park, and lined it with four million gallons of white sand, pumped up from the Florida earth. They built a four-lane parkway running almost five miles from the main entrance to the Magic Kingdom, and constructed three and one-half miles of twin-rail monorails to speed visitors around the park. They fabricated, under Gen. Potter's direction, an environmentally friendly energy plant that captured waste heat for everything from space heating to domestic hot water to cooking.

To finance all this, they floated federally subsidized municipal bonds to pay for the infrastructure, such as their roads and water and sewer lines. But the buildings and attractions were privately financed, aided by Disney's then-soaring stock values. The company's $320-million investment came from two bond offerings in 1968 and 1969, a common stock issue in 1971, and a credit line from Bank of America. Disney vice president Card Walker reported in early 1971 that they would open the park virtually debt-free, though costs had exceeded projections by 40 percent.[21] By opening day, they had invested almost $400 million in the project.

The greatest challenge for the Disney juggernaut was organized labor. Hubbard Construction Co. had the contract for the park's massive excavation work. A nonunion employer, they were paying $2.25 an hour when union scale was $4.60. Elmer Sevor, the business manager for Operating Engineers Local 673, began talking with Hubbard's sixty or so workers, and eventually won their support. Because there were no buildings in the area, the workers met in a field, under the illumination of car headlights, and voted to strike for recognition of the union and union-scale wages.

Their strike began in mid-January 1968 and lasted several weeks. Fifteen job entrances had to be covered, so the Operating Engineers turned to members at other job sites to work the picket lines. On several occasions, contractors tried to go onto the property to get their equipment so they could use it on other projects. "We persuaded them it would not be in their best interest to do that," explained Sevor, winking as he told the story.[22] When negotiations between Disney and the Operating Engineers officials broke down over whether the company would agree to use the union's hiring hall, the building trades from Orlando to the Space Coast called a one-day general strike. An estimated 8,000 workers and their supporters rallied at Orlando's Tangerine Bowl, now the Citrus Bowl, disrupting construction projects throughout central Florida.[23]

Soon, Disney agreed to the hiring hall, and the strike was settled. After another strike the following summer, the company and the AFL-CIO reached agreement covering all construction and maintenance work on the project. This agreement paved the way for the Services Trades Council, representing six different unions, to represent service employees when the park opened for business in 1971.

Meanwhile Orlando was metamorphosing too. In 1969, it became one of the nation's ten fastest-growing areas. Measured in terms of jobs attracted from other areas, it ranked sixth nationwide. By the same measure, interestingly, the metropolitan area surrounding Anaheim, California—home to Disneyland—ranked second. At the same time, a small renaissance was occurring in downtown Orlando. Having declined as a retail shopping area, it experienced a modest revival as a financial center for the building and tourist industries emerging around it. For example, the Hartford Insurance Group and CNA Financial Corp. erected downtown office towers of fourteen and nineteen stories, respectively. Meanwhile, suburban housing developments were popping up like dandelions, including one named Williamsburg that William Levitt of Levittown fame built. To house so many construction workers and theme-park ride operators, apartment houses were springing up in one-to-one ratio with single-family homes. An eight-mile strip known as "apartment-house row" was emerging on S.R. 436, which runs along two sides of Orlando.

This growth was stimulated not only by the lure of Mickey Mouse. It also arose from the movers and shakers' success in securing several large installations for the area, most of them government-related. Other than I-4 and bending Florida's Turnpike to Orlando, their biggest success was bringing the Glenn L. Martin Co. (later Martin Marietta) to Orlando in 1956. The missile company was initially attracted to central Florida by the opening, in 1955, of the U.S. Missile Test Center at Cape Canaveral, forty miles east of Orlando. But it was Billy Dial and Linton Allen who brought Martin to Orlando. Allen, who preceded Dial as president of First National Bank, used $2,500 of his own money to option 6,400 acres of land, south of the city, as a site for their missile works.[24] Then Dial won state approval for two access roads to the Martin property, along with circuit court approval for a special sewer district that served only them. In all, the deal making took twenty-two days.

Another success was landing a naval training center for the area. *Sentinel* publisher Martin Andersen knew Lyndon Johnson through their common mentor, Charles Marsh. After first endorsing Johnson in his aborted 1956 presidential try, the publisher organized a motorcade for him during a 1964 campaign visit.[25] Delighted by the turnout, Johnson offered to organize a testimonial for the publisher, who purportedly responded, "What I'd really like, Mr. President, is a military base." After the visit, the President called Andersen and said, "I'm sending you a naval base."[26] The Naval Training Center soon replaced a deserted Air Force base in Orlando.

Still another coup was landing a state university for Orlando. As Dial explained in an interview, "We needed a university where [the] Martin [Co.'s] engineers could earn an advanced degree." The task was getting state support. "We had to fight that thing through the legislature and through the Board of Regents," said Dial.[27] Even after the legislature authorized the university, the Regents refused to carry through until the local group secured a deed for the property. "So a hundred of us put up $10,000 a piece—a million dollars—to buy the property where the university is today," said the banker-attorney. Founded as Florida Technological University, the new university broke ground in April 1967, just as the Disney charter cleared the legislature.

In addition, Orlando mayors Robert Carr and Carl Langford negotiated with the air force to permit use of McCoy Air Force Base. Under Mayor Carr, the air force agreed to allow commercial use of one of their two runways.[28] In 1969, Mayor Langford negotiated a better deal: a twenty-year lease for one dollar, with Orlando collecting all commercial landing fees. Then, in 1974, McCoy Air Base was officially closed and the property sold to the city for one dollar.

The movers and shakers continued their preference for politically insulated bodies like the State Road Board. Their working model was the Orlando Utilities Commission, founded in 1923 as a municipally owned public utility, providing water and electric service to Orlando and adjoining portions of Orange County. The OUC was a perfect example of why American socialists at the turn of the century favored municipally owned utilities, as it provided relatively cheap service and returned a tidy profit to the city. Yet, a self-perpetuating business elite controlled the utility company, rather than the ratepayers lionized in socialist theory. Following this model, the Orlando-Area Expressway Authority was created in 1963 and the Orlando Airport Authority in 1975. Both are self-financing through tolls and lease arrangements, relatively autonomous from local government, and dominated by gubernatorial appointments, all diminishing voter control.

While the movers and shakers succeeded in these endeavors, they reached their limit when voter approval was required. In 1964, for example, Orlando voters decisively rejected an urban renewal plan supported by this leadership group. At the time, downtown was decaying as shops moved to the suburbs, and local leaders hoped to use the federal urban renewal program to rejuvenate Orlando's central core. As another example, local business leaders tried to streamline the Orange County commission in the mid-1970s. "With five independent commissioners and no elected chair, we had a vacuum of power with no leadership," said County Attorney James Robinson.[29] But county voters overwhelmingly rejected a proposal to create an elected county chair in 1974.

There were other limits to the informal system of private governance. For one thing, the task of molding business consensus became more difficult as Orlando grew and diversified. In 1964, Tom Brownlee, then the president-elect of the national association of chamber directors, was hired to revitalize the Orlando Chamber of Commerce, which was then little more than a travel bureau. "Back then," said Brownlee, "Billy Dial and Martin Andersen and Linton Allen made all the decisions, but Orlando was growing too big and too diversified, and they were growing older."[30] For another, the growth issue was becoming more complicated, requiring a more selective business recruitment strategy as well as new efforts to manage growth. One of Brownlee's first acts was to organize an advertising committee to market the city. The group was led by Buell Duncan, a First National Bank vice president. As he explained, "Our focus changed in the mid-60s. We realized we had tourism. It was industrial development we needed."[31] Duncan gave speeches all over town using a three-legged stool to illustrate that, in his words, "we had agriculture, we had tourism, the weak leg of the economy was industry." After Disney opened, Brownlee worried publicly that Orlando's economy had become imbalanced in favor of tourism.[32]

Managing growth required, among other things, synchronizing public and private development, so that roads, schools, and sewers were available to meet the demands of new private development. This task went beyond the capacity of the old system of private governance represented by the movers and shakers. It required action by government in the form of regulation and planning, as well as new public facilities and the means to pay for them. It also went beyond the capacity of the caretaker-style government of the day, with its orientation toward municipal services and keeping government small and taxes low.

How different it was for Disney, which was not encumbered by voters or elected officials or even traditional property rights. There, one man—Gen. Potter—controlled their governmental arm, which built the utilities and public works, while another man—Adm. Fowler—supervised construction of the theme park, hotels, and other private works. Since Potter was simultaneously a Disney employee and president of the Reedy Creek Improvement District, public and private development could be coordinated. From the roads and utilities to the rides, shops, and hotels—it was all Disney.

Not quite appreciating these differences, Martin Andersen encouraged city and county officials to emulate Disney's planning. His advice echoed David Brinkley's remarks at the beginning of this chapter. "As Disney has planned, we, too, must plan," he wrote in a front-page editorial that was titled, "The Man in the Engine Toots, Toots, Toots; What Say We Back in the Caboose?" He wanted government leaders to go to maps, charts, and changes in their *modus operandi.* "You cannot dump 50,000 tourists a day into this community along with 50,000 new jobs and build 40,000 new homes without putting some-body out of joint," he wrote in his avuncular style. "Disney has taught us that, knowing the facts of life as to what is to come, we should plan for the great confrontation."[33]

What Andersen overlooked was that local government could not control development as Disney had done. True, they could do more to coordinate among themselves in developing regional transporta-tion and waste treatment systems; to assess the impact of large-scale developments before approving them; and to regulate subdivision lay-out and the location of shopping malls and other commercial com-plexes. But, unlike Disney, they did not own everything. Hence they were continually in a reactive posture, responding to growth forces originating in the marketplace. They lacked the resources to build all the infrastructure and provide all the services that a tourist economy required. And not least, they were constrained by Disney's immunity from state and local regulations.

Harlan Hanson played a key public planning role during this pe-riod of Orlando's transformation. As director of the Orange-Osceola-Seminole County Planning Commission, he understood the need for compact development to conserve the cost of extending roads, sew-ers, and other public services. "We are discouraging spotty growth in favor of concentric growth," he told the *St. Petersburg Times* in 1969, "because development adjoining development is so much less costly."[34] The problem was, his agency's powers were advisory only. Thus, the *Times* reporter noted a "communications gap" between planners and those who had invested in peripheral land with an-nounced plans for ambitious, costly development. "The developers seem unaware," she wrote, "that the compact development project of Hanson and the commission, if followed, could scuttle their plans."

As Hanson said in an interview, it was Disney's control over the building process that distinguished their planning, rather than their creativity. He called their design work "something that any B-student could do."[35] They succeeded because they listened to their planners and implemented their plans, which they could do because they were private, he said. Public planning, on the other hand, was hampered by cities' lack of power to control development at their edges, by politicians' unwillingness to be guided by planning, and by property owners' resistance to regulation. Hence public planners needed continually to "marshal their forces," lining up support from individuals, neighborhoods, and public agencies, whatever worked. In his own case, he drew upon his master's thesis on education in planning, written at the University of North Carolina. Keeping the message simple, he created eight-page summaries of each of the four elements of the plan: land use, transportation, recreation, and water and sewer. As well, he gave almost 400 speeches before retreating to the private sector in 1970, frustrated by the limits of public planning.

Hanson's counterpart at Orange County was Don Greer, a graduate of the Georgia Tech planning school, hired in 1964 to organize a county planning department. One of his first acts was to hire David Johnston, fresh from planning school at the University of North Carolina. Greer and Johnston, ages 32 and 28 respectively, and a draftsman named Jim Smart, were Orange County's planning staff when the Disney charter passed in 1967. At the time, they had an atlas of land uses, which Greer had prepared by driving around the county, and a transportation plan that "amounted to improving a few roads and making some connections," said Greer.

There was a regional planning council, the East Central Florida Regional Planning Council, formed in 1962, but it was headquartered in Titusville, forty miles away on the Atlantic coast, reflecting the emphasis on the space program. The planning council had commissioned a study by noted planner Carl Feiss, recommending a compact pattern of development to reduce public service costs.[36] Their recommendation was advisory only; the planning council served mainly as an information resource. However limited, the planning powers in the region were vested in the cities and counties. By 1969, every county in the region had a planning department, as did most cities. Yet none of the counties had comprehensive plans, and most cities lacked even subdivision regulations, said Hanson. Moreover, capital improvement budgeting for such things as roads and sewers was unknown to governments in the area.[37]

"It wasn't heard of in those days to try to control growth to keep it where you had water and sewer service," said Greer. "The idea of paving all the streets when you did a new subdivision was a new thing, too."[38] About the only way to accomplish anything was to get landowner cooperation, he added. That solved a legal problem, since the county lacked adequate authority to control private development. It also solved a political problem, since county commissioners loathed taking on property owners, especially large ones. In the early 1960s, Orange County's zoning ordinance required landowner approval before a change in zoning, a stipulation removed before the Disney building-boom. Still, the zoning code back then was "full of holes," said Greer, who left the county in 1968 to work for Joe Potter at the Disney government.[39]

Advance planning was a resource problem, too. "Orange County had no money to build roads," explained Greer. "The only way you could ever build a road was to get the state to build it, [which meant] you had to lobby the State Road Department." The county did not even have money to purchase road rights-of-way, not without increasing taxes and revealing the costs of growth. Planners would therefore ask landowners to grant rights-of-way for roads, and landowners would sometimes get together on their own to dedicate land for roads. The drawback, said former county planner Dave Johnston, was that landowners in these situations felt justified in "developing their property to the max."[40] This happened, for example, along Orlando's inner beltway, S.R. 436, a jumble of apartment complexes, strip malls, and fast-food joints.

A reliance on private development also prevailed with water and sewer. In Orlando and the immediately surrounding area, the city-owned Orlando Utilities Commission provided water. Elsewhere, water was typically supplied by private companies, most of them small and undercapitalized. Developers in "leapfrog areas," as Greer called them, often built their own package plants for water and sewer— facilities that frequently reverted to county control after developers ran them into the ground. Standards for these package plants were "none too high," said Greer.[41] Not only was environmental quality threatened, but the reliance on package plants and septic tanks, rather than on public utilities, deprived local officials of an important growth-management tool.

At Disney, on the other hand, there was only one landowner and one government; public and private were fused. Their combination of public and private powers let them synchronize public facilities— such as roads and water and sewer lines—with their private facilities—their attractions, stores, and hotels. Public facilities did not lag behind private ones. They were close to achieving the ideal of their 1966 planning grant proposal: a city "freed from the impediments to change, such as building regulations, traditional property rights, and elected political officials."[42] There was no division among property owners, no conflict over taxes, land use, or public services. Nor were elections needed to define the collective will; that was done instead by corporate fiat. In all these respects, they enjoyed advantages over public-sector planners. As seen below, their powers and immunities, along with their deep pockets, also distinguished them from other private developers.

International Drive provides a case study of speculative private development under conditions of fragmented land ownership and weak government. Spawned by the Mouse's arrival, I-Drive (as it is known locally) runs parallel to I-4, lying partly in Orlando and partly in unincorporated Orange County. The antithesis of Disney World's ordered aestheticism, the popular tourist strip is a jumble of sports bars, outlet stores, fast-food restaurants, and souvenir shops of every description, usually mired in traffic congestion. Its initial two-mile stretch was built, on the south end, by an assortment of individual and corporate investors and, on the north, by an overextended real estate company. In different ways, each fell victim to land speculation.

The man who started I-Drive was Finley Hamilton, a dapper fellow well known in Orlando's Country Club district for his chauffeur-driven limousine. He had the good fortune of owning the Hilton franchise in Orlando when Disney came to town. He also had the foresight to build a hotel near the interchange of Sand Lake Road and I-4, the first interchange between Disney World and Orlando. "Then it was just a bunch of palmettos," he said of the land. "I couldn't get any of my investor friends to go in with me. They all called it Finley's folly."[43]

Finally, he persuaded local sign-company owner Jack Zimmer to be his 40 percent partner, and together they purchased ten acres from Jim Morgan, a Florida Ranchlands salesperson who had purchased the land on speculation following the Disney announcement. Hamilton and Zimmer then built a 114-room Hilton Hotel, later expanded to 400 rooms and now a Ramada Resort.

Needing an access road to reach their property, which fronted on I-4, the two men built a quarter-mile road, naming it "International Drive." It was a good name choice, since, today, I-Drive attracts millions of international tourists a year along its twelve-mile length. Hamilton disclaims credit for prescience, however. "I wanted to call it 'Hamilton Drive' but the name was already used," he says. In then-parochial Orlando, the name "International" was still available.

Convinced that more growth was coming, Hamilton and Zimmer bought twenty-eight acres north of their property, paying $10,000 per acre as they had for their hotel site. They then divided the land, selling the last ten acres to a Kuwaiti group for $200,000 an acre; their lowest price was $100,000 an acre. There was no master plan for the overall property; instead, Hamilton and Zimmer divided it to suit the needs of individual buyers, some of them speculators who resold the land. "That was 30 years [sic] before all this plan stuff came about," Hamilton said in a 1998 interview.[44] They got the water from a neighboring development and installed the sewer lines themselves, using bank financing for the utilities. In contrast, the Disney Co. used tax-free municipal bonds to finance their infrastructure. "It would have been nice to have their bonding power," commented Zimmer, adding "our interest costs were about twice theirs."[45]

After Disney World opened in 1971, Hamilton and Zimmer extended the Hilton's access road to the north in a deal with Major Realty Co., whose property abutted theirs in that direction. These two properties are shown in Map 5. The only problem was that the south section of I-Drive built by Hamilton and Zimmer was two lanes, and the north section built by the better-capitalized Major Realty group was three lanes. Public service coordination was also complicated because the Major property lay in Orlando, and Hamilton and Zimmer's land in the county. The Orlando Utilities Commission provided power in Orlando and buried its lines, while Florida Power had the county franchise and refused to bury its lines.

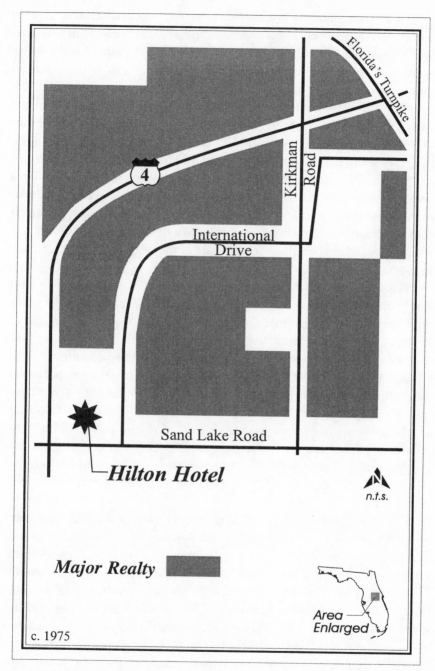

Map 5   Hilton and Major Realty properties

These coordination issues reflected the problem of fragmented landownership, an endemic problem in capitalist cities, but one that Disney with its centralized landownership could avoid. On the other hand, the Major Realty property at the north end of I-Drive proved that centralized land ownership and strategic location were no panacea. Their development sounded good on paper as advertised in the early 1970s. "Major Center," it was called, a master-planned community for 100,000 persons located at the "crossroads of Florida." The property spanned the junction of I-4 and Florida's Turnpike, just five miles from Disney. As developed, though, it was a mishmash of land uses, unattractive, with no unifying features. It was a victim of bad management and a sour economy—of a company that leveraged itself into a corner, buying too much land without the cash flow to service its massive debt when the energy crisis of the mid-1970s sent tourism into a tailspin.

As sales slowed, the company went into a "survival mode," said real estate writer Jack Snyder, liquidating properties to meet their debt service.[46] David Winter, vice president for residential property at the company, said that "the difference between us and Disney was that we used the banks' money and they used Disney's money."[47] The Disney Co. had their revenue from movies and theme parks to weather market downturns, Major had only its land sales. That difference also explains why Major failed to adopt land-use restrictions that would make their overall property more coherent and attractive. As company consultant Gary Jarhaus explained, architectural and design standards would hurt land sales: "Someone who would be willing to pay $100,000 per acre might offer only $50,000 because of [such] restrictions."[48]

The Disney advantage was that, having bought their land cheap, and having a steady cash flow from their other operations, they could endure a bad market. And having their own government, they could create a rational utility network. A case in point was the requirement for every room to have a fire sprinkler linked to monitors in fire stations. None of the original hotels on I-Drive was built with fire sprinklers. That changed only in the 1980s in response to a state mandate. The cost of retrofitting older hotels was "enormous," says hotelier Harris Rosen, who knows from experience.[49] And maybe it was for naught: Reedy Creek administrator Tom Moses questions whether

I-Drive has the water pressure to support so many sprinklers, should a major fire occur.[50]

Likewise with mass transit, Disney World was built with an integral monorail system, whereas I-Drive must be retrofitted for mass transit, a daunting task that continues to elude property owners and politicians in the new millennium. Rosen, now a competitor of Disney's, acknowledges their superior planning capacity but is less charitable in describing their power to inspect their own buildings, which he sees as their biggest advantage. "It enables them to fast-track everything. So what if their standards are high, they still control it. I'd rather have high standards with my own inspectors than lower standards with somebody else looking at it," says Rosen. Lending support to this view, Todd Mansfield, the head of Disney's development arm in the early 1990s, said of Reedy Creek inspectors: "They gave me fits, but at the end of the day I knew we worked for the same company."[51]

Disney's ability to get its way extended to its dealings with other businesses. Finley Hamilton, who started I-Drive, complained that the Disney Co. took advantage of him and partner Jack Zimmer. When his Hilton Hotel opened in 1968, it was the only large hotel close to the Disney construction site. The California company approached them and offered to manage the hotel, saying they wanted a place to train their staff to run the Contemporary and Polynesian hotels, scheduled to open in seventeen months. "This will bring you a lot of business," they told the two men, in what was a handshake agreement. Instead during this time, "we lost hundreds and thousands" said Hamilton. It was an eye-opener for Zimmer and him, since "Disney was like apple pie then, and we thought we would be treated fairly."

Among their complaints: the Disney Co. hired an expensive chef whose real job was preparing fancy meals for company executives flying in from California. Hotel maids were used to clean homes the company had purchased in ritzy Bay Hills for their visiting executives. More distressing to Hamilton and Zimmer, the company let employees sign chits in the hotel restaurant, chits that the owners were unable to collect and that the company refused to honor. Hamilton wrote a detailed letter to Disney president Donn Tatum itemizing their complaints and requesting reimbursement.[52] Under Disney management, the hotel had lost approximately $50,000 in sixteen months, despite a room occupancy rate of 70 percent. That occupancy rate compared favorably with a 68 percent rate for the Southeast over the same time period, Hamilton noted.

Tatum never responded, however, displaying an attitude of aloofness bordering on arrogance that was seen before in Disney's treatment of Nelson Boice and would be seen again in their dealings with Orange County. As county officials would later do, Hamilton decided to let the matter rest, fearing the consequences of more aggressive action. "We didn't feel we could sue," he said, "because we had that hotel, and another one under construction, and we knew Disney could be a source of business."[53]

What a proprietary government combined with centralized land ownership and a steady revenue stream could do well, Disney did extremely well. With these qualifications, David Brinkley's opening comment was right: the Disney Co. excelled at "getting things done." As the Disney designer commented above, they had an advantage not possessed at Disneyland. Because they owned so much land and could plan and equip it with their private government, they could incorporate positive amenities into the overall plan of development. But the reverse was also true: they could impose the costs of development on the surrounding community—the cost of building roads and schools and sewer lines; the cost of social services for a massive low-wage workforce; the cost of synchronizing public facilities and services with their private development.

On the costs of building infrastructure, politicians from Governor Kirk on down were bemoaning the shortage of roads and road funding. As one indication of the increased traffic as Disney opened, the oil industry predicted that 150 new service stations would be needed in the next five years.[54] Likewise, schools exceeded capacity in Orange County. "A school we put on the drawing boards today is overcrowded yesterday. With 119 families moving into the Orlando metropolitan area each week, our opening day enrollment was 75,000; but by the end of the school year, there'll be 90,000 students," said a county school official.[55]

On the costs of providing social services and housing, the regional planning council sounded a warning soon after the Magic Kingdom opened. "There are several complicated problems associated with tourist industry workers, and several reasons why government spending may need to be higher than normal in an area based on service industry employment," they advised in 1972. One problem, they said, was the cost of providing social services for so many low-wage workers. Another was providing adequate and affordable housing. Mobile homes, they said, would be "lifesavers" for the tourist workforce, and more mobile home parks were needed. It was a visual image—overflowing mobile home parks—at odds with what local leaders had thought Disney would bring.

But the larger problem, they said, was making people aware that this workforce existed. "A large number of tourist industry employees remain out of sight, occupied as kitchen help, chambermaids, maintenance workers, janitors, watchmen and the like. Many of these workers are not highly paid. They can remain invisible at a tourist attraction, but they must reside in the community and, as residents, they are not invisible," said the planning council in a prescient warning.[56]

On coordinating public facilities with new Disney development, the company's view was, "It's your responsibility," said former county planner David Johnston. He recalls getting that message in a meeting with Disney representatives, including Gen. Potter, just before the theme park opened. "They were saying 'you'd better be ready for all this traffic that is going to be generated,'" said Johnston, who became Winter Park mayor in 1987. "Their attitude was, 'We'll build this here and generate all this need, but you'd better build the infrastructure to service this need.'"[57]

In fact, Disney's attitude was shortsighted. As events in the 1980s would make clear, they were part of a mutually dependent relationship with the local community. If the area's transportation system was burdened, they were burdened too. If local leaders called them bad neighbors, their public image was threatened. It was a lesson that the Disney Co. under Michael Eisner would learn the hard way, as their honeymoon with the local community ended and a period of open conflict with Orange County officials began.

six   Conflict

T he Disney Co. chose an auspicious setting to announce their plans for Epcot, the first big expansion of Disney World since the Magic Kingdom opened in 1971. It was the meeting of the Southern Governors Association at Disney's Contemporary Hotel on September 15–17, 1975. On hand were major government officials, from governors to congressional leaders to federal agency heads, including Secretary of State Henry Kissinger, the featured speaker. These dignitaries in turn attracted a small army of news reporters to record their reactions to the Disney presentation. Gaining more exposure, company executives simultaneously delivered personal invitations to thirty foreign embassies for a second presentation on October 10–13.[1]

On a lower profile, the Disney Co. offered a preview presentation on the day before the governors conference to Cliff Guillet, executive director of the East Central Florida Regional Planning Council.[2] Accompanying Guillet to the preview was his director of planning, Carl Gosline, who would later work for the Disney government. When the two planning officials arrived at the Contemporary Hotel, they were cordially greeted by a dozen Disney executives and ushered into the hotel ballroom, where they viewed angled models of Epcot's buildings and attractions. At the center of the room, reserved for them, were two big chairs facing a large movie screen. As they took their seats, the lights dimmed and Walt's image suddenly appeared on screen. It was the Epcot film, the same film shown to the Florida legislature in 1967, the film in which Walt described Epcot as a living, breathing community.

After the presentation, Guillet and Gosline were shown an audio-animatronic display of three talking heads, representing Thomas Jefferson, Ben Franklin, and George Washington. The figures were talking about Epcot's impact on the world, not just Florida. Emblematic of that impact, the globe-traveling secretary of state arrived in Orlando the same day. He was met at the airport by Florida Governor Ruebin Askew, host of the governors conference, and Card Walker, president of the Disney Co. Askew had brought Walker along so he could invite the secretary to a special presentation on Epcot. "Card, I can see you tomorrow morning," Kissinger told a relieved Walker, who had assembled a VIP cast for the governors conference presentation.[3] As arranged there, Kissinger came to the Contemporary Hotel the next morning for an Epcot preview—just like the one Guillet and Gosline saw.

As Guillet recalls, he was enjoying his morning coffee with his wife when he opened the *Orlando Sentinel* the next day. There, he read that Secretary Kissinger had said Epcot would enhance world peace more than all his shuttle diplomacy. "Holy cow," Guillet exclaimed to his wife, "we may have to disapprove it," referring to the possibility that the regional planning council would reject the Epcot project. At the time, he and Disney officials were unsure whether Chapter 380 of the Florida Code applied to Disney World. Chapter 380 was a 1972 planning law that subjected "developments of regional impact"—big development projects affecting more than one government jurisdiction—to review by regional planning bodies like the one Guillet headed. The plan-review requirement was significant because the agency could require developers to mitigate impacts for a long list of facilities, from roads to sewers to affordable housing. If a developer failed to comply, a project could be stopped.

During the planning phase of Epcot, Disney officials were solicitous of Guillet and the planning council, said the planning director. They came to visit him regularly and even hosted a planning council meeting a month before the Epcot announcement. Guillet, a veteran of many planning battles, assumed that Disney was being nice because they feared the council's regulatory hand. He also knew that the council's actions needed political acceptance, and, accordingly, he felt trapped by Disney's adroit use of Kissinger and the other dignitaries at the governors meeting. How could his agency disapprove Epcot because of its traffic impact, a comparatively minor issue in the larger scheme of things, when Secretary Kissinger proclaimed that it would foster world peace?

In fact, the face-off never occurred. The Disney Co. had been seeking an advisory ruling from the Florida attorney general on whether Ch. 380 applied to Epcot. They succeeded in May 1977 when Attorney General Robert Shevin ruled in their favor. At issue was Sec. 23(1) of the Reedy Creek charter, which read in part: "The jurisdiction and powers of the Board of Supervisors [of the Reedy Creek Improvement District] provided for herein shall be exclusive of any law *now or hereafter enacted* providing for land use regulation, zoning, or building codes, by the State of Florida or any agency or authority of the State and the provisions of any such law shall not be applicable within the territorial limits of the District" [italics added]. Florida's Division of State Planning, the agency responsible for administering Ch. 380, had concluded that the law did *not* apply to Disney, based on the charter's "now or hereafter enacted" provision.[4] Now, Shevin's short, five-paragraph opinion had sustained the agency ruling; in the absence of a court decision, his opinion was legally binding. "After that, we didn't hear from them again," Guillet said of Disney.

In the Epcot era, Disney's relationship with the local community would change considerably. Before, the company had made demands on government, securing their semiautonomous political district, their powers and immunities, and their interchanges on I-4. In the mid-1980s, however, Orange County would begin making demands on them. It marked a new period in the Disney–Orange County relationship, one of conflict but also of growing interdependence. A new social contract was being formed as both sides grew aware that neither could flee the other. Like the plight of women in many nineteenth-century marriages, the opportunity to "exit" was blocked. The remaining alternatives, in the terminology of economist Albert Hirschman, were "voice" (to complain) or "loyalty."[5]

Epcot, as announced, scarcely resembled the going community that Walt described on film to the Florida legislature in 1967. Back then, Epcot was heralded as a fantastic—yet real—community in which "20,000 people would live and work and play."[6] The Disney Co. said they needed powers and exemptions to ensure their "flexibility" to plan for the future of this real-world community. In contrast, the announced Epcot was more like a permanent world's fair. It would have a World Showcase in which various nations exhibited their products and cultures, separated by a man-made lagoon from Future World, where major American corporations displayed the latest advances in technology. Germany, Mexico, Canada, France, the United Kingdom, Japan, and Italy agreed to build pavilions for World Showcase. The industry exhibits were sponsored by a roll call of corporate giants: General Motors, Kodak, Exxon, Kraft, United Technologies, General Electric, Sperry, American Express, and Coca-Cola. The exhibits included World of Motion (sponsored by GM), Journey into Imagination (sponsored by Kodak), Land (sponsored by Kraft), Communicore (sponsored by Sperry), and Flagship Earth, whose spherical ball became the Epcot symbol.

In all, Epcot was an amazing feat of imagination and coordination that few corporations could have achieved. Yet it was hardly a functioning community, hardly the prototype community that Disney once claimed they would build. Guillet and several planning council members had raised this issue when the Disney Co. hosted a meeting of the regional planning council just before the September 1975 announcement. Where were the citizen-residents? they asked. Why did they use the original Epcot film since their concept had obviously changed? The Disney representatives had no real response, said Guillet. Publicly, marketing vice president Jack Lindquist characterized the model city concept "as only one visual depiction of one way to go."[7] Also, Disney president Card Walker suggested that International Village, constructed for foreign students working in Epcot's country pavilions, was like Walt's model city. In words mimicking Walt's description of Epcot, he called International Village a place where students would "live and play and learn."[8] Of course the foreign students could not vote, which was precisely what Disney wanted to avoid.

So much for their presentation to the Florida legislature. For legal reasons explained in Chapter 4, the Disney Co. needed to say they were building a city. Only a popularly elected government could exercise planning and zoning authority and gain exemption from land-use laws. Having won that authority, they felt free to redefine Epcot—without renouncing the powers and exemptions derived from the original concept. Amazingly, they were not called on it. The *Orlando Sentinel* editorialized that the new Epcot was "the same dream" that

Walt described.[9] Governor Askew seemed captivated by how the project would contribute to world peace and the Florida tourist economy. Local congressman Richard Kelley, later snared in the Abscam scandal, called Epcot an example of what free enterprise could do without government help[10]—overlooking the interchanges built for Disney on I-4.

This failure to call Disney on re-visioning Epcot is more striking given the abundant media attention it received. When it opened on October 1, 1982, about 150 press organizations were present, averaging three representatives each, from across the country and abroad.[11] Only half as many covered the Magic Kingdom's opening. All three major networks broadcast the opening live between 7 a.m. and 9 a.m., and CBS taped a two-hour special for airing in November. It was part of a pattern in which news organizations, taking advantage of free theme-park passes and Disney's special brand of lavish hospitality, provide soft coverage of Disney openings, typically sending their entertainment and travel reporters to cover these events.

Whatever it was supposed to be, Epcot crystallized Orlando's status as the world's major tourist destination. Astonishingly, more people came to Orlando's fiberglass swathed theme parks than to the Eiffel Tower, the Taj Mahal, the Tower of London, and the Egyptian Pyramids combined. Overall attendance at the Disney complex soared 81 percent in Epcot's first year, jumping from 12.56 million in 1982 to 22.71 million in 1983. These attendance figures reflect clicks of the turnstile, however, rather than the actual visitor count. The number of people coming to central Florida had not skyrocketed, but those who came were staying longer. Nonetheless, Orlando experienced a surge in hotel construction, reflecting the increase in "room-night" demand as tourists prolonged their stays. In 1982, Orange, Osceola, and Seminole counties had 33,800 hotel rooms, while just two years later the area boasted 44,500 rooms. In its first year, Epcot was credited with generating $500 million in new hotel construction,[12] and hoteliers were jubilant over their 83 percent occupancy figures, a performance unparalleled in the country.[13]

As well, Epcot started a shakeout in the tourist industry, spawning new attractions and killing others. One change was the emergence of dinner-show attractions, providing a nighttime diversion for theme-park visitors.[14] On the casualty side, Circus World at the edge of Polk

County south of Orlando changed hands several times, was renovated and turned into Boardwalk and Baseball, then finally closed for good in 1990. Of course, many attractions died aborning from the start of the Disney era. Said former Orange County Administrator Jim Harris, "For every 'It's a Small World' (at Disney) there were a dozen that didn't make it."[15] Among the start-up casualties were Hurricane World, World Peace Expo, Bible World, Roy Roger's, and Marco Polo Park.

Orlando's International Drive tourist district really took off after Epcot opened. The state had adopted a county-optional tourist tax in 1977, a so-called bed tax that applied to hotel rooms but not theme park admissions. Orange County voters promptly adopted a 2 percent tax on hotel rooms and approved the construction of a 700,000-square-foot county convention center on a two-mile extension of I-Drive. These developments marked the county's deepening dependence on tourism. Not only was the county dependent on Disney tax revenues; when the convention center opened in 1983, it went into the tourist business itself. The bed tax fueled this dependence, since its revenues could be used only to support the tourism and convention business. These revenues were used to expand the convention center in 1989 and again in 1996, giving Orlando almost as much convention space as New Orleans and Atlanta.

Meanwhile Disney was expanding too, and not just in Orlando. By 1983, the entertainment company had sunk $1.7 billion into their Orlando complex. As well, Tokyo Disneyland was slated to open in early 1983. The $400-million park would be owned, operated, and paid for by the Oriental Land Co. of Tokyo. Yet Disney supervised the planning, design, and construction of the project, as well as employee training, and would receive royalties on admissions as well as on food and merchandise sales. Back in Orlando, the company was poised to build more hotels. In 1982, they had 3,100 new hotel rooms on the drawing boards, including three new hotels plus additions to existing hotels.[16] These plans awaited approval from top corporate management, however.

Locally, the benefits were mixed. As population and tourism increased, so did the pressure on roads, schools, water and sewer facilities, and police and fire services. Said Aaron Dowling, assistant executive director of the East Central Florida Regional Planning Council, in 1983: "A dozen years ago, we thought growth was good because it produced new taxes. We didn't consider the cost of the services that went along with it."[17] The kind of jobs being created was a problem, too. Despite record employment growth, personal income in Orange County remained below the state average, a phenomenon that *Florida Trend* magazine attributed to "the county's heavy concentration of employment in low-wage occupations such as tourism and hotel service."[18] The new emphasis on convention trade—in which the county was now a partner—was unlikely to improve this record, said the magazine. In passing a bed tax linked to tourism and the convention center, the county created a "low-wage job machine," as county planner Bruce McClendon would say later.[19]

It was after Epcot that growth problems began to generate political reaction. Bill Frederick, Orlando's mayor from 1980 to 1992, aptly characterized the growing friction between Disney and the surrounding community. "We were like two families sharing a house with one bathroom," he said.[20] Like a marriage, there was mutual dependence—but also conflict. Political scientist Paul Peterson has approvingly written that a pro-development consensus underlies policy making in most large cities.[21] This was essentially the attitude toward Disney and the growth it spawned at least until Epcot opened in 1982. Except for minor skirmishes over road financing, there was widespread support for "the Mouse," as Disney is known locally.

As Peterson recognizes, institutions often blunt conflict over growth, which happened with Disney's private government, the Reedy Creek Improvement District. Later on, it became a source of conflict, but more conflict would have occurred, and sooner, had the Disney government not existed. Without it, county taxpayers would have been saddled with building Disney World's entire infrastructure, and county government would have borne the administrative burden of regulating and inspecting the theme park's construction. As a special-purpose government, Reedy Creek lifted this responsibility from county shoulders.

Yet urban growth seldom remains uncontroversial. As "regime theorists" in political science have written in response to Peterson, the consensus on growth often breaks down over subsidiary issues—like how to finance growth, what kind of growth to pursue (tourism, manufacturing, etc.), and who will be inconvenienced by growth.[22]

These issues are subsidiary in that they presume an acceptance of growth, yet they nevertheless spawn sharp controversy. For cities have choices about how to grow, though those choices are constrained by the weight of past decisions, producing a blend of underlying stability and incremental change.

Thus conflict erupted in the mid-1980s over who should finance the public facilities needed to support Disney's growth. This conflict, which altered the Disney–local relationship, arose from changes in the company's top leadership.

In the early 1980s, the Disney Co. faced a leadership crisis. After Walt died, his brother Roy took charge until his own death just three months after Disney World opened. Then a triumvirate directed the company, consisting of Walt's son-in-law Ron Miller, Donn Tatum, and Card Walker, though it was Walker who called the shots. Finally, in early 1983, the company was put under the single reins of Miller, a former professional football player. By 1984, the company was struggling financially. Epcot had been built way over budget, generating massive corporate debt. The movie division had produced a string of family-fare box-office failures, theme park attendance had fallen for two years running, and profits were down 30 percent in three years.[23] Compounding the problem, corporate raiders Saul Steinberg and Irwin Jacobs were buying stock in the company, preparing separately to make takeover bids.

In response, Disney's corporate board of directors fired Miller in September 1984 and started searching for a replacement. Disney World president Dick Nunis offered himself as a candidate and was spurned by the board, even though the theme parks represented two-thirds of the company's revenue. Instead, they turned to the movie industry for leadership, hiring the team of Michael Eisner as chairman and Frank Wells as president. Eisner was the boy wonder who had turned around Saturday morning children's TV at ABC before becoming a Paramount executive. Wells, a Rhodes scholar, was an entertainment lawyer who had become president and co-chief of Warner Brothers before taking a sabbatical in 1982 to climb the world's tallest mountains.

To obtain these positions, as Ron Grover explains in *The Disney Touch*, Eisner and Wells needed to appease Texas oilman Sid Bass, a major company stockholder.[24] Bass, who invested heavily in real estate as well as oil, cared little about movies but saw an untapped gold mine in the company's 28,000-acre Florida property. Under Walker's leadership, no new hotels had risen on the property since 1973. In that time, almost 40,000 hotel rooms had been built around Orlando, only a fraction by Disney. For Walker was a "Walt man," harking back to when Walt and Roy were running the company, when there were Walt-men who were entertainment oriented, and Roy-men who were business oriented. Walker was bound by Walt's vision, seeing their business as entertainment rather than hotels. No more. Under pressure from Bass, who upped his stake in the company to 25 percent to ward off corporate raider Irwin Jacobs, Michael Eisner would move headlong into hotel building.

From a business perspective, the company's more aggressive strategy made sense. The business press universally said so, as reflected in Grover's subtitle, "How a Daring Management Team Revived an Entertainment Empire." Why not profit from their mountain of Florida real estate? Why not build hotels for the visitors they attracted to Orlando? From a public perspective, however, this new strategy violated an implicit social contract. Before, the company had failed to carry through in building the Epcot residential community that provided the rationale for their governmental privileges and immunities. Now, under Eisner, they were using those privileges to build something very different: a hotel empire.

By yielding to pressure from Sid Bass and others in the company to turn toward real-estate development, Eisner was restructuring the company's interest in the Orlando market. It was like one party in a marriage taking a new job without consideration for the relationship. Once Disney became a major hotelier, they would want to keep visitors on their property; they would oppose mass transit schemes that might take their patrons off property, to spend their money elsewhere. In altering the terms of the company's economic development marriage with Orlando, Eisner sowed the seeds of discord with local officials.

For Vera Carter, an Orange county commissioner from 1980 to 1992, the tipping point was a traffic accident. Carter, a Democrat, was a reluctant politician who had run for office on the platform of making growth pay for itself. She lived in Windermere, a scenic lakefront community just north of the Disney property, and counted many top Disney executives among her friends and neighbors. Overall, she thought their entertainment complex had been good for the community. At least, she thought the community could have absorbed Disney if county commissioners had acted courageously, using the Disney tax dividend to build the roads and water and sewer systems that were needed to support growth.[25]

A fatal auto accident had occurred on Reams Road, a dangerous two-lane road leading to the employee entrance at the north end of the Disney property. Carter, who knew friends of the victim, made an appointment to talk with Disney World president Dick Nunis about the condition of the road. She believed that the road should be the company's responsibility, not the county's. It unnerved her that Disney had permission to do "all sorts of things on its property," yet no responsibility for addressing off-site impacts as other developers did. When she met with Nunis, he insisted on showing her a promotional film and related that his own daughter had been killed in an auto accident. Unfazed, she told him that it was unconscionable that Disney cared so little for their own employees. "They are our friends and neighbors," she said. "But he just refused to accept that I had a valid point of view. We did not part on good terms."[26]

For Nunis it was an old issue. In the mid-1970s, he had started an "Arrive Alive on 535" campaign. Like Reams Road, S.R. 535 was used extensively by Disney employees; both roads were narrow and curving, without adequate shoulders or even turn lanes. Nunis had erected billboards along 535 with the "Arrive Alive" message, telling employees it was the county's fault the roads were so dangerous. "It was obviously an unproductive situation," commented Orange County Administrator Jim Harris.[27] He took umbrage that Nunis blamed the county when it was Disney's choice to put their employee entrance where they did. Though the signs would come down, Orange County Commissioner Paul Pickett never got over it. Pickett, who served on the commission in the 1970s, refused to visit the theme park, saying "If you have seen one carnival, you've seen them all."[28] But he was fairly isolated on the county commission as a Disney critic. Before the mid-1980s, little open conflict occurred between Disney and commissioners.

For County Commissioner Lou Treadway, transportation was like-wise the galvanizing issue.[29] Elected commission chairman in 1983 and again in 1984, he pushed through a transportation impact fee, the county's first attempt to make developers pay for growth. He came to his pay-to-grow philosophy by a different path from Vera Carter, however. Winning office as a Reagan Republican in 1980, Treadway was a retired Army lieutenant colonel who served two tours in Viet-nam and another in Europe, where he commanded a nuclear-armed artillery platoon. After leaving the army, he returned to Orlando where he had lived as a teenager and got involved in the local GOP, soon becoming county chair. Within the party, he was valued as a mediator between moderates and religious conservatives, while on the county commission, he was anything but a mediator. His forma-tive experience in the military made him sensitive to a larger public purpose but also made him accustomed to barking orders.

In August 1984, the county appointed Harry Stewart as county attorney. An expert on land-use law, Stewart had been the county at-torney of Ft. Lauderdale's Broward County. He not only wrote Brow-ard's first impact fee ordinance but also tried Florida's first case approving impact fees. Soon after Stewart arrived, Treadway told him he wanted a transportation impact-fee ordinance prepared and adopted before the November election. "I told him you can't do that," Stewart said in an interview. "It takes about a year to do one of these things."[30] Recalling the meeting, Treadway says he told the attorney: "Damn it. Don't come in here and tell me we can't do this."[31]

"I didn't say we couldn't do it," Stewart responded. "I said we couldn't do it this way." He said that the courts would demand a law that passed the "rational nexus test"—in other words, the ordinance would have to establish a clear linkage between the fee and the impact of the new development being assessed.[32] The fee needed to be linked to facilities required because of that impact. Otherwise, the courts would view the fee as a tax that unfairly applied only to developers. This conversation spawned a relationship in which Stewart the legal tactician advised Treadway on making growth pay for itself.

While the impact-fee struggle continued, Treadway took the lead-ership on another transportation issue: building a light-rail system between I-Drive and Disney World. The plan involved a co-partner-ship with Matra, a French high-tech conglomerate, to build a computerized, driverless train like one in Lille, France. It would be financed with a combination of private investment, bank loans, industrial bonds, federal and state grants, and an annual service fee to be paid by Orange County and the city of Orlando. In the end, the plan died— as another would three years later—because Disney refused to go along. Seventy percent of the projected riders would be tourists; without a stop at Disney, the plan was dead.

Treadway was furious with Disney. "We brought them in from the beginning," he said, referring to the planning process for the train. "They sat on all the committees."[33] He was especially angry that Disney World president Dick Nunis would not even respond to his letters after disapproving the project. The rail planners were not asking Disney for money, only for a fifty-foot right-of-way and land for a station. In Treadway's view, the station was the problem: the company opposed mass-transit access to their property. In the preceding twenty-four months, Disney had announced plans to build the 900-unit Grand Floridian hotel and the Pleasure Island nighttime entertainment area, and there was talk of adding 20,000 moderately priced hotel rooms on the property—all part of the Eisner-era wave of new construction. A rail stop on property would let their hotel guests escape, to spend their money elsewhere.

Eisner-era expansion sparked a critical series of *Orlando Sentinel* articles in mid-1985. Disney was accused of adopting a strategy to dominate and control visitors from the time they arrived until they left—at the expense of the area's non-Disney hotels and attractions. The capstone editorial was descriptively titled "Magic Kingdom of Aloof."[34] It offered tepid criticism, urging Disney executives to become more involved on county boards and commissions. Yet the company's response was anything but tepid. On the morning the editorial appeared, a Disney employee began removing *Sentinel* newsracks from Disney property, and a *Sentinel* delivery truck was refused admittance to Disney property.[35] Five more *Sentinel* articles labeling Disney "A World Unto Itself" appeared in early 1986. This unusual outburst of criticism signaled a breakdown of the anything-goes consensus favoring Disney.

The pot boiled over for Treadway and Carter on January 28, 1988, when Michael Eisner announced plans for two new projects: a $30-million shopping plaza and a $375-million convention center complex. The 200,000-square-foot convention center would connect with two giant hotels, the Swan and Dolphin, and have a total of 2,270 rooms. When construction began, Disney would have almost $1.4 billion in projects under way on its property—more than the $1.2-billion price tag for Epcot on opening day. In addition to the Grand Floridian Hotel and the Pleasure Island nighttime entertainment complex, the company was building a Norway pavilion at Epcot; Typhoon Lagoon, a water-thrill park; the 1,344-room Caribbean Beach Hotel near Epcot; and the $400-million Disney–MGM Studio Tour.

From a distance, it was remarkable that Eisner's announcement proved controversial. It was not like an auto plant shutdown in the Northeast; the Disney Co. was investing in, not abandoning, Orlando. But there were extenuating circumstances arising from Disney World's unique history. Treadway and Carter were not rebelling against growth in general or Disney World in particular. They were rebelling, rather, against the terms of the Disney charter, against the pre-nuptial agreement signed with the Disney Co. in 1967, the agreement that protected their immunities into the future. The Disney charter was written to attract growth. "Now [the Disney Co.] is using that law to build hotels and shopping centers and leave the tab to others," editorialized the *St. Petersburg Times*, calling this "growth management in reverse."[36] From an inducement to invest, the charter had been transformed by the growth it sought to encourage, into a constraint on managing growth. It was the contradiction of deregulation: it failed once it succeeded, becoming the problem where once it was the solution.

Treadway moved swiftly, firing off a memo to fellow commissioners the same day as Eisner's announcement. He had met with Stewart, his legal tactician, to ask what could be done. Framing their response to the Disney announcement was their impact-fee experience. Pushed by Treadway and crafted by Stewart, an impact fee had finally been adopted by commissioners in December 1985, requiring new development to pay 52 percent of the cost of needed road improvements. Treadway thought that figure was too low, but it was the best he could get politically. He had paid the price with his developer constituency for advocating the impact fee. At one public hearing he told developers to "go develop somewhere else" if they did not like the proposed fee.[37] Now, Disney was announcing a spate of new projects that were immune from impact fees. Transportation impact fees alone on their hotel and shopping complex would be $2.6 million. It just was not fair, thought Treadway and Stewart, not after all their work, not after the political fallout from imposing the fee, not when other developers had to pay up.

Treadway's January 29 memo recommended using the legal system to challenge Disney's government charter. "To my knowledge, the courts have never examined the implementation of the enabling act by the board of supervisors of Reedy Creek. Maybe the time has come to test these legal waters," he wrote. The memo was quoted in the Sunday *Sentinel*, setting the stage for a pointedly anti-Disney county commission meeting two days later.[38] At the meeting, Treadway complained—rather than praised Disney, as they no doubt had expected—about the 3,000 new jobs being created.[39] The regional economy was already at full employment, so the employees would have to come from somewhere else, he said. "That means they are going to need housing (and) transportation facilities, and I think we need to question all the exemptions Disney claims." Vera Carter added that "Disney needed to have some accountability for off-site impacts." With the other commissioners joining in criticizing Disney, they voted unanimously to pursue a two-pronged strategy that involved preparing a lawsuit against Disney while trying to negotiate with them on impact fees.

After the meeting, Treadway received a call from Jeno Paulucci, founder of the Chun King frozen-food brand. Paulucci had relocated to Florida from Minnesota and was developing an upscale residential community, Heathrow, twenty-five miles north of Disney in Seminole County. The frozen-food magnate had a stake in the clash since, when the California company developed their property, they utilized road capacity that otherwise might go to Heathrow. He believed "the powers that were bestowed on the Disney people were unconstitutional," and he had retained a University of Florida law professor, Fletcher Baldwin, who agreed with him.[40] But Paulucci's wife did not want him to "sue Mickey Mouse," in his words, and Professor Baldwin had concluded that the county had better standing to sue. When Paulucci called Treadway, he told the commissioner: go after them.[41]

Like Paulucci, Treadway and Stewart were troubled by Disney's competitive advantage in developing their property. They had observed Disney's race with Universal Studios in the mid-1980s to open the area's first movie-studio theme park. Universal was hobbled in this competition by having to comply with land-use regulations and building inspections. They also had to pay Orlando's impact fees. To Stewart it was not fair. "Michael Eisner announced that thing on a Saturday and Monday they had their people out there building it," said the attorney.[42] In the end, Disney won the competition, opening their Disney–MGM Studios in May 1989. They beat Universal Studios by thirteen months, about the same time it took Universal to go through the land-permitting process.

Disney's local leadership contributed to their political woes. Their top executives in Orlando had been Nunis and Bob Allen, known locally as Mr. Inside and Mr. Outside. Nunis was officially president of Walt Disney Attractions, Allen their vice president for public affairs. But Allen had died prematurely in 1987, at age 55. Nunis sought to consolidate the two roles but was unsuited by personality for the external relations job. People described the ex-Marine and former University of Southern California football player as hard-nosed and sometimes tyrannical. They said he did not like being challenged, had little use for government, and saw the world in us-versus-them terms. The same people also usually expressed admiration for him, saying these traits were probably necessary to build Disney World in record time and manage it successfully.

Faced with the challenge of Eisner's plans and Nunis' personality, the company commissioned a consultant report on improving relations with the local political community. Submitted in December 1986, the report by Orlando public relations consultant Jane Hames marked a turning point in their relationship with local government. In the 1960s, their corporate consultants advised them to gain autonomy from local and state government, which they did. Legally, they were an island, immune from most forms of nonfederal regulation. But their legal powers existed in a political context. As the events of the mid-1980s suggested, they needed to maintain good relations with the local political community to preserve those powers.

The Hames report was mailed anonymously to a county commissioner, probably by a friend within the company.[43] Among other things, it advised Disney officials to "stop sucking up to [Mayor] Bill

Frederick." They often used Frederick on ceremonial occasions, as when foreign dignitaries visited the park. They also took him on foreign missions, such as to Tokyo and Paris, where they sought local approval for building new theme parks. Frederick was a wise choice as ambassador, in part because he was the area's top elected official. (This was before Orange County began electing a chairman countywide in 1990.) In addition, Frederick, a Duke graduate, was handsome, articulate, and urbane—the picture of what many would expect a mayor to be. The county commissioners, by contrast, were cut from rougher stock.

Disney executives should see the county commission as "five mayors," said the consultant report. Maybe the commissioners did not act like mayors, but in the county's headless political system, with a county chair appointed by fellow commissioners on a rotating basis, they were like little mayors. (Sometimes they were called the five dwarfs.) In profiling individual commissioners, the report described Treadway as pro-development and well-versed on transportation issues; Carter as smart but prone to tangents; newcomer Linda Chapin as influenced by Frederick; and then-Chairman Tom Dorman as pliable and a possible spokesman for Disney interests. The report also encouraged Disney to woo Osceola county officials. Build something there in a year, ask them for help and be specific, offer to assist them in solving their transportation problems, and even promise to help them get elected, Hames recommended. Above all, Disney needed to combat the image that "they were only interested in themselves."

Disney even experienced friction with Bill Frederick in this period. The Orlando mayor was rejuvenating downtown and asked Disney to contribute a redesigned bandshell on Lake Eola, at the center of downtown. It was part of a long list of improvements, including a streetscape project on the center-spine Orange Avenue and an NBA sports arena. A Disney bandshell—by name—was symbolically important to Frederick, who was peeved that tourists came to Disney World and set foot in Orlando only when passing through the airport. When the Disney Co. demurred, Frederick sent Nunis a hot letter. "I wasn't prepared to take no for an answer," he said.[44] The letter so incensed Nunis that he called Frederick out of a city council meeting, telling him that he was about to write a $1,000 check for his re-election campaign when he got the mayor's letter. "Now I don't think I'm going to write it," said Nunis. After a spirited conversation, Nunis reconsidered. As a result, the Disney Co. lent their name to the Lake Eola bandshell and gave $80,000 for its construction, agreeing also to support an annual "Disney Days" weekend at Lake Eola. Though touted by the company as major contributions to the community, these gifts were made only under pressure.

Disney responded to its political problems by creating a high-profile new position. The title said it all: Senior Vice President for Community and Government Relations. They appointed to the post a smart and attractive ambassador for the company, Dianna Morgan. Like Nunis, who started as a ride operator at Disneyland, she rose through the ranks from her teenage days as hostess at the pre-opening Orlando Preview Center. In selecting Morgan, the company was plying the old-girl network. She had left the company two years earlier to start a public relations firm with Glenda Hood, an Orlando city commissioner in line to succeed Frederick as mayor. As well, Morgan had become a friend of County Commissioner Linda Chapin, who was preparing to run for Orange County's new office of county chairman. Mutual friends, the three women took an annual Christmas shopping trip to New York.

In her new post, Morgan quickly assembled a team of top executives to make Disney's case to county commissioners. She invited individual commissioners to the theme park where they were treated to a tour of the property followed by an individual screening of a special film, as only Disney could create, touting their many contributions to the community. Tom Dorman, the county chairman whom Disney saw as their potential spokesman, said that Nunis drove him around the park after hours and made an effective presentation.[45] Vera Carter refused the tour but met with Nunis and Morgan in Nunis' office. "He talked about all the taxes they paid, and I said, 'But we're talking about your employees, my friends and your friends, and you're doing nothing for them outside your boundary,'" Carter related.[46] Disney, not the county, should pay for needed road improvements, she said. Treadway at first refused to attend the presentation but relented after other commissioners urged him to go. He was surprised that Disney officials showed part of the Epcot film in which Walt talked about building a going community. "I asked them, 'Where are your citizens?'

They shrugged off the question," he said. Nunis and Morgan also talked about all the taxes they paid. He responded: "You're the largest landowner with the most expensive property, so you should pay the most taxes. But your share doesn't take care of all the impact that your development causes."[47]

Treadway soon departed the political scene, however. In September 1988, he was defeated in a Republican primary by Bill Donegan, a relatively unknown Maitland city councilman. Neither the Disney issue nor opposition from Disney defeated Treadway, however. His arrogance, his rudeness to other commissioners, and not least, his alienation of the home builder community that had previously supported him all cost him politically. Vera Carter, who often voted with Treadway on growth issues, admired him from a distance but found him personally unbearable. "He had the courage of his convictions," she said, "but he somehow let his ego dilute his effort."[48] Ten years later, Treadway admits he was probably guilty as charged.[49]

Yet Disney fared only slightly better with Donegan. Though less effective than Treadway, he often flailed at them. For example, he complained about the Silver Passes that Disney gave to elected officials throughout the state. They provided unlimited access to the park for the cardholder, a spouse, and three guests. Based on an adult admission price of $30.65, the pass was worth $153.25 every time it was used. Florida's ethics law, however, required that elected officials declare contributions exceeding $100. Donegan's complaints stirred up reports that many officials had failed to declare the passes as contributions.[50] As a result, the Disney Co. in 1990 stopped sending passes to officeholders as an automatic perk, though officials could still call and ask for them.[51]

Harry Stewart had been negotiating with Disney since the February 1, 1988, commission meeting. Before Treadway's defeat, the two crafted a strategy for attacking Disney's charter on constitutional grounds. In lawyer language, Stewart thought the charter contained "infirmities": he doubted whether such sweeping powers could be granted to a private corporation.[52] Not wanting to reveal his hand, he was never explicit about the infirmities with Disney attorneys. He may also have been bluffing. The company apparently took his vague assertions seriously, however, as their attorneys kept coming back to him. They came back even though the company's lobbying of county commissioners was going well, said Stewart. "I would hint, and they would go off and look, and then come back and negotiate."[53]

In researching this issue, Stewart went to the state capital in Tallahassee to investigate the attorney general's 1977 opinion on Disney's exemption from Ch. 380, the DRI (development of regional impact) law. Absent a court ruling, the opinion was binding. Disney attorneys had waved the opinion in his face; Stewart wanted to be certain of it. When he requested the file, he found two opinions, one going against Disney and the other for them. The opinion against them was written first and was unsigned. Curious, Stewart contacted the assistant attorney general who composed that opinion and asked her what had happened. She said that the attorney general, Robert Shevin, disapproved of her conclusion and asked her to modify it. She refused, and another attorney prepared a different opinion that Shevin signed. During the back and forth, Shevin was visited by representatives from the governor's office and the Disney Co., she told Stewart.

Shevin, now a state appeals court judge, said during an interview in 2000 that he could not recall any of these events.[54] He explained that he had enthusiastically supported the Reedy Creek charter as a senator in 1967, believing it was absolutely essential to get the Disney project off the ground. He said that he was "hardly ever" lobbied when rendering an attorney general's opinion. But Stewart had been told otherwise. Shevin was running for governor in 1977, and if the attorney was pressured to conclude in Disney's favor, then maybe a "court of competent jurisdiction" (in his words) would rule differently about the Ch. 380 planning statute applying to Disney. That was his gambit, his threat to Disney.

Stewart's negotiations were two-sided, involving his client as well as Disney. Because county government lacked a strong head, he met individually with the commissioners to keep them abreast of his efforts. After all, the situation was political as well as legal. Disney was lobbying the commissioners, and the county attorney needed to create a majority consensus that he could represent in his negotiations with company attorneys. Interestingly, Reedy Creek officials were little involved in these negotiations, even though the ultimate agreement was nominally between the county and the Disney government. That was one of Disney's "infirmities," thought Stewart: they had not been careful in their day-to-day operations to maintain the corporate veil between the company and their government.

Soon, the Disney Co. negotiators were talking numbers. They conceded they might owe something; the question was how much. Tom Hastings, the county's director of engineering, generated cost figures using a computer model of Disney's land use and internal transportation system. On July 24, 1989, after eighteen months of negotiations, a tentative agreement was referred to county commissioners. In this government-to-government agreement between Orange County and Reedy Creek, both sides were making concessions. Disney—through Reedy Creek—agreed for the first time to pay for off-site impacts; over five years they would pay the comparatively modest sum of $13.4 million for road improvements near their property. As well, they would submit to the DRI process and pay impact fees on their Little Lake Bryan housing development, located just outside Reedy Creek boundaries in Orange County. And they would give the county forty-five days' advance notice on any new developments on their property. In return, the county agreed not to challenge the constitutionality of the Reedy Creek charter for seven years.

Disney executives and their attorneys watched from the audience as Chairman Dorman pronounced the agreement a "reasonable compromise." Commissioner Carter was unpersuaded, though. She called the $13.4-million payment a "drop in the bucket," saying she opposed "giving up all our rights as a local government" by renouncing the right to sue. Bill Donegan was more acerbic. He called the Disney payment "hush money" and asked Stewart why he was retreating from his private assurances that the county could sue and win. With the Disney attorneys listening, Stewart averred that he could win on Disney's exemption from Ch. 380 but that, on the life or death of Reedy Creek, the odds "were not better than a coin toss." Commissioner Chapin spoke against a protracted legal challenge, saying she worried about the toll upon taxpayers and the county's legal staff.[55] The vote was 3–2 for the agreement, with Carter and Donegan opposing.

To Stewart, it was the best deal they could get politically. Legally, he thought he could win a lawsuit on Ch. 380, and possibly on the Reedy Creek Charter, but it would be risky. It might take four to five years and would be costly in legal fees. He only had two votes—Carter's and Donegan's—to "get what we wanted to get done." He had brought Disney to the bargaining table by threatening to sue, but he could not carry through because, in his words, he had only two votes to "get down and dirty." The other commissioners were torn, said Stewart, between the desire to create a level playing field for all developers, and Disney's research showing they had been good for the community. In that sense, Dianna Morgan's lobbying campaign had succeeded, because it helped to prevent a worse outcome for her company.

Looking back, Vera Carter termed the agreement "the biggest mistake we ever made." The other commissioners lacked the courage to do what needed to be done, she thought. Disney's payment was miniscule in comparison with the need, and most of it "went to benefit them," she noted. It went for roads to their employees' entrance, she said, the very roads that had spurred her conflict with Nunis, the roads whose condition had so angered former Commissioner Paul Pickett. In her view, Stewart was too tame. "I think we had a very good basis for challenging them, because their exemptions were based on their being a city," she said. "How could their lawyers say they were a city?"[56]

All along, it was a clash of principle fused with a conflict of will. It was Gen. Nunis facing off with Col. Treadway, said Stewart. Treadway and Carter wanted Disney to accept the principle that they were responsible for their off-site impacts—as other developers were—regardless of how much Disney paid in taxes. Nunis, on the other hand, found it repugnant that the county would even raise the issue; Disney had done so much for Orlando and was above being treated this way.[57] For his part, Stewart, who admired Nunis' leadership prowess, savored that the Disney World president regarded him as "the junkyard dog."[58]

Temporarily, under pressure, Disney was forced to accept some responsibility for their off-site impact. A social contract was also being imposed. Implicitly, they were being forced to accept their interdependence with the local community. As Jane Hames's report had made clear, they needed the local community not only for roads and infrastructure but also for goodwill. If nothing else, local officials had the power to tarnish their public image. That was Disney's Achilles' heel: their sensitivity to bad publicity. Orange County officials had played upon that weakness to bring Disney to the bargaining table, providing an object lesson for politicians in future conflicts with the entertainment behemoth.

The lesson can be described in the terms of economist Albert Hirschman. As the events of the mid-1980s demonstrated, neither Disney nor the county could "exit" from the other. When elected officials exercised "voice," as they did here, the company was forced to give greater "loyalty" to the Orlando community. While a social contract of sorts was achieved, it was part of a continuing struggle, of an unstable equilibrium in the changing power relationship between the Disney Co. and the surrounding political community. As the stories that follow make clear, the Mouse was hardly tamed.

SEVEN

Abuse

On September 27, 1989, Sam Tabuchi flew with five of his advisers from Orlando to Tokyo for consultations the next day with Japanese investors regarding a train, predicted to reach 300 mph, that would run between Disney World and Orlando International Airport. The superfast train would ride on an electromagnetic cushion of air created by magnets on the train and track that repelled each other. This new technology was called "mag-lev," combining magnetics and levitation. The train would not only save time for Disney-bound passengers, who could check their baggage through to their Disney hotel room, it would also remove thousands of cars and buses from the roads. For this, a consortium of Japanese investors, including Dai-Ichi Kangyo Bank of Japan, the world's largest bank, was prepared to invest up to $800 million.

Jane Hames, the Orlando public relations consultant who had previously advised the Disney Co. on dealing with Orange and Osceola counties, accompanied Tabuchi to Tokyo. Having arrived near midnight, she had just poured a cup of tea to soothe the jet lag when Tabuchi knocked at her hotel-room door. Looking devastated, he related the phone conversation he just had with Disney World president Dick Nunis.[1] For months, Tabuchi, 37, had tried to get an answer from Nunis: was Disney willing to support the mag-lev train and allow a terminal on their property, near Epcot? "I need an answer, I need an answer," Tabuchi had told the Disney executive. In particular, he needed an answer before flying to Japan to confer with his investors.[2] Nunis had come through in part, leaving a message that awaited

Tabuchi at his Tokyo hotel. Returning the call, Tabuchi heard the Disney World president say: "We can't support the Epcot location, but we have another location in a cow pasture, three miles south of Epcot, where we'd agree to a terminal."[3]

This was not the response that Tabuchi wanted to hear. He told Hames to assemble their group in the hotel restaurant, where they conferred until morning. The group included representatives from Mag-lev of Florida, the Tokyo-based company formed to promote the train project, and Transrapid International Corporation, a West German firm that would build the trains. At first light, Hames and the Japanese members of the group went to the slick, glass-walled offices of Akio Makiyama, the chairman of Mag-lev Transit, Inc., and one of Japan's largest developers. As the investors met through the day, their Japanese was broken by the words "Nunis" and "Disney" and "cow pasture," reported Hames.[4]

For Tabuchi, who worked four years to broker the Mag-lev deal, it was a tremendous loss of face. He had sold his investors on what they called a "Miss America idea," an idea so good and pure it was bound to succeed. After all, they were solving a public transportation problem with private Japanese money, building a high-tech train that fit Epcot's futuristic image, and exploiting Disney's drawing power to showcase their train technology to millions of tourists. They had assembled tentative financing, secured land options, and passed legislation to expedite the permitting process. They had won almost everything but Disney's blessing—and now Nunis was offering them a location in a cow pasture, a location that would increase construction costs by $100 million and reduce tourist ridership. It was obviously a deal-breaker.

Back in Orlando, Nunis was distributing a press release that ended months of suspense about Disney's participation in the project. There just was not enough room at Epcot for the train terminal proposed by Tabuchi, said Nunis. Instead, they would permit a terminal on Disney pastureland located about three miles south of Epcot, near the intersection of I-4 and U.S. 192 in north Osceola County.[5] In truth, the site was where Celebration—Disney's then-secret model community—was planned. For months, Nunis and Dianna Morgan had been telling Jane Hames they had big plans for the company's Osceola property.[6]

Thus the Disney Co. wanted to use Mag-lev to serve their residential real-estate project, not to solve a regional transportation problem. This plan raised the question of what they were: a community player befitting their public powers, or just another for-profit corporation. Said regional transportation planner Dave Grovdahl, a public entity would be expected to help solve a public problem, in this case, a regional transportation problem.[7] Like air pollution, traffic congestion spilled over municipal boundaries and required cooperative efforts by area governments. Mag-lev offered a solution; it would provide the profitable first leg of an areawide transportation system, in addition to removing thousands of cars and buses from the roads between the airport and Disney property.

In failing to support Mag-lev, Disney's actions suggested they were public only when they wanted to be; they wear their public hat or their private hat, depending on what best serves their corporate interest. In the first of the three stories that follow, we see Disney wearing their private hat to sink the Mag-lev train once it became a means of escaping, rather than accessing, their property. In the second story, they don their public hat to win tax-free revenue bonds to support their hotels, using bond money that area governments wanted for affordable housing. In the third, they put on their private hat, using private security guards who masquerade as public law enforcement while refusing to cooperate with police investigations. In all, we see how the Disney Co. operates, as well as the consequences of an economic development strategy built on privatization and deregulation.

For Disney's ability to be selectively public arose from their economic development deal with the state of Florida. In sanctioning Disney's government charter, the state not only gave them government powers (exceeding Orlando's) and immunities (exceeding other developers'). As the following stories relate, it also enabled them to switch hats, to decide when to be public and when to be private, all on their own initiative. Said former Orange County Commissioner Lou Treadway, "They [Disney] sit out there and play a shell game with their public and private powers."[8] In marriage terms, it was like one party deciding when to be single (the private Disney Co.) and when to be married (the public Reedy Creek government). That is the "abuse" referenced in the title of this chapter. Their powers enabled them to switch roles, from private to public and the reverse, depending on their corporate interest. To show how Disney's actions fit this description, this chapter makes a more overt argument than previous ones.

The Florida Mag-lev project began with Sam Tabuchi. A boundary crosser, he sought to bridge the gap between Japan and the United States and the public and private sectors. He was a Japanese citizen and a converted Baptist whose idea of globalism was using Japanese investment capital, and eventually German technological know-how, to solve an American transportation problem. Schooled in public-sector approaches to providing transportation, he earned a masters degree in urban planning from Florida State after graduating with a major in industrialization from Rikkyo University in Japan. His masters thesis at FSU was on building Atlanta's public transportation system. Yet he was trying to broker a commercial train project in Orlando, involving complex financial dealings with a consortium of for-profit corporations.

After FSU, Tabuchi went to work for the Florida Department of Commerce, where he came to the attention of Florida Governor Bob Graham. During Graham's administration, the young planner took trade missions to Japan in 1982 and 1983. On the second trip, Graham, wearing a helmet and a cross-strap harness, rode a mag-lev train at a top speed of 140 mph on a Japan National Railways (JNR) test track, outside Tokyo. The demo train combined two advances: magnetic levitation for increased speed, and superconductivity to reduce energy consumption. Enthused by this experience, Governor Graham asked the Florida legislature to create a High Speed Rail Commission to launch a public-private venture that would be capable of building a bullet train to run from Orlando to Tampa to Miami.

In late 1985, Tabuchi left the commerce department to work for JNR, which was competing for the Florida high-speed rail project. However, JNR soon withdrew from the project after concluding to the dissatisfaction of state officials that the train would require a $600-million public subsidy. At the time, Tabuchi was familiar with a federal Transportation Department report that the Orlando airport-to-Disney route was one of the two most-traveled corridors in the nation. Using this information, he and JNR executives crafted a plan for an airport-to-Disney train, financed by a consortium of Japanese banks, including IDK. Demonstrating their seriousness about the project, they created a company, Mag-lev of Florida, with an office in Talla-hassee and a home office in Tokyo. The company was technically an arm of Japan Railway Technical Research Institute, one of seven com-panies formed when the Japanese government broke up the state-run JNR in 1987.

Needing legal advice, Tabuchi turned to the politically connected law firm of Messer & Vickers in Tallahassee, where he received advice from lawyer-lobbyist Bob Cox about how to contact Disney.[9] Cox's former law partner Bob Rhodes, who lobbied for Disney, had recently taken a job with Arvida, the real estate development company Disney had acquired from major stockholder Sid Bass. Rhodes knew which way the Disney Co. was headed and, at Cox's request, he arranged for Tabuchi and Cox to meet with Disney officials in late 1985.

The meeting was held in the Sun Bank building on Disney prop-erty and included, in addition to Tabuchi and Cox, Richard Weiden-beck, vice president for design and engineering at Disney, and Judd Perkins from the Bombardier Corp., which had built Disney's mono-rail. As Tabuchi knew, the Disney Co. had considered running their monorail to the Orlando airport; they had even talked with Delta Air-lines about a treaty arrangement so passengers could check their bag-gage all the way through, from plane to monorail to hotel. That idea had been scrapped, in part, because the monorail was too slow. His train, however, would reach 300 mph; it would be like an "E-ticket ride," he told the executives, referring to the tickets for special rides in the early years of Disneyland.[10] Some tourists would pay the pre-dicted $8 fare just to go that fast, he thought. From all accounts, how-ever, he sold the concept better than he explained the details of the futuristic train.

The Disney representatives expressed cautious interest in the proj-ect at this first meeting. They urged the Mag-lev group to follow their own model by forming a dummy corporation to buy land options; to postpone a public announcement until business arrangements were complete; and to secure special legislation for help in condemning land and easing government regulation.[11] According to Cox, Disney also advised them to hire Tom DeWolf as their Orlando counsel, which they did. DeWolf, who provided legal counsel to Disney World and chaired the Reedy Creek board of supervisors, was retained to represent the project to Orlando interests and handle land negotiations. He was well qualified for the latter task since, as Paul Helliwell's partner, he helped to engineer Disney's original land purchase. With his partner Max Morris, a self-described "dirt lawyer," DeWolf set up a dummy Tallahassee corporation, Environmental Resource Services, and began securing land options in early 1986.

Meanwhile, the Mag-lev group continued to confer with Disney representatives, eventually meeting with Disney World president Dick Nunis. Early in these meetings, Disney executives expressed concern about cost and revenue projections, saying, according to Tabuchi, they would be involved only if the project paid for itself. In response, Tabuchi brought an engineering team from Japan in summer 1986 to make detailed cost and ridership estimates. To complete their analysis, they had to know the western terminus of the line at Epcot; otherwise, they could not estimate construction and land costs. According to Tabuchi, it was a settled issue at the time that the train would run to Epcot, contrary to Nunis' statement in his September 1989 press release.[12]

By late 1987, Tabuchi and Mag-lev were ready to pursue their legislative strategy, having secured options on most of the land and completed their engineering studies. Before the 1988 legislative session, Steve Metz, Cox's associate at Messer & Vickers, invited Republican state Rep. Richard Crotty to lunch at the posh Governor's Inn in Tallahassee. Crotty was then ranking member of the House Transportation Committee and head of the Orange County legislative delegation, making him a good choice to sponsor the Mag-lev legislation. As Crotty recalls, he got a tutorial over lunch on mag-lev technology and the merits of the project. He liked its public policy aspects, since it would be privately funded and help solve a local transportation problem "with very little downside."[13] He agreed to sponsor a Mag-lev bill in the House and offered political advice to Metz, and later to Cox, on speeding up the legislative process. He also helped get support from the Orange County legislative delegation.

On March 4, 1988, the Mag-lev story broke in the Orlando-area news media. Aside from a brief article in 1986, when Tabuchi appeared to be working on the bullet train project, the Mag-lev group had kept the project under wraps while Morris assembled the land. For that reason, Tabuchi and Cox had avoided approaching Orlando airport officials regarding a train terminal on airport property. The airport's governing body, the Greater Orlando Airport Authority (GOAA), was nominally public and its meetings were open to the media; hence Tabuchi and Cox feared that information conveyed to GOAA would surface in news reports. As news of Mag-lev was made public, Disney's Nunis made statements that were conditionally supportive. "It excites us," he said about the plane-like train. "The technology is really unbelievable."[14] Yet Nunis said he wanted to see whether Tabuchi could win political support and raise the money.

In April, the Mag-lev bill was introduced in the legislature. Cox and his associates modeled the bill on power plant siting legislation and Florida's High Speed Rail Transportation Act. Fearing that multiple agency reviews would subject the technology to duplicitous rules, they created a one-stop permitting process so all objections would be submitted at a single hearing. In addition, the legislation allowed condemnation of about a dozen pieces of property, gave the airport and Disney the power to veto a terminal on their respective properties, and specified that no public money be used on the project.

For the advocates, the legislation made perfect sense. Like Disney's 1967 charter, it protected a desirable project from unnecessary regulation and nurtured new private investment, in this case a projected $500–$800 million. But the political and economic landscape had changed since 1967. Disney now had large economic competitors, including Sea World, Universal Studios, and the I-Drive hotel owners, all of whom felt threatened by the single-destination train. "This is ridiculous," said William Jovanovich, president of Harcourt-Brace Jovanovich (HBJ), which then owned Sea World. "Who needs a 300-mph train to go 10 or 15 miles? If it were built, it would make Orlando and most of its hotels and other retail businesses a ghost town."[15]

With the bill in committee, the opponents held a series of meetings in HBJ's conference room in the CNA building in downtown Orlando. Sea World and Universal Studios were the moving forces in these meetings, said Jim Harris, who joined HBJ after retiring as Orange County Administrator. "Our strategy," he explained, "was that we could not be successful and be negative about Mag-lev."[16] Instead, they decided to kill the project by inserting a small provision in the legislation, playing on Disney's desire to keep their park guests on property. The provision simply required an easement and "unfettered public access" at all transit stops. Then, said Harris, "we had to stand back and let it come to Disney's attention." Publicly, it seemed justifiable—requiring public access to cabs, buses, light rail, and other conveyances, in return for one-stop permitting. For Disney, as Harris suspected, it was a poison pill.

Universal's attorney, Richard Swann, worked through Rep. Sam Bell of Daytona Beach to get the amendment inserted. Mag-lev attorney Bob Cox admitted to being outfoxed: the amendment was added in committee unbeknown to him, and he initially failed to anticipate the trouble it would cause Disney.[17] For Richard Crotty, the bill's House sponsor, the amendment was acceptable. He was caught between his support for the high-speed train, which seemed like a good idea but had no political constituency, and his need to avoid opposition from powerful I-Drive interests. He also thought the unfettered public access rule was good public policy, among other reasons, because it "flushed Disney out." They had to decide, said Crotty, "whether to become a community player and take a public policy issue into account, or just look at [Mag-lev] from a corporate viewpoint."[18]

Additionally, the I-Drive group sought to force a Mag-lev stop on I-Drive. For this they created an organization, Efficient Transportation for the Central Florida Community, and hired former state Rep. Dick Batchelor as their lobbyist. As Batchelor said of their strategy: "We knew there was a high-stakes risk that it would kill the thing, or else force them to stop at I-Drive (instead of Disney) as their terminus."[19] The *Sentinel* called this a "clever demand" intended to stop the project."[20] According to Tabuchi, the I-Drive proposal was a deal-breaker for Disney: "They said you can't come to Disney if you stop somewhere else."[21] Now that they were heavily invested in hotels, they wanted to hold onto their guests. With unfettered access, tourists could stay off property and hop a train to the Disney theme parks, or stay on property and commute to I-Drive for shopping, dining, and entertainment, neither of which Disney wanted.

Aiding I-Drive hotel owners, another mag-lev train proposal came into the picture while the Mag-lev bill was before the legislature. HSST Corp., a subsidiary of Japan Air Lines, proposed a slower train that used magnetic levitation but eschewed superconductivity to electrify its magnets. With a top speed of 150 mph, their train could make multiple stops—at the airport, Disney, I-Drive, and downtown

Orlando. Local politicians were immediately drawn to HSST, since its multistop system better solved the local transportation problem. Hence the legislature amended the Mag-lev bill to allow the High Speed Rail Commission to decide which technology, and therefore which company, to authorize for the project.

Through spring and summer of 1989, Disney remained coy on Mag-lev, defending it against the HSST alternative but stopping short of supporting it publicly. Disingenuously, Nunis said he supported an I-Drive stop, provided it did not keep the train from reaching 300 mph—as it surely would.[22] Likewise, he said the train should receive no public funding, an oddly political caveat until one considers that the Disney-to-airport ridership made that route uniquely profitable. The more stops the train made, the more subsidy it would require. Privately, Disney officials were offering conditional support to the Mag-lev group. According to Cox, they said, in effect: "This is doable and we want you to do it, but you have to pull it together. We're not going to stake our credibility on it."[23]

Under Tabuchi's leadership, the Mag-lev group had cleared numerous hurdles. They had gained tentative financing, completed engineering studies, secured land options, and passed the needed legislation in June 1988. They also bested the HSST group, which failed to post the $500,000 performance bond required by the High Speed Rail Commission on March 2, 1989. When the Japanese government balked at licensing Mag-lev's superconductivity technology for export, Tabuchi negotiated an amazing turnaround, getting the German Transrapid Co., which had licensed its slower mag-lev technology to HSST, to license the same technology to Mag-lev. In the spirit of globalism, Japanese and German technology was now poised to build the world's first commercial mag-lev train in Orlando.

But Tabuchi could not overcome Disney's non-support. Though the project lingered on, Nunis' rejection of the Epcot terminal destroyed the train's economic rationale. It could not be profitable without ferrying Disney-bound passengers. Disney officials persisted in saying there was no room for an Epcot terminal—an explanation at odds with Tabuchi's story that Epcot was the approved terminal site since the summer of 1986. For Jim Harris of HBJ, who helped prepare the poison pill requiring unfettered public access, the explanation was obvious. "It is frankly understandable that if you have hotel properties, you're not going to open the property up to [I-Drive hotel owner] Harris Rosen with $30 rooms. There is no motivation to support mass transit," he said, referring to Disney. Why would tourists pay for cost-lier Disney hotel rooms if they could stay in a $30 room, on I-Drive, and speed to the theme park on Mag-lev?

Befitting a public power, the Disney Co. could have made Mag-lev happen, supporting the first leg of an areawide train system. They viewed it from a corporate perspective, however, and refused to swal-low the pill of unfettered public access and an intermediate stop on I-Drive. Having once given the project qualified support, they aban-doned Mag-lev when it became a means to escape, rather than access, their property. Acting as a private corporation, they sought to main-tain a tourist bubble, keeping their hotel guests on property. Their actions arose, in part, from Michel Eisner's decision to move head-long into hotel building. In part, too, they arose from the powers they were granted by the state legislature—powers that enabled them to switch hats from public to private, depending on their corporate in-terest. In the next story, it was more convenient to don their public hat.

Ray Maxwell, director of finance and planning for the Reedy Creek Improvement District, was meeting with Lisa Fisher, head of Orange County's housing finance authority, in early January 1990 to explore how Reedy Creek might support local housing initiatives. At the time, the Disney government was under state pressure to address housing issues in its 1990 comprehensive plan. Putting more pressure on Dis-ney, an Orange County task force had recommended in September 1989 that "major employers be persuaded to participate in employer-assisted housing programs." The report cited Disney World, or rather Disney salaries, as part of the problem, noting that over three-quarters of their employees needed housing assistance.[24]

While in Fisher's office, Maxwell got a call from a Disney attor-ney relaying the good news: the State Division of Bond Finance had awarded Reedy Creek its requested private activity bond allocation. As background, the Reagan administration in 1986 asked Congress to limit the private activity bonds issued by local governments. These are bonds issued to assist nongovernment entities, mainly for eco-nomic development and housing initiatives. Local governments liked these bonds, since interest on them was tax-exempt, making it possible to sell the bonds at below-market rates; but the IRS regarded them as costly giveaways that fueled the federal budget deficit. After hearing stories of abuse, of local governments issuing bonds for K-Marts that would locate in their communities anyway, Congress voted to cap the amount of bonds each state could issue. Important for Disney and Orange County, the downward-sliding cap—set at $150 per capita in 1987, $75 in 1988, and $50 in 1989—was based on population. Florida implemented the cap by carving the state into districts and allocating bonding capacity in proportion to each district's population. Within the districts, however, the state would allocate the bonds on a first-come, first-served basis.[25]

Sitting in Lisa Fisher's office, Maxwell told her that Reedy Creek had won its bond request.[26] As he recalls, she congratulated him—though she doesn't remember it. If she did congratulate him, she was unaware that Reedy Creek's win was her agency's loss, since the Disney government had captured all the bond money available in central Florida. In District 14, consisting of Orange County, Reedy Creek's application arrived before her agency's, so they got the entire allocation. Reedy Creek also applied in District 6, which encompasses Brevard, Lake, Seminole, Volusia, and Osceola counties, because their jurisdiction reaches into Osceola. Their application arrived the same day as Brevard's housing agency, and, in accordance with state rules, lots were drawn between Reedy Creek and the Brevard agency. The Disney government won the drawing and received the entire District 6 allocation. Altogether they garnered $57.7 million in bonding capacity—$19.4 million from District 14 and $38.3 million from District 6.

Fisher was stunned and angry upon learning her agency had lost to Disney. "I'm sore about this," she told a reporter, "but I don't know that there's a damn thing we can do about it."[27] The conflict was not just between competing entities—one a housing finance authority, the other a special-purpose district, one clearly public, the other private. It was also between competing uses. In the three counties affected, the bonds would have leveraged the construction of 1,200 homes in the $24,000 to $27,000 price range, about $20,000 less than the median home price in the area. According to Orange's housing finance authority, the typical beneficiary was someone in the $20,000 income range, including many of Disney's then 31,000 employees.[28]

In contrast, Reedy Creek would use the money to expand their sewage treatment plant—to support the Eisner-era wave of new hotels. As Ray Maxwell said in the press: "We're responding to the needs our public has. It disturbs us that people are expressing concern, but all we did was follow guidelines set up by state law and apply for bonding authority. There's no more public purpose than sewage treatment."[29]

"Excuse me," Orange County Commissioner Linda Chapin recalled thinking at the time. "We need to build affordable housing for our citizens."[30] Like Fisher, who had briefed her on the issue, she was amazed by Disney's "presumption" that their private needs took precedence over the county's housing need—especially when Disney had contributed to that need. Said Fisher, who had a reputation for blunt talk, "I felt they were doing an in-your-face to Orange County. It was so blatant that a private purpose was taking advantage of public-purpose bonds. They had the wherewithal to finance their [sewage treatment plant] without putting it on the backs of people needing affordable housing."[31]

In Fisher's mind, Reedy Creek officials had purposely circumvented the county in filing their application. The protocol in District 14 was for applicants to coordinate their applications through the county administrator. She had not submitted her agency's application before January 1, because she assumed that any competing applications would be routed through the county administrator. If the applications exceeded the district's bond cap, the competition would be resolved by the county, based on public interest considerations, not by the state's indiscriminate first-come, first-served rule. The state did not require this protocol, however, and, because of the decreasing cap, bond money ran out for the first time. If Ray Maxwell and other Reedy Creek officials did not know the protocol, their bond counsel and financial advisers surely did, Fisher reasoned. Tom Lang, bond counsel for the housing authority, agreed. "That's how they make a living," he said, referring to Reedy Creek's financial advisers. "They sit down and strategize how to get those things."[32] Hence Fisher's and Lang's conclusion that Disney/Reedy Creek had knowingly taken advantage of the process.

Ironically, on January 8 the Orange county commission voted to accept the report of their affordable housing task force, the same meeting at which they addressed Disney's bond coup. There, Commissioner Linda Chapin presented a qualified defense of the Disney Co., saying "Disney corporate" was unaware of Reedy Creek's application. Commissioner Donegan, however, was incensed, complaining that "we've got a private enterprise using a governmental body to further its own ends."[33] He wanted legislative action to end Disney's privilege. Following the meeting, the *Sentinel* ran an unusual opinion article by business writer Dick Marlowe. He conceded that Disney had been first in line, but that was not the issue, he wrote. "The question is how in the heck one of the biggest money-making machines in the nation gets to compete with revenue strapped, non-profit municipalities and counties in the race for tax-exempt bonding capacity?"[34]

Following the commission meeting, Linda Chapin held a meeting in her office to flesh out the issue. A former Junior League and League of Women Voters president, Chapin, then 49, shied away from controversy and constantly sought "win-win solutions." She had co-chaired the county's affordable housing task force and cared deeply about the issue, regarding herself as "the Joan of Arc of affordable housing in Orange County," in her words.[35] It was an issue that would figure prominently in her successful campaign, later that year, for the new post of elected county chairman. At the same time, Chapin was friendly with Disney; she had known Dick Nunis for years and was a close friend of Dianna Morgan, their community and government relations vice president. She had sought, at the January 8 commission meeting, to shield "Disney corporate" from the public-relations fall-out of Reedy Creek's actions. And she asked Orange officials to co-ordinate all their media statements on the controversy through her, leading one participant to say she was "running damage-control for Disney."

Joining Chapin in her office were Orange County Attorney Harry Stewart; Phil Brown, the county administrator; Lisa Fisher; Dianna Morgan; Ray Maxwell; and Frank Ioppolo, Disney's corporate counsel. As Stewart recalls, there was a lot of posturing at the meeting, with Fisher saying "How dare you" and Maxwell responding "But we played by the rules and won."[36] Yet Stewart and Brown observed a difference in attitude between Reedy Creek and Disney officials, one of the few times they were not totally in sync in public, said Stewart.[37] Morgan and Ioppolo were searching for a face-saving solution, while Reedy Creek officials were defending the propriety of their actions.

As Maxwell confirmed in an interview, company officials clearly disliked the bad publicity.[38] Though no solution emerged from the meeting, Disney officials said afterwards that they might be willing to contribute some money to Orange County rather than return the bonds, a proposal the *Sentinel* called unfair to Brevard County, which also lost bond money to Disney.[39] Still, Disney refused to return the bonds, as the county commission requested on March 16.

A week later, the commission adopted a resolution calling on the Orange County Housing Finance Authority to investigate all legal means, including legislative action, to recover the bonds. The suggested legislative remedy was interesting. Devised by Stewart, it proposed that Reedy Creek be limited to its "pro rate share of District 14's allocation based on the special district's share of the county's population."[40] After all, Florida's bond allocation from Washington was based on population. If Reedy Creek received its "pro rate share," it would get $50 per person for its forty-seven permanent residents— or $2,350—not the $57.7 million it captured in 1990. The stratagem exposed the contradiction of Reedy Creek's claim to having a "public."

Suing to recover the bonds proved impossible, however. When the housing authority took up the issue, their counsel Tom Lang posed the question: "Is a public purpose being served" by Disney's use of the bonds?[41] As finance authority board member Joe Eagan, an attorney, pointed out, that question was preempted when the state legislature approved Reedy Creek's charter in 1967. In essence, the state created a "public agency doing private business," said Eagan, who felt Disney had abused its powers.[42] One option might have been to challenge the Reedy Creek charter, but the 1989 interlocal agreement eliminated that possibility. Harry Stewart, who negotiated the interlocal agreement, advised the housing board about the seven-year restriction against challenging Reedy Creek's charter.[43] Since the housing authority was part of Orange County government, the restriction applied to them, too.

That left the option of a legislative cure, which Disney supported, though their cure was vastly different from Orange County's. They wanted to separate bond funding for housing and sewage plants so the two uses would not compete.[44] No such legislation was introduced, however. Instead, Senate Tax and Finance Chairman Tim Deratany, a Republican from nearby Brevard County, submitted a bill requiring special districts to gain county approval before applying for such bonds. Chapin urged support for Deratany's bill at a March 19 commission meeting, though she never contacted him about it; and no one from the county's legislative delegation offered to co-sponsor his bill, said the senator. "They gave lip-service but never provided support," Deratany said of Orlando politicians. "I thought the bill was a good idea, then I realized everyone went to Disney's [promotional day for legislators at WDW] and nobody wanted to alienate them."[45] The bill died for lack of action.

The face-saving solution for Disney and Orange County was a bond refunding, an idea that occurred to Lisa Fisher in early May while she was in New York trying to refinance a 1980 bond issue. Basically, Disney agreed to invest $1.8 million to buy the residual—the profit a bank stands to earn over the life of the bond issue—from the institution owning the 1980 loan.[46] This enabled Chapin and Disney to claim a win-win: the housing authority could use the refinanced loan for mortgage assistance to lower-middle-income families, and Disney could say it did something for affordable housing. As Fisher explained, the refunding was not philanthropy on Disney's part. With her involvement, the bond firm Bear-Stearns evaluated the deal three times to assure Disney they would not lose money.[47] In addition, Reedy Creek officials agreed to forgo applying for bonds—for one year. They have applied in subsequent years and won, however.

According to Chapin, the whole episode was a learning experience. "Family relations between Disney and Orange County were sorely strained," she said. But when the brouhaha became a national news story after the *Los Angeles Times* and ABC's *Prime Time* got hold of it, county officials and the *Orlando Sentinel* closed ranks with Disney, said Chapin.[48] Apparently someone forgot to tell Michael Eisner about the *rapprochement*, though. On May 11, while officials were negotiating the re-funding, he traveled to Columbia, South Carolina, to speak at a university commencement. Asked by a reporter about the bond fracas, he commented that "Orlando is incompetent as a government."[49] Realizing he had confused Orlando and Orange County, he sought to retract the statement, telling reporters, "I can't believe I said that."

It was all part of a continuing saga of Disney switching hats back and forth between public and private, depending on which role best served their interest. In the third story, this time concerning law enforcement, Disney again abused their power to switch roles. Here, though, it was more convenient to slip on their private hat.

On December 20, 1995, Eric Faddis and Ron Davis were departing the postmodern "Team Disney" headquarters building when they spotted a company security van idling in the parking lot. "There's one of them there," Faddis said to Davis, pointing to a white van with lights and markings like an Orlando police vehicle.[50] Faddis, a former criminal prosecutor, was the plaintiff's attorney in a wrongful death suit filed against the Disney Co. Accompanied by Davis, a former traffic homicide investigator with the Florida Highway Patrol (FHP), he had just interviewed Susan Buckland, a Disney "security host" who had allegedly engaged in a high-speed chase on Disney property, resulting in the death of 19-year-old Robert "Robb" Sipkema, III. An issue in the pretrial proceedings was whether the Disney Co. improperly used private security guards to perform a nondelegable police function.

Faddis told Davis, who worked for him as a private investigator, to photograph the security van. Davis tried to comply, but security host Jim Weaver rolled down his window and shouted, "Hey, what are you guys doing?" Faddis responded: "We're in the process of suing Disney, and we're taking pictures." Weaver shouted, "Get out of here," and then raised his window and spoke into his radio.[51] Davis noticed a radar device on the van's dashboard and attempted to photograph it, whereupon Weaver covered the device with his clipboard.

Robert Phillips, another security host, heard Weaver's call to Disney's Communications Control Center as he patrolled at the Pleasure Island entertainment complex across the street. Weaver said he had "two gentlemen making trouble," and his voice "sounded like he was in distress," said Phillips.[52] Spotting Faddis's car headed in the opposite direction on Buena Vista Drive, Phillips responded in an emergency mode. Making a U-turn across the median, he activated his revolving red lights, known as "takedown lights" since they are used by police to pull over motorists. With Weaver's security van behind him, Phillips proceeded to follow Faddis down Hotel Plaza Blvd., off Disney property, and onto S.R. 535. But Faddis did not stop, did not pull over, for he knew as an attorney that private security guards have no more power to make traffic stops than ordinary citizens do.

The Sipkema death was tragic, no matter what caused it to occur late that night on August 31, 1994. According to security host Buckland, she responded to a radio call reporting that a man was standing atop a moving truck in the Contemporary Hotel parking lot.[53] Arriving at the scene, she observed a pickup with a person lying spread-eagle on the shell top. She followed the vehicle out of the parking lot and tried to stop it by flashing her lights. What happened next is disputed: she says she followed the vehicle without speeding and without leaving the property, while the driver of the pickup, Kevin Blazack—who was convicted of manslaughter while driving under the influence in the accident—says she chased his pickup through several traffic lights, at speeds reaching 90 mph. In either case, his vehicle careened through the Disney employee entrance at the north perimeter of the property and onto Reams Road, a two-lane public road off-property. A short way down the road, as Blazack glanced over his shoulder to check the location of Buckland's van, he lost control and left the road at approximately 75 mph, striking a tree and instantly killing Robb Sipkema, whose body was consumed in the resulting fire. Buckland maintains she did not follow Blazack off-property.

The problem of Disney's private police force arose during the crash investigation. When FHP trooper Scott Walter, a traffic homicide investigator with seventeen years of experience, arrived on the scene, he was told that Disney Security had been involved in the fatal crash. As part of his preliminary investigation, he tried to contact Buckland to find out what she knew about the accident and whether Disney Security could put a driver behind the wheel. "I made appointments with her through Disney Security. I tried contacting her. She was never available to me," said Walter.[54] He also tried several times to get a copy of the dispatch tapes of her radio conversation with Disney's Communications Control Center. "The first time they said they would make arrangements to get a copy for me," he said, referring to Disney Security. "The second time they said it was being prepared. They also told me that two copies had been made for individuals at Disney and that they shouldn't have any trouble getting me one. When I tried again they said it was unavailable, that it had been taped over," he reported.[55]

When the parents of Robb Sipkema filed suit against the Disney Co. and Reedy Creek in 1995, Faddis asked both entities for copies of their traffic citations, accident reports, and crime incident reports for a five-year period. He also requested a copy of Disney Security's Standard Operations Procedure Manual that was in effect when the accident occurred. The attorney reasoned that Disney Security was performing a police function in regard to traffic control and crime prevention and interdiction, a police function that only a public agency could perform. Accordingly, Disney and Reedy Creek were bound to produce pertinent "public" records—just as the Orange County Sheriff's Office and the FHP must do. But Disney and Reedy Creek refused, claiming Reedy Creek had no such records and that Disney Security had no obligation to comply, since it was part of a private company. In other words, when it came to policing, a seemingly public function, they donned their private hat to shield themselves from public oversight. The stage was set for a protracted legal battle.

As background, Disney's 1967 charter legislation treated law enforcement different from other public powers. Their Reedy Creek government was authorized to perform a long list of public services, from road building to fire protection and building inspections to energy production. Because policing is a special power that impinges upon citizen liberties, it could not be granted to a landowner-controlled government. Instead, it was assigned to the City of Bay Lake as part of a peculiar arrangement, in which Bay Lake would police the entire Disney property, including another city, Lake Buena Vista, in part of Osceola County. Disney never implemented these police powers, though, either because their constitutionality was uncertain, or because private security guards protected their corporate interests better, or for both reasons. Rather, the Reedy Creek government contracted with the Disney Co. to provide security for it.

Whereas Reedy Creek claimed park guests as part of their "public" in the private activity bond controversy, in arranging security they claimed only the forty-seven permanent residents of Bay Lake and Lake Buena Vista. With such a small population, the district required only minimal "night watchmen services," such as checking doors and turning off lights, said district manager Tom Moses. "Where there's no crime, you don't call the police," he explained.[56] With one major exception, the four-lane roads on Disney property are regarded by Reedy Creek as "public," the exception being the World Drive entrance to Disney beyond Epcot Drive, at which point it becomes an access road to private property. The Disney government regards the two-lane roads and property inside the toll gates as private; within these areas, the "landowner" (as Reedy Creek officials say) provides security. For this purpose, the company employs over 800 "security hosts," compared with Reedy Creek's 240 total employees, of whom half work in fire protection.

As attorney Faddis demonstrated in court, Disney and Reedy Creek tried to have it both ways, claiming that their security hosts were private but giving them uniforms, vehicles, equipment, and duties like police officers. Asked in court to describe their uniform, Susan Buckland called it a "costume" and said they were Disney "cast members" (just like Mickey and Pluto). The costume—with shields, caps, name tags, belt-holstered radios, and other indicia of police authority—matched their assigned duties. Relating to traffic control, they were authorized to issue traffic citations to Disney and Reedy Creek employees for moving and nonmoving violations without notifying law enforcement; to issue traffic accident reports for purposes of auto insurance claims; and to utilize revolving red bar lights (aka police takedown lights) when making traffic stops. For this they were given security vans with markings like the Orlando Police Department; radar speed-measuring devices; and the flares, traffic cones, wands, and chalk commonly used by traffic cops. Relating to criminal investigations, security hosts receive and disseminate BOLO ("be on the lookout") bulletins, perform surveillance, conduct investigations, and interview witnesses regarding crimes against both persons and property.

There was even a special arrangement between local law enforcement and Disney Security hosts regarding traffic tickets. If an Orange County deputy sheriff stopped a Disney or Reedy Creek employee on Disney property, including the four-lane "public roads," the officer radioed a security guard who issued what was called a "driving record." Security host Buckland explained how this arrangement worked during her fifteen years at Disney: "They [sheriff's deputies] would tell me that they stopped the vehicle in question, what he was doing wrong, about how fast he was going, and where they pulled him over."[57] Buckland then issued a driving record, which looked identical to a Uniform Traffic Citation. The driving record was placed in the employee's personnel record but was not sent to the state, and did not add "points" against the individual's license. In addition, security guards investigated traffic accidents on Disney property and issued accident reports, the same blue accident reports used by public law enforcement. This occurred even though Florida law requires that accidents be reported immediately to the nearest law enforcement agency.

In several ways this cooperation benefited the public. Informally, Disney Security agreed to be the "eyes and ears of law enforcement." In addition, their patrolling of the property and their issuing of "driving records" and accident reports saved sheriff deputies and FHP troopers from these time-consuming tasks. All this enabled the FHP to focus on higher-priority tasks, such as speed control and accident investigation on I-4 and other major roadways, said FHP district commander Robert Flemming.[58] In deferring to Disney Security on theme-park property, FHP was only treating Disney like other "municipalities" and other "law enforcement," said the officer. Flemming offered this assessment as if Reedy Creek were a municipality and security hosts were really police officers.

In other respects, Disney runs their police force to serve their corporate interest rather than the public interest. One example is their operation of the 911 system. Calls to 911 on Disney property go to a Reedy Creek "public" employee, who refers calls involving a reported crime to the Disney Co. Communications Center. A Disney employee rather than a Reedy Creek official decides whether to call outside law enforcement, said Kenneth Kincaid, assistant operations chief at Reedy Creek.[59] Orange County undersheriff Rick Staly is generally happy with the 911 arrangement, which saves his agency from responding to unnecessary calls, though he admitted that "they sometimes miss on forwarding 911 calls."[60] Incident reports regarding serious crimes—including burglary, rape, and robbery—have been generated by security hosts but not reported to any law enforcement agency.[61] The desire not to alarm Disney's guests is the rationale in some of these cases. "We have a good working relationship," says

Staly, explaining how Disney Security helps sheriff deputies make arrests for offenses such as shoplifting. "They stop suspects and interview them," says Staly, "then we make the arrests." The convenience for sheriff deputies, he acknowledged, is that security guards need not read suspects their rights before interrogating them.

Another example is discouraging concentrated DUI patrols. When FHP troopers have conducted these patrols on public roads inside Disney property, company representatives have called to ask "why were we out there and what were we doing," said Flemming, who supervises approximately 110 officers. In addition, Reedy Creek EMTs (emergency medical technicians) refuse to draw blood from suspected drunk drivers when requested to do so by highway patrol troopers, even though state law requires all certified EMTs to comply with such requests. Apparently the company does not want a DUI arrest to mar a park guest's vacation. To address this issue, Flemming's supervisor raised the issue with Perry Doran, the ex-FBI agent who supervises Disney Security, by going through the Central Florida Criminal Justice Council, which brings together law enforcement and security personnel to discuss common problems.[62] The approach of FHP to this issue is curious, since the EMTs work for Reedy Creek and Dolan works for Disney. If Doran could control the EMTs, as implied by their contacting him about an EMT issue, then the company must control Reedy Creek.

Disney goes to great lengths to make their guests feel safe. When law enforcement is present on the property, they are discouraged by company representatives from using their emergency lights or sirens, asked not to park their marked cars in highly visible areas, and prevented from wearing their weapons inside the park or Disney hotels. One FHP trooper in the Sipkema evidentiary hearing said he was repeatedly asked by Disney Security to keep a low profile when investigating crashes involving their hotel guests. "You would normally pull up in front of the hotel and immediately Disney Security would come out there and ask me to park around back and they would bring me in the back way," Trooper Randolph Bush related. Asked if a reason was given, he said: "They stated they didn't want the profile of the vehicle out front for the guests to see. They would rather have it hidden in the back."[63] Trooper Bush was also asked numerous times to remove his weapon before entering Disney hotels. Likewise, Trooper Terry Hoops was escorting visiting Japanese dignitaries associated with the Florida high-speed rail project into the Magic Kingdom when he was approached fifty feet beyond the turnstiles by "gentlemen in suits" from Disney Security who said they did not permit firearms in the park. "He instructed me to either give the firearm or release the firearm to him or to secure it in my vehicle," said the uniformed officer. Trooper Hoops declined the request and was asked to wait outside the turnstiles for the dignitaries to return.[64]

To the Sipkemas' attorney, Disney was playing a shell game in using private security guards to perform a public police function. "Walt Disney World performs a governmental police power function in attempting to make a traffic stop and then when FHP investigates they avoid responsibility and they have purposely withheld information from FHP," said Faddis.[65] As he told Judge Belvin Perry in closing arguments, the roads on Disney property where the hotels are located, roads on which FHP troopers in fact issue citations, are public in their use and should hence be governed by applicable public records law.[66] The Disney Co. had implicitly acknowledged this fact by removing the red lights from their security vehicles, inasmuch as Florida law says only law enforcement officers may display such lights on public roadways, said Faddis. The lights were removed after he complained about them to the State's Attorney, who raised the issue with Disney.

It was not only a public records issue, argued Faddis. There was potential harm to all those who found themselves on Disney property, from tourists to Reedy Creek employees to bus drivers and vendors—a daily population exceeding 100,000 persons. Within the 27,000-acre property, the Sheriff's office maintained only two full-time liaison officers; police protection was primarily the work of Disney's 800-person security force. What about the constitutional rights of citizens who become crime victims on the property—their First Amendment right to redress for any injury; their Fourth Amendment protection against unreasonable search and seizure; their Fifth Amendment guarantee against being deprived of life, liberty, or property without due process of the law; their Fourteenth Amendment right to equal protection of the law; and their Supreme Court–sanctioned guarantee for victims of crimes to be informed and present and heard at all crucial stages of a criminal investigation?[67] For their own reasons, the Disney Co. decided to rely on private security guards, rather than creating the public police force authorized in their charter. The inherent flaw in this arrangement was that the profit motive of the private entity might override the fundamental rights of citizens.

On whether Disney Security should release the dispatch tapes and other records requested by Faddis, the Circuit Court ruled in Disney's favor in May 1996. The legal issue, wrote Chief Judge Perry, was whether the Disney Co. was acting as a public agency in its policing activity. Since it was neither created as a public agency nor acting in one's behalf, it had no inherent obligation to release such records, the judge concluded. Without comment, Florida's Fifth District Court of Appeals affirmed Judge Perry's decision, as did the Florida Supreme Court.

For the Sipkemas' attorney, the legal issue was frustrating, since he claimed Disney controlled Reedy Creek, not the reverse. He had advised the court of a recent federal court ruling, in a sexual harassment case brought by female Reedy Creek firefighters, that Disney controlled Reedy Creek.[68] He also presented evidence from that case showing the two entities' interconnection. Tellingly, that evidence included an internal corporate memo, on Disney stationery, to top corporate officials requesting approval of Tom Moses' job classification, and a letter from Moses to a Reedy Creek employee inviting her to attend a program, at the University of Walt Disney World, to "study the philosophy and organization of our Company."[69] Owing to the peculiarities of the Sipkema case, the courts now demanded that Faddis prove the opposite pattern of influence: that the special-purpose district controlled the corporation, that the Disney Co. was Reedy Creek's "agent."

It was another example of Disney's ability to take advantage of their governmental charter: here they were married; there they were single. Here they were a public entity eligible to receive bond funding; there they were a private firm, unwilling to permit public access for a Mag-lev train on their property. Here their private security guards masqueraded as real cops; there they stiff-armed external law enforcement to protect their corporate public image. Such were the results of the economic-development deal struck between Disney and the state of Florida in 1967. The deal invited abuse not only in granting public powers to a private business corporation. It permitted Disney to switch roles at will, abusing the power to decide when to be public and when to be private. In the following chapter, we see another type of switch, as Disney shifts its development to Osceola County, where local officials prove more pliant.

EIGHT

Negotiation

I t was early 1989 and Osceola County Property Appraiser Bob Day
was having icy dinner conversation with Disney attorney Rick
LaLiberte in the Italian Pavilion at Epcot. Day had requested the
dinner meeting with LaLiberte, saying he had something important
to discuss.[1] They had met on Hotel Plaza Boulevard at Lake Buena
Vista, just inside Disney property, and drove from there in LaLiberte's
car across the back property to Epcot. Over dinner, Day gave the Disney attorney the bad news. He had decided to deny the company's
agricultural classification on their 11,000 vacant acres in Osceola
County.

At the time, Disney's developed land as depicted in Map 6 was
all in Orange County, where the company paid $30–40 million in *ad
valorem* taxes annually. In Osceola County to the south, where almost one-third of their property lay, they paid only about $400,000
in taxes. Yet, Disney's impact on Osceola was enormous. U.S. 192,
originally the Magic Kingdom entrance road, had become a tacky
tourist strip outside Disney property; county roads teemed with tourists and theme park workers traveling to and from the park; and Disney's low-wage workforce exhausted the county's meager mental
health and social service budgets. Before Disney arrived, the county's
bovine population exceeded its human population of 40,000, but the
latter figure would double by 1980 and again by 1990.

As long-time County Commissioner Larry Whaley said of the
county's woes, "We got the traffic and crime while Orange County got
the tax base."[2] For years, Osceola politicians had complained to Dis-

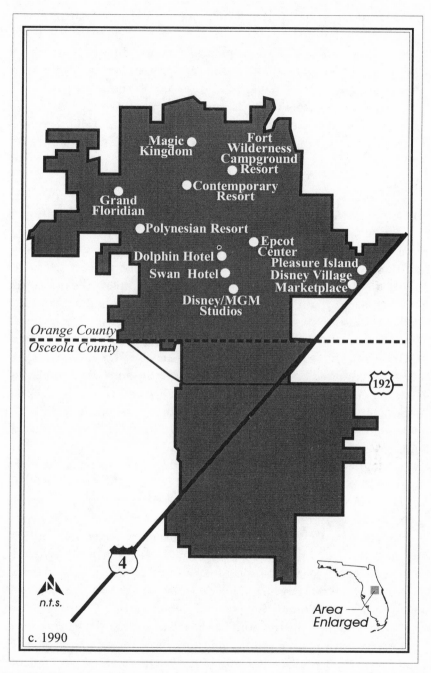

Map 6   Disney property, 1990

ney about not getting taxable development. "We kept hearing promises," said Whaley. "Disney vice president Bob Allen would tell us privately that something big was planned for us. 'Just be patient,' he said. The problem was that he was talking long-term and we were talking next year," said Whaley, who served on the county commission from 1978 to 1996. Finally, in 1989, the company got more specific: Dick Nunis briefed commissioners on a proposed 1.5-million-square-foot regional shopping mall, plus an exclusive residential community, slated for south of U.S. 192, across I-4 from the Magic Kingdom entrance.

Nunis' shopping mall presentation "sort of rang a bell in my head," said Property Appraiser Day.[3] "If they were planning to develop the property, then it should be taxed as commercial," he thought. That was the tipping point in his decision to challenge Disney's agricultural land classification. He had worked in the appraiser's office for ten years before his appointment, in 1984, to complete the unexpired term of the previous officeholder. In that time he had developed a cautious philosophy regarding the agricultural classification. In his view, a property owner deserved it only if engaged in bonafide agricultural operations for the long haul. The Disney Co., he thought, was in the theme park and hotel business, not the cattle and timber business. True, they leased property to a cattle rancher and contracted with a timber company to harvest pine trees on part of their land. But state law called for taxing property at its "highest and best use," and, as Nunis' presentation revealed, their land's highest use was commercial, not agricultural. In his opinion, they were using their agricultural classification as a "tax dodge," burdening Osceola County's infrastructure and services with their theme-park operations in Orange County while avoiding their fair share of Osceola taxes.

"Here's what I've decided to do," the property appraiser told Disney attorney Rick LaLiberte as they dined. Hearing that Day would deny their tax classification, LaLiberte responded in a huff. "If you do, we'll pull all our land back inside Reedy Creek and you won't get a penny," Day remembers him saying. "No you won't," he told LaLiberte, "you couldn't take the political heat." In his mind, Disney's powers were constrained by public opinion. The company traded on its favorable public image, and anything that threatened that image, threatened the company. It was also bad timing for Disney, since they were then quarreling with Orange County over impact fees.

But LaLiberte continued his threat. As the two men verbally jousted, their conversation grew more heated until, finally, Day got up from the table and walked out, fuming. It was late in the evening because the laser light show announcing the closing of Epcot had started, and Day was stranded. His car was back on Hotel Plaza Blvd., miles away, and he was unsure how to get back there. Lacking a park pass, he mingled with a group of foreign tourists as they boarded a bus, hoisting a small child up the bus steps, and rode with them back to the hotel area. It was two years after that before he spoke with LaLiberte, who has since left the company.

"I really shook things up," Day said of the political fallout from challenging Disney. While there was no pitched conflict between him and Disney officials—their dealings remained businesslike and professional—he was violating a norm in "taking on the Mouse." His denial of their agricultural classification effectively raised their tax bill from $395,000 in 1988 to almost $1.4 million in 1989. For this he received letters of support from the cities of St. Cloud and Kissimmee and from the county commission, and he garnered favorable publicity in the *Miami Herald* and *Insight Magazine,* among other publications. Yet he also endured subtle pressure from Disney. He did not receive the freebies that other county politicians routinely got, such as golf invitations to one of their five courses, and he worried about their "dropping $100,000 on one of my [election] opponents," he said. Was it a coincidence, he wondered, that two county commissioners who urged him to settle the lawsuit Disney filed over the matter had received campaign contributions from either Disney executives or their attorneys?[4]

In all, the controversy lasted two years. Day denied Disney's agricultural classification each year and the company sued to stop him, tying up the issue in court. Meanwhile, Disney paid its *ad valorem* taxes at the lower rate. Then in 1990 the editorial stance of the *Osceola Sentinel,* an arm of the *Orlando Sentinel,* suddenly changed. They opined that Day should sit down and negotiate with Disney, saying "neither side wants a court battle and a bunch of expensive legal fees."[5] Said Day, "I could see the writing on the wall and decided to settle." In return, he got an agreement that Disney would pay $600,000 in taxes for 1989 and $600,000 for 1990; that the county would tax land fronting U.S. 192 and I-4 at the commercial rate; and that Disney would release a certain amount of land from the agricultural classification each year.

The agreement, besides increasing county tax coffers, signified that local officials could exercise some power over the behemoth company. Osceola, with its weak government and small staff, was not totally at their mercy. As the company switched their development into Osceola County with the Celebration project, this was a timely lesson for local officials to learn. For, at the time, the state was starting to implement growth management legislation, adopted in 1985, giving new controls to local government. Disney faced not only these controls, requiring that they work with local officials in the surrounding community. As they developed Celebration, which, unlike Epcot, had real residents, they faced the controls that citizens with rights of citizenship can exercise. It made this the era of negotiation for Disney.

The Eisner era at Disney spawned the Celebration project. Eisner had a mandate from the Bass brothers to develop the company's real estate holdings, and the company had purchased the Arvida real estate company from the Basses. In response, Eisner tapped Peter Rummell to invigorate Disney Development Co. (DDC), the real-estate arm of Disney/Arvida. Rummell, then 40, was well chosen. He had helped develop Amelia Island off the coast of Jacksonville and had headed Arvida's operations in Jacksonville and Atlanta before leaving the company in 1984 to manage New York's Rockefeller Center. He in turn recruited Todd Mansfield, a Harvard MBA then 29, to spearhead the company's evolving commercial real-estate operation. As Rummell's duties expanded—he moved to California in 1993 and assumed worldwide responsibility for Walt Disney Imagineering (the company think tank) as well as DDC—Mansfield took over DDC-Florida.

Before Rummell and Mansfield joined Disney, planning for the Osceola property was dormant. "The pre–Eisner era management was not prepared to invest capital in such things," said Mansfield.[6] One of Rummell's first acts was to execute a total master plan for the company's nearly 30,000 acres in Florida. "What we found," he said, "was that based on practical transportation capacity, and practical mass of tourists, we could do everything we could dream about [related to our core business] and still stay north of (U.S.) 192."[7] This finding—that their property south of 192 was excess and could be developed for commercial and residential purposes without jeopardizing their theme-park and hotel business—culminated in Celebration.

Yet Eisner was initially reluctant to approve a community development project. "Michael was smart enough to realize that one of the company's huge untapped veins of value was its landholdings. But he [initially] felt that community development was outside the brand," said Rummell, who left the company in 1997 to become CEO of the Jacksonville-based St. Joe Co., the state's largest landholder. When it was announced in 1991, Celebration was characterized in the media and by company publicists as something that Eisner wanted in order to fulfill Walt's dream for Epcot. "That was press copy stuff," said the former DDC head, explaining that the Epcot comparison was actually a negative in his discussions with Eisner. "One of the things he and I were concerned about was that people would draw out the comparisons." If so, Eisner apparently changed his mind after Celebration left the drawing board. In his *Work in Progress,* he wrote that Celebration was built, in part, "to make good on Walt's unrealized dream for a city of the future."[8]

In Rummell's mind, the decision to build in Osceola was driven totally by economics. He had commissioned the consultant report in 1986 that called for building something in Osceola to soothe relations there. At the time, Orange County was complaining about Disney overdevelopment, while Osceola politicians wanted more taxable development in their county. The 1986 consultant report by Jane Hames dovetailed with Walt Disney's much earlier advice to Bob Foster, the company attorney who oversaw the original land purchase. As related in Chapter Three, Walt told Foster they should always deal with two governments at once. That was the reason they wanted land in both Orange and Osceola counties.[9] Consistent with that advice, the Osceola Project served twin purposes: it appeased Osceola politicians and reminded Orange County that Disney could go elsewhere. Still, Rummell avers that economics, not politics, drove the project; the Hames report was a "happy coincidence," he says.

Meanwhile, Florida Governor Bob Graham was securing passage of important new growth management legislation. Supported by major newspapers throughout the state, the 1985 Growth Management Act provided a statewide framework for managing growth. It required, among other things, that public facilities be provided "concurrent with the impact of new private development." This so-called concurrency provision took effect in 1990, shortly before Disney announced their Celebration project. Unlike earlier planning legislation, the new law specifically applied to Disney, or rather, to their Reedy Creek government. In fact, Reedy Creek is the only special district (among some 700 in the state) required to comply.

Contrary to popular belief, even in high political circles,[10] the law was not applied to Reedy Creek over their opposition. According to Casey Glucksman, a Sierra Club lobbyist who participated in drafting the legislation, "the language just appeared in the draft overnight," and even the chairmen of the House and Senate committees that wrote the legislation could not recall how it happened.[11] Actually, Disney chose to come under the law, though it was a preemptive strike on their part, demonstrating their strategic sense as well as their political skill. Said Reedy Creek District Manager Tom Moses, "I wanted to be darn sure that at no time would we be subject to the Orange and Osceola county plans."[12] He worried the counties would claim such power under the law unless the Disney government was allowed to formulate its own plan. Hence their lobbyist, Bob Rhodes, of the firm Steel, Hector, and Davis in Tallahassee, inserted language in the bill making it apply to Reedy Creek.[13]

The Osceola Project continued this erosion of Disney's autonomy. Having decided to build a residential community, the company faced a vexing choice: they could de-annex Celebration from Reedy Creek and make it subject to the DRI process, or they could keep it in the District and avoid the review process altogether at the expense of further alienating Osceola politicians. Keeping Celebration in the District also imperiled Disney's political control of the Reedy Creek government, which hinges on the carefully selected residents of their two mobile home park "cities," Bay Lake and Lake Buena Vista. If Celebration residents lived in the District, they could vote there, weakening company control of their vassal government.

Unsurprisingly, the company chose to de-annex Celebration. According to Rummell, they could have "threaded the legal needle" and remained in the District, but they decided not to begin a twenty-year relationship with Osceola County that way. "Why invade a government concerned about theme parks?" he asked rhetorically, as though nothing else was at stake.[14] To Osceola politicians the company's political motivations were transparent: "They didn't want voters out there controlling their destiny," said Larry Whaley. "All the commissioners understood that."

Thus it was a new era in Disney's relationship with the outside community. For the first time, they faced regulation by a government not their own. Before, Disney World's top brass—notably Dick Nunis—handled government relations, going straight to the top in state government, as they could do because of the jobs and tax base they represented. Executives at lower rungs were seldom involved in government or the outside community, and they were almost paranoid about releasing information to the outside, revealed a former Reedy Creek official.[15] But now, as the concurrency law took effect and Celebration underwent DRI scrutiny, a new cast of executives would be negotiating with government regulators.

The Osceola story is not just about the Disney Co. learning to cope with government controls, however. It is also about their developing a new modality of power, relying less on the authority vested in their private government and more on conventional forms of corporate influence, like lobbying and media relations and armies of consultant-experts. As well, this story reveals the limits of privatization and deregulation, showing how these strategies were compromised once real residents and public institutions such as schools entered the picture, as happened at Celebration.

Florida's concurrency law tried to stop growth from lowering the quality of public services. The 1985 growth management act required local government to set service standards for public services, including roads, sewers, solid waste, recreation, drainage, and mass transit. These service levels, measured from A through E, were to be growth-resistant. If a new strip mall would reduce the service level of nearby roads from a C, which was deemed acceptable, to a subpar D, local officials would negotiate a plan to repair the resulting deficit. Practicing "concurrency management," they would phase in improvements as the project was built out.

Importantly, the law did not say who should pay for new facilities, nor did the state increase funding for this purpose. The funding choice—whether to tax residents or impose impact fees on the developer—remained largely a local matter, though the state Department of Community Affairs (DCA) monitored local plans to see whether cities and counties had infrastructure funding to support their projected growth. Under these circumstances, the Disney Co. could no longer ignore their fiscal impact on surrounding jurisdictions. Having acceded to the concurrency law, they were ineluctably drawn into tax and spending controversies in Osceola County.

One of Disney's most costly impacts was on transportation. The concurrency provision required that local authorities build and expand roads to accommodate new development like Disney was planning for Osceola. To fund concurrency, they strove to shift costs to taxpayers, pursuing a three-pronged strategy. First, they worked to raise the county sales tax to finance more road building; second, they secured county funding for road improvements in front of Celebration and intersection enhancements on I-4; and third, they formed a public-private partnership to build Osceola Parkway, a toll-road linking Florida's Turnpike and their property.

To raise the sales tax, Disney had to overcome their reluctance to being involved in local politics. In 1990, the Osceola sales tax was 6 percent. However, state law made possible a voter referendum on raising the tax one cent to fund infrastructure needs like roads, sewers, waste disposal, and parks. Interestingly, this local-option tax—to support growth—controverted the frequently heard claim that growth paid for itself. Under the banner of "Citizens for a Better Osceola County," the Disney Co. participated in a coalition of groups—developers, builders, real-estate interests, bankers, and the Kissimmee/Osceola County Chamber of Commerce—to raise Osceola's sales tax.[16] As a gift in kind, their publicity shop printed 45,000 postcards and 15,000 glossy pamphlets that were distributed in four mailings to selected voters. The mailings outlined the reasons for supporting the tax, arguing that tourists would pay 40 percent of the proceeds. In addition, the company provided ten employees for a telephone bank to call likely voters in the last week of the campaign.

Osceola car dealer Alan Starling, a foe of the tax initiative, complained that "their phone bank called my elderly mother and told her that her property taxes would go up if the sales-tax initiative failed."[17]

He saw another revenue option: to tax Disney's land at the commercial rate. At the time, Disney's lawsuit over Bob Day's denial of their agricultural classification in Osceola lingered in court. The General Motors dealer admittedly had a bias in this matter, since raising the sales tax hurt his auto sales. Still, he thought it was disingenuous for Disney to campaign for the tax by saying tourists should pay more. It made more sense for the tourist magnet—the Disney Co.—to contribute its fair share in taxes. As he told a Disney executive before the vote: "People who don't pay their fare share of *ad valorem* taxes shouldn't be urging other people to pay higher sales taxes." The June 5 referendum passed 70–30 with 16 percent voter turnout.

As a second prong in their strategy, Disney sought county help in paying for road improvements needed to support their Celebration planned community. Because of concurrency, they needed funding to widen two small sections of U.S. 192 and to improve two intersections on I-4. The total price tag was $66.6 million. After first asking the county to pay the full amount, they negotiated a two-thirds, one-third split, with Disney putting up $44 million through Reedy Creek and the county contributing about $22 million. It was a good deal, said then-Commissioner Jim Swan, because the county's share would come from property, sales, and gas taxes paid by Celebration residents and by Disney's new All-Star Resorts hotel project.[18] Another commissioner, Chuck Dunnick, representing the eastern side of the county, questioned the deal, asking why Disney's road needs took precedence over other pending road projects. To Property Appraiser Bob Day, however, it was a travesty. Disney was capturing the growth dividend—the tax revenues from developing Celebration—to benefit themselves, he complained. The whole county millage then was about $20 million, Day pointed out, adding, "Disney's a rich corporation. You know they could have found another way to build that."[19]

As a third prong, the Disney Co. gained county funding for Osceola Parkway, running 12.5 miles from Florida's Turnpike to World Drive on Disney property. Costing $153 million, it was Osceola's most expensive public works project ever. It would enable Disney to satisfy concurrency requirements for projects in the pipeline: Celebration, Wide World of Sports, and eventually Animal Kingdom, their fourth Orlando-area theme park, launched in 1998. It would also open thousands of acres of raw land for resort and commercial development, benefiting five major non-Disney landowners. And it would give Osceola residents a faster means of east-west travel through the congested tourist corridor. Summarizing the road's impact, County Commissioner Mary Jane Arrington said, "The county needed it but Disney needed it more."[20]

The bond deal to finance the Parkway was sold to Osceola residents as essentially costless. Jim Swan, a fishing guide who preceded Arrington on the commission, frequently said it would not cost the county "one red dime."[21] County Administrator Bill Goaziou, who negotiated the financial agreement with the affected property owners over three years, stated publicly that it would take "an unholy act of God to even expose the county to any financial cost."[22] The complex deal involved two governments—Osceola County and Reedy Creek—and six private companies, including the Disney Co. It called for Disney and the other companies to pay money up front, the county to issue $153 million in revenue bonds backed by gas tax revenues and toll proceeds, and Reedy Creek to guarantee the bonds. Because no property taxes were pledged, the county commission could approve the bond package without a voter referendum.

When the bond deal was signed, the participants called it a "unique public-private partnership," a model for other governments to follow. Tom Lewis, DDC vice-president who negotiated the deal for Disney, handed out toy front-end loaders with Mickey Mouse at the wheel, plus "Let's Make a Deal" hats for the commissioners. Prematurely, the *Osceola Sentinel* called it "a pretty savvy deal negotiated by folks who are still seen in some Central Florida circles as a bunch of rubes."[23] For in fact, the Parkway has been a money loser from the start. The toll proceeds barely cover operations and maintenance, and, unless the bonds are refinanced successfully, the county will make annual payments of $1.375 million for the next twenty years to cover the shortfall. In 1998, county auditor Doug Martin told a stunned county commission that they had assumed $1.07 billion in liability, stretching to the year 2055, for a $125-million roadway.[24]

The fault in the financial arrangement—the ridership estimates were off by half. The engineering consultants, URS-Greiner, admitted that they failed to "ramp-up" their estimates by taking into account the time it takes motorists to learn to use a new road.[25] Gary Lee, who manages an Osceola ranch property and closely followed the Parkway project, asked, "Where were the professionals who were supposed to advise the county?"[26] Arrington, who replaced Swan on the commission, asks why Goaziou, a CPA, did not have someone "re-run the ridership estimates." In one case there was proven wrongdoing. Larry O'Dell, the public works director who helped negotiate the deal, pled guilty to taking a $1,000 bribe to include a Little Rock, Arkansas, brokerage firm in the consortium marketing the bonds.

Commissioner Robert Guevara, who was elected after the deal was consummated, blamed the problems on Disney's tricky style of bargaining. "They give you one thing and take away another," said the commissioner, who represented Osceola's fast-growing Hispanic community before his death in 2000.[27] Indeed, the bond covenants are contradictory. Reedy Creek guarantees the bonds—to reassure the bond market, not to protect Osceola taxpayers. Disney steps in with the other five landowners to fund a shortfall—but the county must repay them with interest. The Parkway is a toll road—but no tollbooths may be located on Disney property. Guevara complained that the $1 toll is too steep for Disney workers in his district making little more than $6 an hour—but the bond covenants mandate an initial $1 toll and increases every four years.

For Disney, however, the Parkway victory marked a transition in their means of power. In this era of negotiation, they were forced to work with politicians and government officials on the outside, rather than providing for themselves through their private government. Their resource: the divisible benefits of growth, from bond deals to engineering contracts to enhanced land values. As one example, the $150-million bond deal included $25 million for expenses related to bond financing, and the 12.5-mile Parkway was divided into seven segments, each with its own engineering contract. With these resources they forged a powerful Parkway coalition comprising attorneys, engineering firms, construction companies, bond bankers, land owners, politicians, and government officials. Yet their victory caused Osceola County to deplete its financial capacity to fund growth. The county had raised the sales tax—with Disney's help—and pledged its gas-tax revenues for the Parkway bonds—to benefit Disney. As a result, it had diminished capacity to fund concurrency for other growth

projects. Disney's Celebration, heralded as a boon to economic progress, had locked up the county's prime tax resources for funding
growth.

Celebration was also subject to DRI review, because the property
had been de-annexed from Reedy Creek. That meant that regional
planners would evaluate the project for its consistency with regional
plans. In 1975, regional planning director Cliff Guillet had thought
Epcot would go through DRI review, but the Florida attorney general
had ruled in Disney's favor, eliminating that possibility. Now, for the
first time in Florida history, a Disney project was subject to regional
plan review. If the project had adverse impacts, the regional planning
council and the state DCA would recommend so-called mitigations.
On the important affordable housing issue, however, Osceola County
would decide what level of mitigation was required.

Seemingly, the DRI review would be a cinch. What urban planner
would not love Celebration? It drew from the tradition of "new urbanism," combining cutting-edge urban design with a historically sensitive approach known as Traditional Neighborhood Development,
which tried to appropriate the best of pre–World War II town planning. The plan embraced pocket parks, buildings grouped around a
green, narrow streets and front porches, a mix of housing types, a
walkable downtown, abundant sidewalks, and de-emphasis on the
automobile. According to Mansfield, he and Rummell were not pre-
committed to new urbanism. "None of us were into it," he said of
DDC executives. "We considered the pros and cons—it was more expensive—but at the end of the day, it was the most progressive idea
and the most historical."[28] Its nouveau association also appealed to
Eisner, who wanted something inventive, befitting the Disney enterprise.

Influenced by the work of Miami architects Andres Duany and
Elizabeth Plater-Zyberk, who designed Seaside in the Florida Panhandle, the Celebration design departed from new urbanism in
several respects. Its streets are curvilinear rather than rectangular
in design, and the office park is removed from the downtown
and residential area, requiring a commute by car. In other respects,
though, the principal designers—architects Robert Stern and Jacqueline Robertson—followed the new urbanism mantra. Besides striving

for a walkable town, the residential areas were built dense while, to nurture civic life, public areas were conceived generously. As Michael Pollan wrote in *House & Garden:* "The central premise being tested at Celebration is that a sense of community can be created by dramatically shrinking the private realm of the home while at the same time expanding the amount and quality of 'public' spaces."[29]

For regional planners and the state DCA, the homes were the problem. To Disney's credit, Celebration was a mixed-income project. Unlike most suburban developments, it offered a wide range of housing prices, from $900,000 custom homes and $140,000 town houses to rental units starting at $850 a month. But most developments are not towns in themselves, much less an "international prototype community," as Disney described Celebration. Planning officials were concerned that Celebration provided no on-site affordable housing. It neither responded to the existing housing deficit created by Disney's theme-park operation, nor provided affordable housing for those working in Celebration.

Previously, Disney has resisted state pressure to address their affordable housing impact. When their Reedy Creek plan was rejected in 1992 by DCA because it failed to address their housing impact, they responded by proposing to make a film that would encourage other employers to address their housing impact. They then used a Reagan-era tax law that enabled them to claim affordable housing credit for purchasing tax credits to support affordable housing projects. In fact, the housing projects would have been built anyway; Disney merely underbid another investor when the tax credits were auctioned off. But the credits, for which the company expected a 15 percent rate of return,[30] enabled them to take credit for two housing projects, one in Winter Garden and the other in Kissimmee, both within ten miles of Disney, providing a total of 464 housing units.

At one point during the planning of Celebration, they considered building a Funky Town (their name) offering affordable housing for Disney employees. The idea was scrapped because, according to Peter Rummell, it was too "market-limiting"; non-cast members would find the concept a turnoff, DDC concluded.[31] So Celebration was built without affordable housing. According to a mail-in survey of Disney World employees, done for the company by Fishkind & Associates, only 10 percent of cast members could afford the minimum $140,000 home price.[32] The "model" community, like the theme park, left affordable housing to the surrounding environs.

Housing specialist Susan Caswell from the regional planning council met frequently with Disney planners and attorneys to discuss the Celebration DRI application. At one meeting, their attorney accused her of "social engineering," an ironic term, she thought, given their community-engineering goals at Celebration. Her agency also learned that negotiating with Disney could be tricky. "We caught on that they were saying to us that they had talked with DCA and been told something was fine," said Caswell. "They were doing the same thing at DCA, saying we'd said it was fine."[33] At the state level, DCA attorney David Russ had similar concerns. The Disney team would meet with different DCA planners and "sometimes things would come up that I thought had been resolved." Consequently, he sat in on the meetings and wrote memos summarizing what was said to "make sure everyone had the same information," in his words.[34]

For Caswell the elemental issue was whether enough affordable housing existed nearby to Celebration. Disney wanted a 20-mile/30-minute target zone while she and her agency defended a 10-mile/20-minute zone. The zone mattered because, at 20 miles, the deficit for very-low units was 98 and, at 10 miles, it was 269 units.[35] Caswell also revised their housing inventory list. To avoid double counting, she eliminated almost half their units, other DRI applicants having already counted them. In addition, the state DCA urged Disney to provide on-site affordable housing for Celebration's workforce. By Disney's own numbers, almost two-thirds of the eventual 15,000 employees at Celebration could not afford to live there. In the first of its four phases, one-third of the town's non-construction employees would earn less than $14,999 and another third would make $15,000 to $24,000.[36] All would need to find housing elsewhere.

This jobs–housing imbalance troubled DCA's planning chief Thomas Beck, who observed in appraising the Celebration DRI that an "international prototype for communities" should offer housing for all income classes. On one side, it was a housing issue. "The provision of on-site affordable housing for persons with low and very low incomes who are employed at the Celebration DRI would provide quality employment/living features," wrote Beck. On the other, it was a transportation issue. On-site affordable housing would "decrease the number of external project transportation trips, decrease energy consumption, and decrease the amount of air pollution created by vehicle exhaust," his report continued.[37] Celebration was supposed to de-emphasize the automobile; that should mean reducing external trips as well as internal ones, Beck maintained.

Finally, after more than two years of wrangling with state and regional planners, Disney signed an affordable housing agreement with Osceola County that resolved the issue for Celebration Phase 1. Though the state and regional planners had the power of appeal, Osceola was the permitting government; it could sign the development order approving Celebration. The housing agreement called for Disney—through the Celebration Co.—to pay $100,000 for three years into Osceola's Housing Assistance Plan (HAP). This HAP fund provides downpayment assistance to income-qualified Osceola home-buyers, regardless of where they work. Not on-site housing, but $300,000 paid into a trust fund to support affordable housing else-where in the county was Disney's response to the housing affordability problem created by Celebration's workforce.

Anna Pinellas, the county's housing grants administrator, explained how the deal was struck.[38] She said that her supervisor, Mike Kloehn, the county planning director, stuck his head in her office before attending a meeting with Disney and asked: "How much would you like to have from Celebration for housing assistance?" Without much thought, she responded: "$100,000 for three years." When Kloehn returned he told her, "You're going to be sorry you didn't ask for more." She was. "The county had so many other mitigation issues on the table. Everybody said: 'Don't ruffle the feathers. Just sit back and wait,'" said Pinellas, who did not participate in the negotiations.

Kloehn, who defended the agreement, saying it "put real people in real homes,"[39] admitted that Disney's army of consultants sometimes overran his four-person staff. "They always wanted things at warp-factor 8," he said, using Star Trek terminology to define the sense of urgency that prevailed.[40] Also, political factors constrained the county. As Pinellas explained, the county had no advocacy group supporting affordable housing, so there was no political price for caving on the issue. Osceola leaders may have opposed additional cheap housing anyway. According to Orlando's Fannie Mae head: "The word in the industry is that Osceola doesn't want more affordable housing."[41] An understandable statement, in part. Despite its cowboy culture, Osceola is central Florida's only county with more apartments than single homes—largely because of Disney's impact. Despite tremendous job growth in tourism and hospitality, the county's wages have fallen in real terms between 1979 and 1997.[42]

Disney officials liked the affordable housing agreement. As a DDC executive wrote to Celebration manager Don Killoren in late 1993, "At present, the County would like for us to provide some funding for their Countywide AH (affordable housing) program. I am hopeful that we can get away with a small donation (for which we will get mitigation credit) and the balance of our mitigation requirements will be satisfied via our LITC (low-income tax credit) investments."[43] To state planning chief Thomas Beck, on the other hand, the concept behind the agreement was flawed. The critical need created by Celebration, as he noted in a 1994 letter to Celebration planning official Brenda Eckmair, was for very-low-income units, and the county housing program to which Disney contributed "does not seem to be for very-low-income units."[44] Celebration's Phase 1 deficit was 269 such units (or 98 units using Disney's calculations). In fact, from information supplied by Pinellas, Osceola's HAP funds aided seventy-seven people over three years, of whom only seven were very low income. She estimated that one-third of the beneficiaries were Disney employees.

Yet neither the planning council nor DCA appealed Osceola's development order for Celebration. Dave Russ, who has since left DCA, said the agency was eager to approve projects where "planning agencies had been arguing for a long time." For this prototypical international community, the agency backed away from accepted planning traditions and the state comprehensive plan, "which called for full-service communities, for trying to locate people close to their jobs," said Russ. Philosophically, he added: "The people who live in Celebration get the benefit of these planning ideas, of a mixed-income community. The people who work there don't."

In planning their prototype community, Disney also faced the problem of citizen controls. They were building a community, not another theme park, and it would have real residents, people who could exercise political voice and vote. Disney planners thus confronted the same problem that ERA consultants, attorney Paul Helliwell, and Walt himself had addressed in the mid-1960s: how to exercise company control and still have residents. In the end, these residents would prove a greater threat to managerial prerogatives than the planners and bureaucrats from DCA, Osceola County, and the regional planning council.

As told in Chapter Four, the governance solution propounded for Epcot combined centralized land ownership and private government. This solution promised to free Disney planners, as ERA consultants wrote, "from the impediments to change, such as rigid building codes, traditional property rights, and elected political officials."[45] The governance solution at Celebration was likewise antipolitical but tailored to the reality that, in this case, there were real residents. Todd Mansfield's thinking on this governance issue was shaped by his wife's experiences as an officer of their suburban Orlando neighborhood association, he said. "They used to meet in our kitchen, and it seemed like every little issue degenerated into [a situation of] anarchy, of hostility between neighbors," he related. His solution was to escape democracy and discord, relying instead on centralized control—benign, even paternalistic, based on expertise. "You don't need to vote to decide how to replace a light bulb," he said.

At Celebration, Mansfield's team created a complex web of control devices. In place of the Reedy Creek government that performs public functions at the theme-park property, they formed a Community Development District (CDD) to provide public facilities, including roads and water and sewers, at Celebration. A five-member board elected on the familiar principle of one-acre-equals-one-vote governs the CDD. Disney, as the largest landowner, controls the board; but after 2004, it will be elected by a majority of landowners. That could still be Disney, however, depending on how fast lots sell.

In essence, this CDD has taxing powers. The Disney Co. did not front the money to build public facilities, but instead bonded the infrastructure costs, leaving the CDD to assess residents for debt service as well as for operations and maintenance. In its initial year, 1997, this payment ranged from $650 a year for a townhome to $2,000 per year for estate homes.[46] The debt service is included in the owner's Osceola County property tax bill. Had Disney instead asked Osceola County to provide infrastructure, the county would have gained leverage to use in getting the company to address off-site impacts, such as their housing impact. Hence the CDD protects managerial prerogatives against residents and regulators alike.

There are also two owner associations, one for homeowners and the other for commercial property owners. A Joint Committee, run by five directors initially appointed by the Celebration Co., oversees both. Their control ends when 75 percent of the residential units have been sold or in forty years, whichever comes first. After that, the two owner associations will appoint Joint Committee directors. This faux homeowners association oversees the "Declaration of Covenants," a thick loose-leaf binder of legal documents that every homeowner must sign. These covenants enumerate the multiple rules governing life at Celebration: no parking of boats, mobile homes, or trucks in front of homes; no changes in landscaping without permission; only one small political poster on display outside a residence, and it must come down within two days of the election; no more than two people sleeping in the same bedroom; no TV aerials or satellite dishes visible from the street; and the removal of any cat or dog that the board deems a nuisance.

Offering further protection, Disney retains veto power in perpetuity over any substantive decision by the owner association. As authors Douglas Frantz and Catherine Collins discovered, a clause conferring this power is buried in the legal language of the covenants that homeowners sign.[47] Their veto is good as long as the company owns a single piece of property, which means forever, since they own the entire downtown.

These developer-controlled owner associations arguably intrude on homeowner rights more than typical owner associations do. In *Privatopia,* his thoughtful account of residential private government in the United States, Evan McKenzie concludes that such districts "expose residents to treatment that would be considered unconstitutional had these government functions not been privatized."[48] Yet McKenzie is writing about homeowner-controlled "common-interest developments," such as condominiums and planned-unit developments of single-family houses. In the Celebration's case, the powers of the owner association are wielded for the indefinite future by the developer, not residents. In keeping with Mansfield's antipolitics philosophy, this arrangement maximizes efficiency—substituting management for politics—at the expense of accountability.

Mansfield concedes that these mechanisms confer developer control. "At the end of the day, for many owners and buyers that was an advantage," he maintains. The covenants protect residents from the perils of democracy—the endless meetings, the strife and discord, the difficulty of imposing rules to protect the many from the inconsiderate actions of the few—that Mansfield saw in his own neighborhood association. Like a community constitution, the covenants protect residents, equally, from the developer and fellow residents, imposing mutual obligations. Besides, buyers know what they are getting. "It's all in Technicolor," said the former CDD head, referring to the Declaration of Covenants that homebuyers sign, page after page, as a condition of purchase.

To create a town feeling at Celebration, the Disney Co. made the strategic decision to build the downtown before the residential areas were completed, a costly undertaking. For self-governance of their town, residents must wait until a majority of the land is sold before they can control the CDD, and until 75 percent of the lots are sold (or forty years) to control their (home)owner association. More, these milestones are manipulable since Disney could stall the pace of development, or build more apartments to retain land ownership, in later phases. And further, as already noted Disney retains a veto over substantive decisions. Cynically, one inhabitant remarked on the residents' Web-site message forum, "The only thing the leaders of the town of Celebration are paid by the Disney company to do is to sell houses and make money for the Disney company."[49]

In Celebration's first three years, Disney's control of the town spawned grumbling among some residents and isolated acts of resistance. There are anecdotal reports, for example, of residents waiting until dark to paint their front doors a forbidden color, though most residents appear to accept the rules, for now. Perhaps Mansfield is right that, in Hobbesian fashion, residents and developer share a mutual interest in order. Like Hobbes's *Leviathan*, the Celebration Co. guarantees that order through their web of controls. Douglas Frantz, a *New York Times* reporter who lived in Celebration for fourteen months while researching a book on it, said that the rules were less onerous than the idea of company control.[50] Two recent books, one by Frantz and his wife Catherine Collins and the other by Andrew Ross, recount residents' mixed feelings about the rules.[51] As both books acknowledge, Celebration School proved more controversial than the landowner controls. The difference was that, in the case of the school, the interests of the Celebration Co. diverged from the interests of school parents.

Celebration School was a natural for the Disney Co., said Michael Eisner, because their "primary constituency is children."[52] They made education one of the town's five cornerstones (the others were wellness, community, technology, and place). Whereas the town's architecture looked backwards for inspiration, the school was forward-looking. It incorporated "best practices" divined by educational experts at Harvard and Johns Hopkins, employed high-tech advances in computer networking and educational software, and used open-classroom architecture based on Disney's own research about how kids learn. Among other progressive reforms, students were divided into multi-aged groupings called "neighborhoods," where they practiced "integrated learning," receiving math and science instruction in the context of broader lessons. As well, each student had a "personalized learning plan," and teachers (called "specialists") evaluated their work using "narrative reports" rather than grades.

But how to create this "world class" school in a public school system? As Michael Eisner wrote: "We agreed to work with local county officials to plan and help fund an innovative public school at Celebration—a deliberate alternative to other public schools in central Florida."[53] It was daring: they wanted to keep the school small, recruit a top-notch committed faculty, and employ the latest technological advances—all very costly. That, in a state ranked near the bottom in educational spending, in a county at the bottom in central Florida. More, the school would be administered by the Osceola School District and governed by the Osceola School Board, neither of which felt obliged to support lot sales at Celebration or to make its school better than other county schools. It was a contradiction waiting for an issue to arise. As auto dealer Alan Starling told DDC's Don Killoren after an early briefing on Celebration: "The school part will be very tough."[54]

Undaunted, Disney formed a self-described "unique partnership" with the Osceola School District, built on ingenuity and money and their penchant for control. They got $15 million in construction funds from the county and contributed $5 million for "enhancements" over the first three years, money used for extra teacher training, additional computers, and graduate students who would work as interns. When construction bids for the school building that Disney designed came in over budget, they chipped in $3.5 million for the gym, ball fields, and a playground. In a contract running through 2016, the school board accepted an 80–20 split on the crucial attendance issue. By this agreement, children living in Celebration were guaranteed a slot in the school, and 20 percent of the seats were reserved for students coming from outside the new community. The school, though owned by the school district, has its own semi-independent Board of Trustees responsible for curricular and related matters, with one representative each from the school district, Disney, and nearby Stetson University, which initially agreed to run a Teacher Academy linked to the school.

From before it opened, the school was a flashpoint for criticism. Some critics in national educational circles called it a "boutique school in an elite community"—too small an initiative for a company Disney's size.[55] Others in Osceola, including one school board member, criticized spending $15 million in Celebration when the county had more pressing school needs, such as leaky roofs and faulty wiring, in existing schools.[56] Among Celebration school parents were initial complaints about missing textbooks, unusable equipment, and teacher turnover. Some parents also criticized the school's progressive curriculum, saying among other things that dividing students into multi-age groups was no proven best practice, and that integrated learning meant that children received too few math and science lessons.[57] Part of the underlying problem, said school board member Donna Hart, also a Celebration School trustee, was the school's K–12 concept. "Parents are complaining (in essence) because they don't have a comprehensive high school, but we can't provide that in a small K–12 school."[58] A school serving more students will have better science equipment, she noted.

In the first year, 16 of 21 teachers left and 13 of the school's then 211 students withdrew. Yet withdrawing remained a difficult option. The school was the reason many parents came to Celebration, the reason they paid a premium for their homes. If they withdrew from the school, they might as well sell their homes and move elsewhere (as some did). But many parents had moved cross-country and felt stranded; moving elsewhere meant another job search, among other stresses. In addition, to prevent land speculation, the Disney Co. required that residents live in their homes for one year before selling or forfeit any profit to charity. Practically, that meant home-sellers needed to absorb the real-estate commission if they departed earlier. In some cases, however, the company cut a deal with dissatisfied home-buyers in return for their silence.

The real crisis arose, though, when Disney struck a deal in 1999 with Osceola school officials to build a mega–high school at Celebration. For Disney and the school district, the 2,000-student school was a win-win solution. To meet the requirement of their DRI, the company needed additional school capacity before they could build additional phases of Celebration. At capacity, the Celebration K–12 school would hold only 1,400 students, and 1999 projections called for twice that many slots in five years. The school district, on the other hand, was "cash poor and land poor," as one board member said.[59] To meet projected student population growth over the next five years, it needed twenty new schools by 2020 and a new high school in the high-growth area close to Disney. By donating a fifty-acre school site, Disney could control the school's location. It might not be a K–12 neighborhood school, but it would sit in their development and Celebration could expand.

Left out of the deal were Celebration's true believers in K–12. "We feel betrayed," said Cyndy Hancock, the school's first Parent Student Teacher Association president. "Most of us moved here for the school. The original vision could never have happened in a regular Osceola high school."[60] The new regional high school meant busing hundreds of students into Celebration, violating the town's low-traffic principles. It meant a departure from Celebration School's progressive curriculum, which parents elsewhere in the county would not embrace. It meant abandoning K–12, since the original Celebration School would become either K–7 or K–8. And it meant a breach in the neighborhood-school philosophy, since high school students from Phase 1 would be bused, past their walkable school, to a conventional mega–high school. "They'll be going to a school just like Columbine," one parent complained to the school board, referring to the Colorado high school where thirteen students were slain in 1999.[61]

Whether Disney culpably betrayed residents depends on interpretation of the fine print. All of the Celebration Co. sales brochures warn that they provide only general information and do not constitute a warranty. Also, the disclaimers that Celebration home-buyers signed after November 1997 stipulate that the Osceola School Board, rather than Disney, controls the school. Hence the Celebration Co. is not responsible for "any actions or omissions to act by the Osceola County School Board with respect to Celebration or the Celebration School, or any changes in the manner in which the Celebration School is operated, or any criteria that may be established from time to time by the Osceola County School District relative to curriculum, eligibility for attendance or any other matter relating to the operation of the Celebration School."[62]

Yet not all purchasers signed this disclaimer. It is dated November 17, 1997, and lot sales began in June 1996. In fact, some home-buyers were unaware that Celebration School would be an Osceola County school. "It was a shock to us to discover that Osceola County was in charge of Celebration School," said one early purchaser.[63] Others expected the school to be independent because of Disney's partnership with the school district and the school's separate board of trustees.[64] Perhaps these parents were blinded by pixie dust, yet the Celebration Co. clearly encouraged this view. For example, they prepared a six-minute promotional video, "A Day in the Life of a Celebration Student," that was shown to prospective home-buyers. The video portrays Celebration School as a high-tech mecca offering personalized education, integrated with other Disney facilities such as Epcot and the Celebration Health Center.[65] The clear message is that all Celebration students will enjoy this schooling, not just those who graduate before the regional high school is built. Not mentioned: that Celebration will be part of the Osceola County school system.

Parents also complained about the timing of the decision. In familiar Disney fashion, they negotiated the deal privately and presented it publicly when it was nearly concluded. On May 26, 1999, the school principal sent parents a letter about the deal; the following day, a Celebration Co. official brought it to the Celebration CDD; and on June 6, it went to the school board for approval. Saying they needed more information, the school board delayed action for two weeks before endorsing the agreement. Afterwards, a delegation of eight parents went to Perry Reader, the Celebration Co. vice president who served as the town's general manager and head of its owner association. The parents told Reader that the regional high school conflicted with Celebration's educational philosophy. He dismissed their complaint, said one parent, telling them that they did not represent the community.[66]

In response, some pulled out of the community, including the 1999 president of the Parent Student Teacher Association. Others advocated a high-profile media campaign. Said one resident on their electronic message forum: "I'm not in a position to sell my house at a loss, because my life is invested in it. Large numbers and publicity are the only thing that can slow down this train."[67] To publicize their cause, residents purchased buttons and bumper stickers saying "Keep K–12 in Celebration." Some wore these buttons in the Fourth of July parade, sponsored by the Celebration Co., in 1999. Going further, one outspoken parent erected a banner in her yard, emblazoned in eight-inch letters with "Preserve Celebration School K–12 Program." Within two hours, a Celebration assistant town manager called and asked her to remove it. She refused, saying it was part of her Fourth of July celebration. She received a letter from the same official a week later declaring the banner violated the homeowner covenants and should be struck (she already had).[68]

More proactively, one parent encouraged residents to file Federal Trade Commission complaints; she even posted the agency's Web address on Celebration's electronic message forum. Another parent, Teresa Rosen, the mother of three boys in Celebration School, filed a lawsuit alleging that Disney reneged on a promise to parents. Financed by twenty other parents, her suit said the school change would lower the quality of education, bring noisy buses to the community, and diminish property values. It was backed by a survey of community residents indicating that 96 percent believe Disney should withdraw its land offer to the school board. More ominous for Disney's control of the town, 97 percent of the 450 respondents concurred with the statement: "The Celebration Co. should ascertain the opinions of residents before making community-altering decisions."[69] A judge dismissed the Rosen lawsuit on June 7, 1999, saying that mediation between homeowners and the Celebration Co. might still work. In response, the lawsuit's supporters organized a community organization, WECARE, as an alternative to the company-controlled owner association.

The issue comes down to whether Celebration belongs to the corporation or to the residents. On one side is the corporate vision represented by Michael Eisner. In his biography, he acknowledges the constant war within the company between quality and profits. "No tension is as great as the one between quality and commerce. There is a constant push and pull between the company's good and the greater good," writes the Disney chief. His role, he says, is to decide between these competing goods, to discover the "common ground."[70] On the other side is the vision of a citizen-run community. "People may look back at this period," said resident Pam Morris, as the time when "the residents of Celebration became the keepers of the Disney vision."[71] Her husband, Bob, himself a developer, thinks Disney "doesn't understand what it created at Celebration."[72] Most of the visionaries who started the community—Peter Rummell, Todd Mansfield, Don Killoren, and Charles Adams—have departed. "There is no one left at the management level who understands the power of the vision they created," he said.

Morris' comment points to the irony of Disney's situation. They may succeed in galvanizing community at Celebration. As happened to the utopian planners of the nineteenth century whose failed experiments were recounted in the ERA report of 1966, the residents may come together against them. A related irony: Disney's most serious public relations threat in this episode came from people who, in buying lots at Celebration, seemingly bought into the whole Disney vision. A further irony: the regional high school that so many residents oppose will be built by the Celebration CDD, an entity financed but not controlled by Celebration residents.

In this era of negotiation, the Disney Co. got most of what it wanted. At least they succeeded where politicians and government officials were concerned. Property Appraiser Bob Day was the partial exception—most officials were more yielding. Yet Celebration's citizen-residents proved more unruly, more difficult to satisfy, more perspicacious in assessing the company's every move. Perhaps the Celebration Co. should have heeded ERA's warning, in 1966, that new towns typically founder when based upon an ideology—like

K–12 neighborhood schools—rather than dollars and cents. Or perhaps Walt Disney was right, in his comments on the Paul Helliwell memo, when he vetoed "permanent residents" in his prototype town. Maybe real residents and company control are a combustive mix.

Yet the Disney Co. has an exit option. If Celebration becomes a public relations liability, they can sell it to another land developer, as some predict they will. Short of that, they can also reduce the Disney Co. profile at Celebration, as happened in 1999 when negative stories appeared in the national media about Celebration School and about shoddy construction practices and excessive construction delays on the part of Celebration's third-party homebuilders.[73] In response, the Disney Co. removed their signature mouse ears from the totem-like watertower at the entrance to the town. The company also stopped promoting Celebration as a visit-place for tourists, which has reduced patronage at the town's stores and restaurants, several of which had closed by early 2000. Thus the challenge of mollifying residents continues.

NINE

Therapy

"This is an outstanding example of the kind of partnership that central Florida is becoming famous for," said Orange County Chairman Linda Chapin.[1] The occasion was a June 25, 1996, commission meeting at which Chapin and her fellow commissioners approved a $53-million taxpayer subsidy for Disney's fourth I-4 interchange. Incredibly, the interchange was not even in Orange County, a fact not explained to county commissioners when they voted. As Chapin indicated, the deal was like other public-private partnerships involving area road projects. It was like the "cost-sharing" agreements discussed in the previous chapter to build Osceola Parkway and improve U.S. 192 in front of Celebration. As told below, it was also like an interchange subsidy for Disney's competitor, Universal Studios, a few months earlier, a deal costing Orlando taxpayers $50 million and prompting Disney to seek similar aid from Orange County.

Between 1985 and 1990, Orange County had challenged Disney on impact fees, the constitutionality of their charter, their opposition to Mag-lev, and their access to private activity bonds. That period of conflict had culminated in a new social contract, incorporated in the 1989 interlocal agreement, requiring Disney to pay $13.4 million for road improvements over five years. Now, in the mid-1990s, Disney was asking the county for road money and getting it, instead of the county pressing them to pay more. The county did not—or could not—say no to Disney even when it meant importing more low-wage workers into the community, even when it meant funding an interchange in another county. It seemed to be an economic-development marriage gone awry, a one-sided relationship benefiting Disney to the exclusion of Orlando-area residents, a marriage needing therapy.

What accounted for this new equilibrium in the Disney–Orange County relationship? As a basis for therapy, we first need to see how these interchange deals were consummated, for they model the dynamics of the underlying relationship. Second, we will examine four problems that are potential sources of instability in the relationship. Third, we will examine why, despite these problems, Orange County gave Disney what it wanted in the 1990s. Finally, we will explore how recuperation might occur in this relationship and what alternative courses of action exist for the area.

Universal Studios needed an interchange on I-4 to provide access to the expanded theme park they were building. They were transforming their existing movie–studio park into a complete destination resort, and, like their mouse-eared competitor, Universal claimed city status: the new complex would be called Universal City. The $1-billion expansion would include a second theme park, Islands of Adventure; a nighttime entertainment complex called City Walk; upscale themed hotels, vacation villas, a golf course, and an 18,000-car parking structure. "We saw that Disney had their interchanges paid for by the public sector," said Alan Eberly, Universal's vice president of properties. "'What's wrong with this picture?' we asked. We thought we should get some help too."[2]

After meeting with Orlando mayor Glenda Hood, Universal executives worked with city staff to craft a tax-increment financing agreement allowing Universal to capture part of the growth dividend from its own expansion. The city borrowed $50 million in tax-free bonds, and Universal agreed to make the payments until 2000. At that point, the original bonds would be paid off and replaced with a second borrowing, backed by the extra taxes that the Universal development would generate. Including interest, nearly $108 million would be spent over 25 years to pay off the $50-million commitment.

When Mayor Hood brought the financing plan to the city commission on June 5, 1995, the lone dissenter was Commissioner Bruce Gordy, a frequent critic who later ran, unsuccessfully, against Hood for mayor. Gordy's criticisms of Universal echoed Orange County

Commissioner Lou Treadway's earlier complaints about Disney. As Gordy said at the commission meeting, "I don't think government should be in the business of funding this interchange for a private enterprise. They ought to be able to build a $50-million interchange with their own funds."[3] In response, Orlando finance director Mickey Miller claimed that taxpayers were not really funding the interchange, since the city's share would come from Universal's increased taxes. The implication was that taxes paid by a big corporation still belonged to them. When pressed by Gordy, Miller agreed that tax revenue generated by Universal's expansion "could be used for another purpose."[4] The same logic, of course, applied to the interchange deal struck with Disney.

Jim Harris, president of Busch Properties, which owns Sea World, termed the Universal deal "curious." "Here you have a major entity, not being enticed, that's already in the community, about to make a major investment, and they want this level of assistance," says Harris, a former Orange County administrator.[5] "It kind of griped us," he added. To ensure access to an expanded Sea World, Busch had built an interchange at Central Florida Parkway and I-4, turning the interchange over to the state without even asking for impact-fee credits. Though "griped" about Universal's public subsidy, the Sea World owners remained quiet about it. "We don't complain about our competitors' deals," explained Harris.

For Disney, however, the Universal deal aroused serious interchange envy. At the time, they were planning an interchange at Osceola Parkway and I-4, an interchange that they needed to ensure access to Animal Kingdom, which was already coming out of the ground. Orange County Chairman Linda Chapin recalls a meeting in Tom Lewis' office, where he and Dianna Morgan presented the deal.[6] Although the eventual agreement was with Disney's Reedy Creek government, Lewis from the company's development arm and Morgan from their government relations office made the case—reflecting the ability of Disney executives to alternate between representing the company and Reedy Creek.

As revealed in a "Q and A" prepared by Disney, Lewis and Morgan said their company deserved assistance because it was investing over $1 billion in the county on three projects: the Animal Kingdom theme park and the Coronado Springs and Boardwalk resorts.[7] They also cited the precedent that Universal had received similar help. More, Disney's request offered the county a better return, they said, since the Animal Kingdom would open later that year and start providing additional tax revenue before the county began paying for the interchange. As well, they compared their proposal to the Osceola Parkway "public-private partnership," an interesting analogy since Osceola officials would see that project as a costly boondoggle in another two years. Finally, they asked a telling question—would it be a public relations problem for Orange County to "share in the funding of an interchange partially located in Osceola County"?

Disney's arguments resonated with Chapin. As noted, she and Dianna Morgan had become personal friends in the mid-1980s, a relationship that had "paid off," according to Chapin, during the bond controversy in 1990. That was the flap over the bond money that Reedy Creek got to build a sewage treatment plant—for tourists— when Orange County wanted the money for affordable housing—to assist Disney workers, among others. Back then, she and Morgan were able to talk "off the record," said Chapin, soothing relations between the company and county. Moreover, she admitted a "positive bias" toward Disney, dating back to Disney's "It's a Small World" attraction at the 1964 New York World's Fair, where she met her future husband. Besides, she thought the entertainment company had been good for the area. They had elevated development standards in addition to providing economic benefits, and their charter posed no problem, since, in her view, they paid more in taxes than they received in services.

More, Chapin wanted to put the county's relationship with Disney on a new footing. She believed that governments can have a personality. In the 1980s, the county commission was opinionated, abrasive, and outspoken—a personality she wanted to change. Historically, county government had been Disney's "country cousins," she said, while their real relationship was with Orlando and Mayor Frederick. "He's the one they took on trips," she remarked. The interchange deal was an opportunity to change all that, "to keep the county from being like little kids with their noses pressed to the glass, on the outside looking in," in her words.

One of those assigned to craft the agreement was Mark Fostier, an assistant county comptroller. Unlike the other members of the team, he did not report to Chapin. Instead he worked for Martha Haynie, the independently elected county comptroller. When Fostier was assigned to the team, his supervisor, Jim Moye, told him to "make sure it's in Orange County."[8] Moye had attended an early meeting on the interchange and was suspicious about its location. During the team's meetings, Fostier maintains, he asked three times: "Is the interchange in Orange County?" Supported by his meeting notes, he got the same answer each time: the interchange was mostly in Orange County. "It was supposed to be built in two phases," explained Fostier. "All but a slight physical portion of Phase 1 would be in Orange, and a majority of Phase 2 would be in Orange, too."[9]

The county commissioners were not told these complicating details, however. A five-page briefing memo prepared by an assistant county administrator indicated only that Phase 1 would provide "full access to and from Orange County."[10] It did not say that any part of the interchange was in Osceola. A map included as an appendix to the thick financial agreement was hard to read: it showed Osceola Parkway crossing I-4 but did not pinpoint the interchange. A *Sentinel* article appearing the day before the meeting ambiguously reported that the interchange was "at the Orange-Osceola county line."[11] When Reedy Creek officials met with Commissioner Clarence Hoenstine to discuss the deal the day before the meeting, the interchange location never came up, says Hoenstine.[12] In fact, only a small portion of the ramp work is in Orange County, according to Donald Lepsic, Osceola County's assistant county engineer.[13] (William Baxter, Orange County's public works director, failed to respond to repeated inquiries about the interchange's location.)

Two years after the deal was struck, Hoenstine learned that a majority of the interchange was in Osceola. Embarrassingly, he learned this fact from an Osceola County official. "I was shocked, to put it mildly," said Hoenstine. Commissioner Mary Johnson was in the dark until interviewed by the author in 1999.[14] Like Hoenstine, she said she would have balked at voting for the measure, or at least asked why Osceola was not contributing. Two key staffers involved in the negotiations said that if the commissioners did not know, they should have, implying it was their fault. "We knew all along it was in Osceola County," said Ajit Lalchandani, then the county's public works director.[15] Deputy County Attorney Jeff Newton added, "It was at the confluence of Osceola Parkway and I-4; they should have known from that."[16] Yet Fostier was given a copy of a legal memo from the county attorney's office that said the interchange was in Orange.[17]

Why mislead county commissioners? When asked about the issue, County Attorney Tom Wilkes said the interchange benefited Orange County economically, regardless of where it was located.[18] In an interview, Chapin offered the same assessment.[19] Though not entirely in Orange County, it would serve projects on Disney property that were. Over twenty years, these projects would supposedly generate $32 million more in taxes than the county spent on the interchange. Yet selling all this to the public might prove difficult. The county already faced a transportation-funding crisis, and a blue-ribbon commission was assessing the county's infrastructure needs, preparing for a campaign to raise the county sales tax. Said Moye from the comptroller's office: "Here was Chapin giving away *ad valorem* tax money, the county's most sacred tax resource, to build what was essentially a driveway to Disney's door."[20]

In fairness, the agreement tied the county's $53-million payment to Disney paying increased taxes on the subject properties. It was a tax-increment financing deal, with Reedy Creek issuing the bonds and the county reimbursing 50 percent of their annual bond costs. To protect itself, the county would not reimburse Disney unless the company's taxes on the three properties increased enough to cover the bond cost, plus 25 percent. But that meant Disney would recoup three-quarters of the growth dividend from their new development for twenty years, with only one quarter going to the county to compensate for the impact of their expansion.

To critics, though, it was like a homeowner enlarging his house and expecting government to build him a driveway in return. No homeowner would expect such government largess. There was also the question of whether getting twenty-five cents on the dollar from Disney's taxes compensated the county adequately for the impact of their expansion. They would create 8,000 new jobs, all but 1,500 of them salaried, with a starting salary in 1999 of $6.25 an hour. Further, the county was not leveraging any new investment: Disney was building the three properties anyway and had already designed the interchange. Contrary to the usual logic of economic development assistance, the county was giving a performance reward, not an incentive to act.

At the county commission meeting at which the interchange subsidy was approved, Commissioner Hoenstine asked about the 1989 interlocal agreement between Reedy Creek and Orange County, the agreement requiring Disney to pay $13.4 million for road improvements. Saying the agreement was worthwhile, Hoenstine asked whether it would be renewed before it lapsed, six months later, in January 1997. In response, Chapin said: "That's an item on the agenda after we finish this," referring to the interchange deal. "That interlocal agreement has served our interests and the citizens' interests very well."[21]

In fact, nothing happened. "The Chairman never got back to us on it," said Hoenstine.[22] In his view, under the new system of an elected county chairman, Chapin initiated policy and the commissioners responded to it. Asked about the agreement, Chapin said in an interview: "Honestly, it may have lapsed without our noticing. Our relationship [with Disney] was on a firm footing then; there were no current controversies." If the county pressed Disney too hard on impact fees, they might push back and request more services. You have to maintain a "balance of power," she thought.[23] It would have been the county attorney's job to notify Chapin that the agreement was terminating. In an interview, he said the same: a new agreement was unnecessary.[24] Harry Stewart, the former county attorney, said that Chapin was ultimately responsible. "If the county chairman did not want it to come up, it certainly wouldn't have been raised by staff," he observed.[25]

When the interlocal agreement was approved back in 1989, Commissioner Bill Donegan had called Disney's $13.4-million payment "hush money." With the passage of time, that characterization seemed more apt. By the mid-1990s, with the county chairman system in place and Chapin installed as chairman, the commission was hushed. While, as Chapin said, there were "no current controversies," there were nevertheless underlying problems in the relationship, problems that called into question whether this "new balance of power" in fact benefited county residents. These problems are potential sources of instability and change in the Disney-local relationship.

Four problems exist beneath the surface in this economic-development marriage. One is Disney's immunity from some types of taxes and fees, despite their enormous public impact and despite the area's resource-needs imbalance. Another is the wage problem associated with Disney and tourism. A third is the region's economic overdependence upon tourism—attributable in part to the large subsidies given to tourism. A fourth is the threat that Disney's and Universal's faux downtowns pose to real-world downtown Orlando, the heart of Orange County. These problems differ in the degree to which they are publicly perceived and discussed. For example, there is little public awareness of the urban competition problem or of Disney's avoidance of certain taxes and fees, while the wage problem is widely perceived by local officials but little discussed publicly.

Consider, first, Disney's escape from taxes and fees that other land developers pay. Like other fast-growing areas, greater Orlando suffers from an imbalance of needs and resources in funding infrastructure. In 1996, a blue-ribbon commission found that Orange County had created an infrastructure deficit reaching into the billions as a result of failing to increase taxes. To fund the deficit for roads, schools, parks, and flood-control facilities, pro-growth forces launched an unsuccessful campaign in 1997 to raise the county sales tax from six to seven cents. During that tax campaign, in which the advocates conceded that growth did not pay for itself, the Disney Co. kept a lower profile than in the Osceola County sales-tax campaign two years earlier. They did, however, give $25,000 to the pro-tax side, an amount exceeded only by Universal's $50,000 contribution.

For their part, Disney representatives think they pay ample taxes. They are easily Orange County's largest taxpayer. As shown in Table 3, the taxable value of their property was nearly $5 billion in 1999, compared with $656 million for Universal Studios and $514 million for Cirent/Lucent Technologies, which manufactures computer chips. Disney representatives like to say they are taxed twice, paying for services such as law enforcement that they provide for themselves. Yet they escape from paying some taxes and fees that other landowners pay, a fact not disclosed in the periodic local news stories about their paying Orange County's largest tax bill.

On the tax side, Disney escapes from paying approximately $15 million a year, according to the county comptroller's office.[26] Despite

Table 3. Orange County's largest property owners, 1999

Walt Disney World	$4,985,127,693
Universal Studios	$656,386,107
Cirent/Lucent Technologies	$514,279,977
Bellsouth Communications	$424,273,189
SeaWorld	$298,686,106
Florida Power Corporation	$281,335,860
Lockheed Martin	$272,226,143
Sprint	$256,514,587
AT&T	$231,576,931
Marriott Corporation	$216,013,703

Source: Orange County Property Appraiser

the law enforcement needs they generate off-property, and despite the economic impact of crimes against tourists, such as the slump in park visitors caused by several high-profile incidents in 1994, they invoke their charter immunities to avoid paying a special tax for law enforcement that other landowners in unincorporated Orange County pay. Instead, they pay $1.7 million a year for special sheriff service, gaining a sheriff detail to use almost as a private police force. Likewise, they refuse to pay a special utility tax that landowners in unincorporated Orange County pay. Their immunity from both taxes saved them $15 million in 1999.

Disney also escapes from paying transportation impact fees, despite their enormous road impact. Invoking the immunities granted in their charter, they also avoid paying impact fees for law enforcement and fire protection. The county's loss in revenue is difficult to calculate, since the fees vary depending on the size and use of new construction. A low estimate of what they would owe for transportation would be the $13.4 million, or $2 million a year, that Harry Stewart won from Disney over the five-year period 1989–1994. The estimate is low because it was a negotiated figure that Stewart won when he lacked the full backing of the county commission. Adding $2 million for transportation impact fees to the $15 million for law enforcement and utility taxes produces an annual revenue loss to the county of $17 million.

In lieu of impact fees, Disney makes highly publicized charitable contributions. Their main event is an annual Community Service Awards banquet, a gala affair at which $500,000 is doled out to nonprofit groups in checks of $1,000 to $15,000. The banquet itself, replete with lavish decorations and Disney troupes to entertain the 1,000 or more guests, costs an estimated $100,000. Without offering a breakdown, Disney public relations officials say the company makes $2.8 million in annual cash contributions,[27] a figure that pales in comparison with the $17 million in taxes and fees that they escape from paying each year because of their immunities. Of course, there is an enormous difference between paying taxes and making charitable contributions, since the latter are discretionary and earn favorable publicity while creating patronage ties to area nonprofit groups.

Second, consider Orlando's growing wage problem. "We have an embarrassment of riches," said Orange County Chairman Mel Martinez, who replaced Chapin in 1998. "[Tourism] has a synergy that keeps it growing so dramatically. But what is the labor force that feeds this beast? It's not what we want to have as a community."[28] Martinez, who joined the Bush Cabinet as Secretary of Housing and Urban Development in 2001, thinks that any job is better than no job but knows that low-wage work costs the community. "It's a workforce that is very dependent on the social network that the community provides," he said. Martinez gets support on this issue from a surprising source, Chamber of Commerce president Jacob Stuart. An opponent of raising the legal minimum wage, Stuart nevertheless thinks $10 an hour is the minimum acceptable wage in Orlando. "Anything less and we're paying it anyway in subsidies for health, transportation, housing, and food stamps," Stuart says.[29]

Disney World may have created riches, but area wage earners have not prospered. A 1999 report prepared for the regional Economic Development Commission (EDC) stated: "While the size of the Orange County economy has grown at one of the fastest rates in the nation, the quality of the growth has not kept pace. Growth in annual earnings per worker has been very slow and well below national averages."[30] In Orange County, real wages have been stagnant since 1987. In Osceola County to the south, which is the most impacted by tourism, average annual real wages have fallen in the past two decades. It is the paradox of Orlando's transformation: low wages amidst rampant job growth.

Disney's wages help to explain the paradox. From 1993 to 1998, their starting wage was $5.85 an hour. In 1998, after a new round of contract negotiations with the six unions representing Disney workers, the starting salary rose to $6.25, with workers topping out after five years at $10.43 an hour. For perspective, the U.S. Department of Health and Human Services says the poverty level for a family of three is $13,880, which requires an hourly wage of $6.67. Workers earning less than $8.67 are eligible for food stamps. According to SEIU (Service Employees International Union) local president Mike Duffy, about half of their 25,000 covered workers have dependents, and only about half have topped out at $10.43,[31] making many eligible for food stamps. Yet Disney's wages and benefits are better than the competition's. In 1999, Universal started workers at $6.15 an hour, and SeaWorld at $6.05.

As stated in a 1998 newsletter of SEIU Local 362, "Those who believe in the idea of a 'free market' say that when a commodity is in scarce supply (in this case, labor), the price (wages) should go up. But the free market is only a theory and doesn't really exist, especially in a company town like Orlando."[32] As a short-term measure, the Disney Co. is recruiting workers from distant places. Wanting employees who can speak Spanish, they have recruited in the Texas-Mexican border area and in Puerto Rico, where unemployment is close to 10 percent. Puerto Ricans willing to migrate from the island are offered $900 to relocate in Orlando—if they do not last three months they must repay a pro rata portion of this allowance. Likewise, current cast members who notify the company of potential workers in Puerto Rico receive a bonus.[33] Longer term, the company expects willing workers to migrate to Orlando. "In a labor pool, it catches up over time," says Walt Disney World President Al Weiss. "You outstrip the demand for a short time and the supply will catch up with the demand over time."[34]

The capacity of labor unions to raise wages is limited. The major unions representing Disney cast members are the Hotel and Restaurant Employees, the Teamsters (who represent costumed characters), and the SEIU. In negotiating with the company, these unions and three smaller ones form a Service Trades Union Council and work together. In 1994, they threatened to strike to keep Disney from taking back health benefits, the Council's efforts bolstered by a company document, leaked to the press, that showed the company planned to increase part-time work—to "help defeat the spiraling costs of EB (employee benefits)."[35] In 1998, the Council not only won wage concessions but also capped part-time work at 30 percent of total hours worked. That still left 10,000 part-time Disney employees, divided about equally between regular and seasonal part-timers.[36]

Yet the unions are weak at Disney, as elsewhere in central Florida. In this right-to-work state, the Trades Council unions have only about 9,000 dues-paying members among the 25,000 employees covered by their union contract. These numbers weaken the unions' ability to strike, their most powerful weapon. As the SEIU's Duffy says, "It's hard to take on a $25-billion corporation with its own TV network (ABC). We need an overall strategy to deal with the whole industry—entertainment, hotels, and theme parks." In 2000, the SEIU was less concerned about taking on Disney than about organizing Universal Studios and the area's 50,000 nonunion hotel rooms.

Third, consider the problem of Orlando's industry mix. Mel Martinez, a Cuban-American, compares the problem to Cuba's overdependence on sugar. "All the time as a kid," he says, "I was told that Cuba was too dependent on one crop, sugar. We've got the same problem except that it's tourism." One of the biggest local advocates for diversifying the economy, ironically, is Bill Peeper, president of the Orlando/Orange County Convention and Visitors Bureau. The Bureau's main job is advertising Orlando for tourism and booking conventions at the convention center and area hotels. Yet Peeper, as much as anyone else in Orlando, worries about the economy's over-reliance on tourism.[37]

In part, this vulnerability stems from the tourism recapture rate. Orlando has an 80 percent recapture rate, meaning that 80 percent of area tourists have visited before. Seemingly a compliment to area attractions, this statistic worries tourism officials, who wonder how many more times these same visitors will return. Another concern is the business cycle. When a business downturn occurs, people cut their leisure spending, making the tourist industry acutely sensitive to recession. The buoyant economy of the last decade has forestalled this threat, but the memory of past recessions causes worry about the future. A more specific concern arises from the fast pace of hotel construction. To keep up with hotel construction at the end of the 1990s, the visitor count needs to jump 1.2 million beyond its 1999 level, said Peeper. By this measure, the convention bureau predicts a shortfall of 1 million visitors in 2002, raising the possibility of a hotel-generated recession.[38]

In Orlando and Orange County there is much talk of stimulating high-tech employment. In addition to Lockheed Martin, which manufactures missiles and related components, Orlando has a growing laser-optics industry, a spin-off from Lockheed-Martin. It also has a simulation and training industry largely oriented toward the military. More recently, it has acquired Cirent, a silicon chip manufacturer that employed 1,700 workers earning an average salary of $40,000 in 1999. Between 1996 and 1999, Orange County gave $22.8 million in incentives to Cirent.

Despite these high-tech incentives, manufacturing employment in the county declined throughout the 1990s. A 1999 study for the EDC said that only 12 percent of the new jobs created in Orange County over the previous ten years paid a wage higher than the local average. The study described an economy diluted by "the rapid creation of low-paying jobs in the service and retail sectors without a corresponding increase in high-wage jobs, reducing the level of the economy."[39] Only Las Vegas, said the report, has a higher percentage of total earnings concentrated in the amusements sector of the economy. Compounding this problem, tourism's share of the regional economy is growing. In 2000, tourism is expected to account for 25 percent of the area's employment, up from 20 percent in 1998.[40]

Tourism's expanding share of the economy reflects Orange County's incentive practices. Says county planner Bruce McClendon, "We nickel and dime high tech while spending 20 to 30 times that to incentivize the hotel and tourism industry."[41] For example, the $23 million given to Cirent contrasts with the combined $103 million given to Universal and Disney for their I-4 interchanges. Likewise, the 5 percent tourist tax (collected from hotel guests) amounts to a "low-wage job machine," according to McClendon. "We generate it, then we turn around and reinvest in low-wage jobs," he says. Presently, tax proceeds can only go to promote or support tourism, a purpose that Disney defines narrowly. Their representative on the Tourist Development Council, which advises Orange County on tourist-tax issues, has routinely voted against uses that benefit the community, such as funding for the Orlando Science Center.

Fourth, consider the urban competition problem. For Orlando, the comparison between real-world cities and the Disney variety is no abstract issue. Joined by Universal, Disney competes with downtown Orlando as an entertainment venue and, when Celebration reaches buildout, they will compete for commercial office space as well. The very name of Disney's newest nighttime area—Downtown Disney—rankles some, for it sends the message that theme-park world, not Orlando, is the hub of the region, the cultural core. Now Universal competes with the same message: "Come to the City" their ads beckon. Though a submerged issue now, this competition will grow more pronounced.

In the 1970s, downtown Orlando experienced a small renaissance due to Disney and tourism. In 1974, entrepreneur Bob Snow launched Church St. Station, a block-long complex of restaurants and bars. He then added a festival marketplace, Church Street Exchange, with partner James Rouse in 1988. According to Bob Windham, who managed Church Street for fifteen years, 80 percent of their patrons were always tourists.[42] They succeeded for so long, he said, because Disney did not initially compete in the nighttime entertainment market. That changed in the Eisner era, starting with Pleasure Island in 1989 and Downtown Disney in 1997, followed by Universal's City Walk in 1998. "Our slice of the pie kept getting smaller," said Windham. "At present, there's no way Church Street can compete with Disney and Universal." At Downtown Disney, the House of Blues offers a mixture of big names and local acts, while Universal's City Walk has separate venues for reggae, rock, jazz, and Latin music. Faced with such competition, more than twenty-three bars and restaurants closed in downtown Orlando between 1997 and 1999.

In Windham's opinion, Disney's biggest advantage is their 30,000 hotel rooms on the property. That gives them a large, captive market inside the Disney tourist bubble, whereas downtown Orlando visitors get exposed to the grittiness of a real city. To Tom Kohler, the head of the city's Downtown Development Board, Disney also possesses a governance advantage. "It's a lot easier when you own everything. The less democracy, the easier to decide," he says, citing the problems in downtown Orlando of decaying properties and passive, nonlocal ownership.[43] Orlando nightclub owner Mark NeJame sees numerous state-granted advantages for Disney—roads to the doorstep, signs up and down the interstate, and special treatment in state statutes. The latter especially irks NeJame: his Zuma Beach Club must close at 2 a.m., and no one may enter after hours, though neither restriction applies at Disney.

In the late 1990s, Orlando Mayor Hood's plan for rescuing downtown hinged on building a light-rail system running between the I-Drive tourist district near Universal and downtown Orlando. As NeJame was quick to say, the city's plans seemed contradictory. First Orlando subsidized competition with downtown by spending $50 million on an I-4 interchange serving City Walk. Then Mayor Hood, with clamorous support from the *Sentinel,* proposed a $600-million train to ferry tourists from I-Drive to downtown Orlando. "For what?" asks Bob Windham. When Universal got their interchange subsidy, Mayor Hood said they would help on mass transit, and she repeatedly said during the campaign for light rail that Universal would contribute $10 million toward the project. In the end, they failed to carry through, helping to defeat the initiative. To close observers, they backed out because they are building hotels on-site and, like Disney, they want to keep their guests on property, to spend their money there.

These problems—Disney's tax and fee immunities, the wages problem, the area's over-reliance on tourism, and competition with downtown Orlando—are potential sources of instability in the Disney-local relationship. The mystery is why, despite these problems, Disney was able to acquire interchange subsidies from the county and to avoid an extension of the interlocal agreement requiring them to pay even a modest amount for roads benefiting them. Was the county constrained to go along with Disney because of the theme park's economic importance to the county? Or do institutional, political, and cultural factors explain their acquiescence to Disney? These questions are important for understanding the nature of Orange County's path of dependence favoring Disney and tourism. To the extent that politics rather than economics is determinant, a path of recovery may be possible.

The above questions take us back to the work of Paul Peterson. As noted in Chapter One, he believes that cities' economic development choices are highly constrained. Cities depend on private business to supply private investment to produce wages, profits, jobs, and, above all, tax revenues. Local leaders' choices are constrained by intercity competition for scarce private investment; and this intercity rivalry, not political competition within cities, drives the formulation of development policy. Further, cities have a "unitary interest" (widely shared, largely consensual) in attaining prosperity, he believes. As a result, economic development policies tend to be formulated in centralized, closed, business-dominated decision-making processes. (The informal processes used by Billy Dial and Martin Andersen's "movers and shakers" are examples.) Business people tend to dominate such decisions, reasons Peterson, not because they receive selective benefits, though they sometimes do, but because their interests correspond closely with the economic interests of the city taken as whole.[44] (Again, Dial and Andersen fit this description in their tireless promotion of roadbuilding.)

In essence, Chapin and County Attorney Tom Wilkes embraced Peterson's argument. The Osceola Parkway interchange indirectly benefited Orange County regardless of where it was located, they claimed. Wilkes, who drafted the interchange agreement, offered an explicit economic rationale in defending the interchange financing plan. True, he said, it did not leverage new private investment: Disney's Animal Kingdom and their two resorts, Coronado Springs and Boardwalk, were already under construction. But the county's "incentives" were needed to reassure other investors down the road, thought Wilkes. "How could we say no," he asked rhetorically, "when Disney was making that large an investment?"[45] This deference to investor prerogatives matches what Peterson's market competition model leads one to expect.

It is difficult to accept Wilkes's argument, however. As local banker Marshall Vermillion said, "Of course local officials can say no to Disney." Vermillion, the central Florida president of First Union Bank and a respected banking leader, admits to being a purist in these matters. "It's more important for local officials to send the right message to taxpayers," he says.[46] He rejects that spurning Disney would send the marketplace a bad signal. The company was not creating high-wage jobs after all, and, besides, they were building Animal Kingdom anyway. "You can't call that incentivizing," said Orange County Commissioner Ted Edwards, who was not on the commission when the financing plan was approved. "It's not an incentive if they would have done it anyway."[47]

Like the economic-necessity argument made by Chapin and Wilkes, Peterson's economic-determinist model fails to recognize the stages of urban growth. As seen in earlier chapters, Disney's coming to central Florida was good for the area in many ways. At least until Epcot opened in 1982, they were what former Department of Labor secretary Robert Reich calls the community "champion": what was good for them was mostly good for the area.[48] That began to change in the mid-1980s during the period of Eisner-led expansion at Disney. It changed as politicians like Lou Treadway and Vera Carter grew concerned about the costs of growth and Disney's exemption from impact fees. In the 1990s, it was even more difficult to accept Disney as the community champion—at least for those cognizant of the wages problem, the economic imbalance favoring tourism, Disney's avoidance of taxes and fees, and the growing competition between Disney's faux downtown and downtown Orlando. To answer Wilkes' question with another question—why subsidize an employer who imports low-wage workers to the community?

If the economic necessity argument does not explain Orange County's willingness to provide infrastructure subsidies for Disney in the 1990s, what does? This question takes us back to the regime perspective introduced in Chapter One. Regime theorists maintain that cities have more choices about how to grow than Peterson's market-based model of urban politics acknowledges. The issue is not only whether to grow but how to finance growth, what kind of growth to pursue (tourism, manufacturing, etc.), and who will be inconvenienced by growth. In their view, it is the nature of the local regime—the informal network of groups and individuals that dominates local governance—that determines local development policies.[49] In short, politics matters.

With two important caveats, the regime perspective offers a better understanding of the dynamics of the Disney-local relationship. The first caveat concerns the stages of growth argument advanced above. For the pre-Epcot era, Peterson's market model provides a satisfactory account of local policymaking regarding Disney. During that time, greater Orlando was relatively constrained economically and

Disney was the local champion. As growth occurred, however, the constraint of needing to assure growth lessened. Likewise the face of the growth issues changed from how to assure growth to how to manage and finance it. In these changed circumstances, political factors became more determinant in local officials' decisions about growth. Accordingly, the regime perspective with its greater emphasis on political factors and relationships provides a more satisfactory account of local policymaking regarding growth.

The second caveat concerns the role of institutions in perpetuating power relationships arising from earlier economic dependence. That is what the Reedy Creek charter did. It perpetuated the asymmetrical power relationship (advantage Disney) that prevailed in 1967, when Disney could have gone elsewhere and Orlando lacked location advantages. As previously noted, the Reedy Creek charter worked like a prenuptial agreement: with its clever perpetuity clause, it froze in time the unequal bargaining relationship that existed in 1967, making it difficult in the future for the company and the community to bargain as equals over the terms and conditions of their relationship. It is this institutional constraint more than continuing economic dependence that constrains local officials in dealing with Disney.

Still, the Reedy Creek charter did not mandate Chapin's support for Disney's interchange financing plan or her inaction on extending the interlocal agreement that had them making payments in lieu of transportation impact fees. Chapin's motives were in part personal. Throughout the narrative, we have seen how individuals—their beliefs, associations, and personalities—influenced the Disney–Orange County relationship. In the hands of Clarence Stone, the leading practitioner of regime analysis, this approach fails to demonstrate how individuals rather than abstract regimes influence local policymaking. Chapin was a friend of Dianna Morgan and, to a lesser extent, of Dick Nunis, and she had a long-standing favorable association with the Disney Co. Further, she (and Disney) benefited from her institutional position as the county's first elected chairman. As county comptroller Martha Haynie, not a Chapin ally, said of the county's switch to an elected county chairman, "It enabled [Disney] to make their case and bring all their persuasive power to bear on one person."[50] That is the simple explanation: Chapin's personal relationships and her institutional position enabled Disney to get its way.

Yet regime analysis helps to provide a complex, layered explanation of local decision making. It looks for the network of relationships, the ties of loyalty and cooperation, that explain the pattern of local policymaking over time. This perspective helps us to understand why it is difficult for policymakers to decide against Disney. As explained below, Disney benefited from its own system of favors and inducements, its alliance with the local pro-growth regime, and its relative freedom from opposing voices.

For much of its history, Disney remained an autonomous political force, dispensing favors and inducements like an old-time political machine. These selective incentives include catering events, cosponsoring summit meetings where politicians can star, offering free theme-park and golf passes, employing relatives, and, not least, providing lavish entertainment. As County Attorney Tom Wilkes said, "We ask them for more favors than they request from us," citing requests for Disney to support summit meetings as one example.[51] When Euro Disneyland opened in 1992, the company flew a planeload of local political and economic elites to Paris for the occasion. These private resources give Disney direct links to officeholders, creating their own gravitational pull. Moreover, as a regional entity Disney is able to fill the void created by the competing jurisdictional interests in central Florida.[52]

In addition to its selective incentives, Disney benefits from informal constraints against "taking on the Mouse." Beyond the norm "of not making waves," those who want to get ahead fear opposing Disney, at least publicly. This fear was evident in the experience of Bob Day, the Osceola County property appraiser who was wary of challenging Disney's tax classification for too long. In fairness, there is little evidence of Disney acting vindictively toward their occasional foes, save for withdrawing positive incentives for cooperation. But the fear is nonetheless there, the flip side of Disney's mystique. Working like a cultural filter to deter criticism, politicians and civic leaders are uncomfortable in opposing the company that "put Orlando on the map" and that continues to give it worldwide name recognition. Even though Disney's regular pullout feature in the *New York Times* advertises a place called "Disney USA," it still draws attention to Orlando.

When the *Orlando Sentinel* criticized Disney for its aloofness in 1985, prompting the company to remove their news racks from the park temporarily, the paper's editors were offering sound political advice. Historically, the company had been aloof bordering on arrogant in their relationship with Orlando. There were reasons for this, as Todd Mansfield charitably explained: "It was because of the self-sufficiency required to build Disney World. If they needed water, they had to drill their own wells. It was the only way to get things done. And that led to an inward focus, to people distancing themselves from the community."[53] With the passage of the state's Growth Management Act in 1985, however, Disney entered a more interdependent relationship with the governmental community. Now Disney needed friends at court; their aloofness was too risky. The *Sentinel*'s advice was sound.

From when they first came to Orlando, Disney officials had lamented the area's fragmented governmental system. In its place, they relied upon the old system of movers and shakers led by Dial and Andersen. As Gen. Potter, the first head of the Reedy Creek government, said in a remembrance of Dial and Andersen, "they were the two leaders in Orlando who could get things done for you."[54] By the 1980s, that old regime had crumbled. It was replaced by a diffuse, government-centered regime that could better address the planning and infrastructure needs of a growing area. The replacement was only partial, however, because in Orlando's branch-plant economy, in which the newspaper, major banks, and largest employer (Disney) were all externally owned and controlled, a few local hands could not pull all the strings together.

The new regime was no longer all-male. Linda Chapin, who served a brief stint in banking following her volunteer work in the Junior League and League of Women Voters, arrived in office just in time for Disney. She was elected county commissioner in 1986, following passage of the Growth Management Act, and she became the first elected county chairman in 1990, just as the concurrency provision of the 1985 growth act took effect. With Chapin as chair, and with Disney now needing to cooperate with local government, Disney became a partner in the local pro-growth machine, giving them access to subsidies and protection from local government.

These relationships proved helpful in keeping Disney's benefits relatively hidden. When Orange County appointed a Tax Equalization Task Force in 1996, no one wanted to raise the issue of Disney's exemption from special law enforcement and utility taxes, said Comptroller Haynie.[55] Nor, strangely, did this $17 million annual revenue loss ever come up during the rancorous debate over raising the county's sales tax to meet road and school needs. The specific techniques used for economic development have also veiled Disney's perks. For example, the use of tax-increment financing for the Osceola Parkway/ I-4 interchange helped to conceal the $53-million subsidy to Disney. Not revealing the project's location in Osceola County likewise deterred controversy. More subtly, allowing public facility deficits to grow rather than raising taxes has helped keep development politics quiescent. Residents might have been more sensitive to development subsidies and impact-fee exemptions benefiting Disney if their taxes had increased to fund these deficits.

The indulgence of the local news media is crucial here. Most development deals are too complicated for television news to dissect, making the print medium all-important. On key deals, the *Orlando Sentinel* has bought into the rhetoric of "public-private partnerships" and other innovative-sounding descriptions, failing to expose the underlying distribution of benefits. While critical stories occasionally appear, the *Sentinel* has been overwhelmingly protective of Disney. In promoting the Orange County sales-tax increase, for example, the *Sentinel* gave ample coverage to the area's resource-needs imbalance, but without mentioning Disney's tax and fee exemptions, and without exposing the cost to the community of importing low-wage workers to support theme-park expansion. They have been especially protective when outside media descend on Orlando in response to a Disney snafu, such as the 1990 bond fiasco, making it difficult for local officials to use against Disney their most potent resource: adverse publicity.

A contributing factor is the scarcity of independent experts to evaluate Disney's public planning, affordable housing, and infrastructure deals. The company is, by far, the largest employer of planning and economic consultants in the region and probably the state, and they wisely spread their work around, so that few large consultant firms in the area have not worked for them. Importantly, the area lacks an urban planning school that might provide an institutional base for independent experts who could evaluate Disney's deals. Public planning is the alternative to accepting corporate planning initiatives;[56]

but whether that challenge occurs depends on who controls the public planning apparatus.

The nonprofit sector is likewise dependent on Disney, unwilling or incapable of drawing attention to how Disney's workforce burdens the social infrastructure of the community. Besides the informal constraints that deter community actors from "speaking ill of the Mouse," nonprofit leaders are constrained by the fear of losing Disney's patronage. It matters little that the company's charitable giving is small relative to their size, to their corresponding contributions in California, and to the forgone revenue from their tax and fee exemptions. They use their philanthropy adroitly to create ties of loyalty and reciprocal obligation with the nonprofit sector. For example, Disney requires applicants for their community service awards to get the vote of their boards before submitting their applications, and applicants must be present at the gala Community Service Awards banquet to win, thus ensuring a large, appreciative audience for their banquet. Although these measures cause grumbling among association executives and board members, they help to ensure that criticisms of Disney will fall on inhospitable ground among such groups.

So taking a stand against Disney is difficult, requiring a large expenditure of political capital on the part of local officeholders. In this respect, we can see that Chapin's decisions supporting Disney were multiply determined, not just the product of personal relationships. Harry Stewart had shown that it was possible to challenge the legality of their charter and, thus, bring Disney to the bargaining table. For Chapin, however, that would have required not only bucking the ties of cooperation between Disney and the county, but also escaping from the entertainment titan's own formal and informal constraints. Given that politicians can only fight so many battles at once, it should not be surprising that Chapin chose a strategy of accommodation rather than confrontation with Disney.

Thus the path dependence that limits greater Orlando's choices about its economic development future are institutional, political, and cultural rather than economic. Institutionally, Disney is protected on certain issues by their government charter. That is the danger of privatization and deregulation; once they prove effective in generating growth, they become constraints on managing growth. But the Reedy Creek charter is not sacrosanct; as Lou Treadway and

Harry Stewart demonstrated, it is subject to legal and political challenge. Politically, Disney's privileges are protected by their own system of incentives and inducements, which exercise an independent
gravitational pull on local leaders, and by Disney's alliance with Orange County's government-centered, pro-growth regime. Culturally,
they are protected by a cultural filter that deters those who want to
get ahead from "speaking ill of the Mouse." Together, these are the
sources of greater Orlando's dependence on Disney and tourism and
low wages. It is not economic factors but these institutional, political,
and cultural factors that keep the Orlando area on its present course.

How might recuperation occur in the Disney-local relationship?
Hirschman addresses the issue of recuperation in political-economic
relationships in his *Exit, Voice, and Loyalty.* "The chances for voice
to function effectively as a recuperative mechanism are appreciably
strengthened if voice is backed up by the threat of exit," he writes.[57]
In the Disney-Orlando relationship, neither entity can leave the other.
Of the two, Disney is the more trapped, however. The company can
push development to the Osceola portion of their property, and they
can switch investment to their theme parks elsewhere around the
globe; but these options are limited because much of the Osceola portion of the property is wetland, and because Disney World is the company's largest profit center, a proverbial cash cow. The mystery is why
Orange County officials do not use the power advantage that arises
from Disney's immobility.

To appreciate how things could be different, we need a theory of
regime transition, something missing in the urban politics literature.
Such a theory would help to envision how Orlando's governing regime
might alter its relationship with Disney. Stone provides relevant insights in his comments on the importance of equity and effectiveness
to a local governing regime and the related role of social learning.[58]
Regime effectiveness requires that a leadership group pay heed to investor prerogatives to ensure a strong economy, he writes. This concern need not come at the expense of equity considerations, however.
In a "tragedy of the commons" in which development occurs that
harms a community in the long run, it might be possible to maximize
both equity and effectiveness, says Stone. Like a town commons
spoiled by overgrazing, such tragedies may be unforeseen and un-

intended, the result of collective action gone awry. Arguably, greater Orlando faces this situation in its relationship with Disney; the four problems identified above are the downstream consequences of the state's economic-development deal with Disney in 1967.

The question is whether social learning will occur in response to this tragedy of the commons. That is, will the local community apprehend the problems arising from the Disney-Orlando marriage and recognize the need for recuperative action? According to economist Douglass North, social learning is far from certain. Path dependence in economic development often results from the subjective perceptions of important actors in the community, he maintains. These subjective perceptions are part of the heritage that we call culture and provide continuity with the past; thus solutions to growth problems in the past carry over into the present. Further, these perceptions derive from socially transmitted information; they can be altered by information, but there are "transaction costs" involved in acquiring that information.[59] So long as denial occurs, or what Hirschman calls "cognitive dissonance," a psychological term referring to a gap between expectations and reality, social learning is forestalled.[60] For social learning to occur there needs to be a perception, as North and Hirschman concur, that exit is possible.

To revert again to the marriage metaphor, the Disney-Orlando marriage is like the high-school quarterback marrying the homecoming queen—a dream come true. As former Orlando mayor Carl Langford said of the marriage, "Show me a mayor in the United States of America who wouldn't just love to have Walt Disney sitting on his doorstep as a neighbor."[61] Then, thirty years into the marriage, the dream shatters. The homecoming queen wakes up to discover that she is not living with the person she thought she married. The erstwhile high school hero has become demanding and arrogant. He plays his wife against his mistress (Osceola County). And he refuses to contribute his economic fair share to the marriage, offering as justification a prenuptial agreement that, she now realizes, was acquired through misrepresentation. Whether the homecoming queen practices denial or takes recuperative action depends on whether she can envision a realistic alternative.

In the Disney-Orlando case, Mel Martinez, who succeeded Chapin as Orange County chairman, at least recognized the problems arising from this economic-development marriage. Elected in 1998 to a four-year term with solid backing from the local pro-growth regime, Martinez understood the wages problem, Disney's impact on the social service network, and the area's over-reliance on tourism. Moreover, he resented that the larger Disney Co. treats Orlando as a branch plant. "Disneyland (in California) is puny," he said. "Yet they have their corporate headquarters out there."[62] He knows that Disney World is the most profitable part of the company, a reliable generator of profits to finance their acquisitions and motion-picture ventures. In his metaphor, the Disney Co. has "a giant pipeline that pumps profits from Orlando to their California headquarters."

Though Martinez has departed for the Bush Cabinet, his comments suggest that partisanship and ideology matter less than personal background in affecting the chairman's outlook upon Disney. A former personal-injury attorney, he understands that corporations do not always do right. He said of Disney's powers: "Their charter is okay if the corporation performs, but there is no guarantee that a private corporation will behave as a good citizen."[63] Martinez was replaced by Richard Crotty, a gubernatorial appointee, who must run for the chairman's seat in 2002. Whether he or his successor challenges Disney will depend, in part, on whether there is an electoral incentive to do so.

A contributing factor might be the sentiment regarding growth and taxes in the county. In *Privatopia*, Evan McKenzie writes that two issues—taxes and growth—drive suburban politics.[64] The same is true in largely suburban Orange County, where voters have rejected five successive sales-tax increases since 1982. In 1997, the tax initiative was opposed by both the Sierra Club, which advocated smarter growth, and the county Republican party, which is instinctively anti-tax. The prevailing sentiment in the county is more anti-tax than anti-growth. In actuality, the two are much the same, since voters seem aware that growth no longer pays for itself.

Given this sentiment, one can imagine a recuperative strategy that appeals to both conservatives and progressives, a strategy that maximizes both equity and effectiveness, that shares the burdens of growth while promoting a vibrant economy. While a regime must heed investor prerogatives to guarantee a strong economy, Disney's prerogatives are not the only ones in the area. Thus, a political entrepreneur might promote the area's fledgling high-tech sector as the new local champion, eschewing subsidies and protection for Disney. Similarly, a political entrepreneur might raise the powerful equity issue, asking whether Disney's exemptions and immunities are fair. Is it fair for them to create traffic and law enforcement problems yet not pay impact fees as other developers do? Is it fair to create affordable housing needs yet escape from DRI review? Did they play fair in acquiring their charter?

In pursuit of this strategy, local leaders might promote the following policy agenda. First, they might adopt a human-capital approach to development in place of the current practice of subsidizing development costs and allowing the market mechanism to distribute benefits. This alternative policy might include expanded impact fees for everything from parks to education to day care, as well as more employer-assisted affordable housing. Such a policy would ensure that current residents receive some of the benefits of growth.

Second, they might urge the adoption of a living-wage policy as other cities have done, including Los Angeles, Chicago, St. Paul, Baltimore, and San Jose, among others.[65] Typically, these policies entail setting a wage standard higher than the federal minimum for companies doing business with a city or county. Applying this concept to a tourist economy, county government might additionally refuse to provide infrastructure subsidies or regulatory advantages to businesses that pay less than a designated living wage—say, the $10 an hour that Chamber of Commerce President Jacob Stuart thinks is the effective living wage in Orlando. Such policies are motivated at least in part by concern for the fiscal impact of low-wage workers in the community.

Third, they might end the imbalance of incentives favoring tourism ($103 million combined for Universal's and Disney's interchanges versus $23 million for Cirent) and expand the permissible uses of the tourist tax. After all, why incentivize low-wage work? Arguably, those are the ways of the past in central Florida.

And fourth, they might stop subsidizing private-sector competition with downtown Orlando. If market forces favor these privatized urban zones, government need not assist the process. Protecting downtown requires more than streetscape projects and marketing campaigns.

To help create a supportive constituency for this agenda, political entrepreneurs might also promote a larger public conversation about what values to incorporate into urban development and what institutions best produce this result. The importance of these topics—values and institutions—follows from the separate works of John Donahue and Nancy Burns. Donahue, a Harvard economist, writes about how to evaluate the performance of privatization arrangements. The ultimate measure, he says, is whether such arrangements allow for "accountability," understood as "fidelity to the public's values."[66] His remarks parallel those of Nancy Burns in her review of the U.S. experience with special-district governments. Most of these, she writes, are developer—or manufacturer—dominated; hence special-district government "becomes government by this set of private values." Their benefit is that they "can get things done in a fragmented American polity," while their difficulties are that "they do this while no one watches except interested developers, and they are gradually becoming the realm where much of the substance of local politics happens."[67] As a special district, the experience of the Reedy Creek government is therefore pertinent to other areas.

The comments of Burns and Donahue relate to the twin mistakes of the Florida legislature. In their haste to accommodate Disney in 1967, legislators failed to recognize that private values—Disney's—would be embedded in a government institution and that a system of public accountability was therefore needed. A wise political entrepreneur might therefore seek to stimulate public conversation over what values to incorporate into urban development, public or private ones, and what institutions do this best. Arguably that debate is long overdue in the Orlando area and elsewhere in the country. For the growth question is only in part an empirical question about whether the costs of growth exceed its benefits. More provocatively, it is a question about whose values should prevail—those of current residents or future residents, developers or taxpayers, the rich and powerful or the middle and lower classes.

As Daniel Yankelovich writes, "values talk" of this sort is more accessible to the public than factual debate, since the latter can easily be dominated by "experts," including hired ones (Disney's).[68] This book has sought to lower the transaction costs of social learning by providing information about the Disney charter, how it was acquired, the immunities granted to the Disney Co., the subsidies they receive, and the consequences in terms of low wages, over-reliance on tourism, and competition with downtown Orlando. The necessary second step is to stimulate a dialogue, or what communitarian thinker Amitai Etzioni calls a "megalogue," referring to a large-scale, extended public dialogue, regarding the above issues.[69] Such dialogue is the most effective source of therapy in political-economic relationships. It has the potential to transform this one-sided economic-development marriage.

Appendix 1

1954   Disneyland opens in Anaheim, California.

1955   U.S. Missile Test Center opens at Cape Canaveral, east of Orlando.
                 Florida's Turnpike is bent to intersect with Orlando.

1956   Glenn Martin Co. opens a missile plant in Orlando.

1956   Orlando–Winter Park Expressway approved as part of interstate highway program.

1963   Walt Disney makes a tentative commitment to the Orlando area.

1964   New York World's Fair tests Disney's East Coast market.

1964   Disney Co. begins purchasing land options near Orlando.

1965   Walt Disney announces plans for theme park near Orlando.

1965   Florida Technological University (renamed the University of Central Florida) authorized by the state.

1966   Walt Disney dies of complications from lung cancer.

1967   Reedy Creek Improvement Disney charter approved by Florida legislature.
                 Orlando named one of the nation's ten fastest-growing areas.

1971   Walt Disney World opens.
                 Roy Disney dies.
                 International Drive construction started.

1973   SeaWorld opens in Orlando.

1974   Orlando takes control of McCoy Air Force Base.
Church St. Station opens in downtown Orlando.

1975   Revised Epcot plan presented to the public.

1977   Florida Attorney General rules that Disney is exempt from
DRI requirement.
Orange County adopts a tourist tax.

1982   Epcot opens.

1983   Orange County Convention Center opens.
Tokyo Disneyland opens.

1984   Michael Eisner becomes Walt Disney Co. chairman.

1985   Florida Growth Management Act adopted.
Orange County adopts a transportation impact fee.

1986   Disney opposition kills Matra light-rail plan.

1988   Disney announces plans for Swan and Dolphin hotels and a
$375-million convention complex.
Church St. Exchange opens in downtown Orlando.

1989   Disney says no to Mag-lev stop at Epcot.
Disney opens Disney-MGM Studios (their third Orlando
theme park) and Pleasure Island.
Orange County–Reedy Creek Interlocal Agreement signed.
Osceola County Property Appraiser Bob Day challenges
Disney's agricultural land classification.

1990   Reedy Creek–Orange County conflict over private activity
bonds.
Universal Studios theme park opens.
Disney agrees to stop automatically sending Silver Passes
to local and state elected officials.
Osceola County voters approve a sales-tax increase.

1991   Disney announces plans to build Celebration residential
community.

1992   Euro Disneyland opens outside Paris.

1996   Orange County approves funding for I-4/Osceola Parkway
interchange.
Lot sales begin at Celebration.

1997   Orange County voters oppose a sales-tax increase.
Disney opens Downtown Disney and "House of Blues."

1998   Disney opens Animal Kingdom, their fourth Orlando theme
           park.
           Service Trades Council wins $6.25/hour starting wage at
           Disney.
           Universal opens Islands of Adventure, their second theme
           park, and City Walk nighttime entertainment complex.

1999   Osceola County School District and Celebration officials
           announce plans to build a conventional school at
           Celebration.

Appendix 2

Bass, Sid — Ft. Worth oilman and major Disney stock-holder.

Batchelor, Dick — Lobbyist for I-Drive hotel owners involved in getting a Mag-lev stop on I-Drive.

Bavar, Emily — *Orlando Sentinel* editor-reporter who broke the story that Walt Disney was the mystery land buyer.

Beardall, Billy — Orlando mayor and a member of the city's movers and shakers in the 1950s and '60s.

Beck, Thomas — Planning chief for the Florida Department of Community Affairs; involved in reviewing the Reedy Creek comprehensive plan.

Behr, Sam — Orlando shoe-store owner who advised Martin Segal on acquiring the William Goldstein property for what became WDW.

Bergendoff, Rueben — Senior partner of the Kansas City engineering firm Howard, Needles, Tammen, and Bergendoff; defended the through-Orlando routing of I-4 at a raucous public meeting in 1957.

Blazack, Kevin — Driver of pickup truck in which Robb Sipkema, III, was killed just off Disney property.

Boice, Nelson — President of Florida Ranch Lands whose firm acquired the "outs" for what became WDW; later sued the Disney Co. over real-estate commissions.

Bosserman, Chuck — Florida Ranch Lands salesperson who helped acquire "outs" for what became WDW.

Boyd, Alan — Aide to Governor LeRoy Collins, he drafted bill approving the inland route for Florida's Turnpike; later became the first Secretary of Transportation under President Johnson.

Brinkley, David — NBC-TV anchorperson who, soon after the park's opening, lauded WDW as an exercise in urban planning.

Bronson, Irlo — Florida state senator and patriarch of an Osceola County ranch-owning family who sold a key property for what became WDW.

Brown, Phil	Orange County administrator during the conflict with Reedy Creek over private activity bond allocations.
Browning, Norma Lee	*Chicago Tribune* columnist who interviewed Walt Disney in 1966 regarding his "city of tomorrow" concept.
Brownlee, Tom	Executive director of the Orlando Chamber of Commerce, hired in 1964 to revitalize the organization.
Buckland, Susan	Disney security host who allegedly engaged in a high-speed chase on Disney property, resulting in the death of 19-year-old Robert "Robb" Sipkema, III.
Burnham, Daniel	Architect and urban planner who supervised design and construction of the "White City" at the 1893 Chicago World's Fair.
Burns, Haydon	Florida governor at the time of Disney land purchase.
Bush, Randolph	Florida Highway Patrol trooper who testified in the Sipkema lawsuit regarding working relationships with Disney Security.
Carpenter, Eddie	Chief financial officer for Disney World who opposed making concessions on Reedy Creek comprehensive plan.
Carr, Bob	Mayor of Orlando in the early 1960s who negotiated agreement with the air force for joint civilian-military use of McCoy Air Force Base.
Carter, Vera	Orange County commissioner in the 1980s who pressed Disney to address their off-site impacts.
Caswell, Susan	Housing specialist for East Central Florida Regional Planning Council; reviewed housing element of Reedy Creek comprehensive plan.
Chapin, Linda	Orange County commissioner 1986–90 who became the county's first elected chairman, serving two terms, 1990–98.
Chiles, Lawton	As a young state senator, he opposed Governor Haydon Burns's road bond program that

was deemed essential for Disney; later elected U.S. senator as well as governor.

Collins, LeRoy — Elected Florida governor in 1954, initially opposed by Martin Andersen.

Cox, Bob — Lawyer with Messer & Vickers in Tallahassee who advised Sam Tabuchi on the Mag-lev train project.

Crosson, Joe — President of Orlando's First Federal Savings & Loan and a member of the city's movers and shakers in the 1950s and '60s.

Crotty, Richard — State representative from Orlando who supported the Mag-lev special legislation; appointed in 2001 to replace Mel Martinez as Orange County chairman.

Davin, Jack — Real-estate broker involved in selling the Demetree property for what became WDW.

Davis, J. Rolfe — Mayor of Orlando in 1954 who appointed a planning board that laid the groundwork for the Orlando–Winter Park Expressway, eventually part of I-4.

Davis, Ron — Investigator working with attorney Eric Faddis in wrongful death lawsuit against Disney Co.

Day, Bob — Osceola County property appraiser who challenged Disney's agricultural land classification.

DeGrove, John — Secretary of the Department of Community Affairs when Florida's 1985 growth management act passed.

Demetree, Bill — Co-owner of a key land parcel that became part of WDW land purchase.

Demetree, Jack — Co-owner of a key land parcel that became part of WDW land purchase.

Deratany, Tim — Brevard County state senator who wanted special districts to get county approval before applying for private activity bonds.

DeWolf, Tom — Law partner of Paul Helliwell who was involved in the original Disney land purchase, later president of the Reedy Creek Improvement District board of supervisors.

Dial, William (Billy) — Orlando's leading power broker in the 1950s and early '60s, co-leader with newspaper publisher Martin Andersen of the movers and shakers.

Dickinson, Fred Jr. — State comptroller in 1965 who met with Disney officials regarding tax concessions.

Disney, Elias — Walt's and Roy's father, he worked as a carpenter on the 1893 Chicago World's Fair.

Disney, Roy — Disney Co. financial genius, brother of Walt.

Disney, Walt — Co-founder with brother Roy of Walt Disney Productions.

Dittmar, Harris — Attorney from Jacksonville who represented Nelson Boice in lawsuit against Disney Co. over WDW land purchase.

Dobryin, Anatoliy — Soviet ambassador to the United States who wanted to come to WDW for briefing on Epcot.

Donegan, Bill — Orange County commissioner from 1988 to 1996, defeating Lou Treadway; like Treadway, he was often a Disney foe.

Donovan, William — Head of the Office of Strategic Services (WW II forerunner of the CIA), he advised the Disney Co. on WDW land purchase.

Doran, Perry — Ex-FBI agent; supervisor of Disney's security operations.

Dorman, Tom — Orange County commissioner in 1980s who was friendly to Disney interests.

Dowling, Aaron — Executive of the East Central Florida Regional Planning Council.

Duany, Andres — Miami architect associated with New Urbanism whose design for Seaside influenced the plan for Celebration.

Ducker, John — Florida senator when the Disney legislation was approved in 1967.

Duffy, Mike — Head of Service Employees International Union, Local 362, representing Disney employees.

Duncan, Buell — Vice president of First National Bank in 1964; he chaired the Chamber of Commerce's Adver-

tising Committee and was later president of
Sun Bank, which succeeded First National.

Dunnick, Chuck

Osceola County commissioner who questioned the cost-sharing plan for road improvements on U.S. 192 in front of Celebration.

Eagan, Joe

Attorney who served on Orange County Housing Finance Authority board during the conflict with Reedy Creek over private activity bonds.

Eberly, Alan

Universal Studios vice president for properties who played key role in the expansion of the Universal theme park.

Edwards, L. K.

Florida senator in 1967 who compared the Disney Co.'s model-city plans with a company town.

Edwards, Ted

Orange County commissioner in the late 1990s.

Eisner, Michael

Became chairman of the Disney Co. in 1984; he expanded Florida Disney complex with more hotels, Disney Downtown, Animal Kingdom, etc.

Elrod, Robert

Florida senator who co-sponsored the Disney legislative package in 1967.

Faddis, Eric

Attorney representing the family of Robb Sipkema in wrongful death suit against the Disney Co.

Feiss, Carl

City planner with national reputation; he prepared a regional plan for the East Central Florida Regional Planning Council in the early 1960s.

Fisher, Lisa

Director of Orange County's Housing Finance Authority; involved in conflict with Reedy Creek government over private activity bonds.

Fishkind, Henry

Orlando-area economic consultant.

Flemming, Robert

Florida Highway Patrol district commander who testified as part of the wrongful death lawsuit on the practices of Disney Security hosts.

Foster, Robert

Disney Co. general counsel and member of the Project Winter site-selection team; played a key role in the wdw land purchase.

Fostier, Mark

Assistant Orange County comptroller; he participated in crafting the financing plan for the Osceola Parkway/I-4 interchange project.

Fowler, Joe

Chief engineer for Walt Disney Productions; he supervised the construction of both Disneyland and Disney World.

Frederick, Bill

Orlando mayor, 1980–92.

Furth, Helmut

New York attorney who helped draft the government charter that the Disney Co. submitted to the Florida legislature in 1967.

Gay, Clarence

President of Citizens Bank in Orlando and a member of the city's movers and shakers in the 1950s and '60s.

Gee, Col. Herb

Senior partner of Gee & Jensen Engineering in Palm Beach; he advised Disney on water-control facilities and the formation of a drainage district.

Gluckman, Casey

Attorney-lobbyist for the Sierra Club; she helped draft Florida's 1985 Growth Management Act.

Goaziou, Bill

Osceola County administrator; he negotiated the financial plan for the Osceola Parkway project.

Goldstein, William

Bay Lake landowner who initially refused to sell his strategic property for the wdw site.

Gordy, Bruce

Orlando City commissioner who opposed the city's infrastructure subsidy for expanding Universal Studios.

Graham, Bob

Florida governor and later U.S. senator; as governor he was responsible for creating a High-Speed Rail Commission.

Graves, Michael

Architect who designed the post office at Celebration.

Graw, LaMonte

Head of the Citizens Expressway Association, which formed to oppose the through-Orlando routing of I-4.

Gray, Charles	Orlando attorney who chaired the Turnpike Authority under Governor Burns and convinced engineering consultants to approve an interchange linking I-4 and Florida's Turnpike.
Greene, Ray	Mayor of Winter Park in 1956; he fought successfully against the original, easterly routing of I-4 through that city.
Greer, Don	Headed Orange County's first planning department when Disney arrived, later worked for the Reedy Creek Improvement District.
Griffin, J. J.	Former state representative from Osceola County who lobbied for the Disney Co. to win passage of their 1967 legislation.
Grovdahl, Dave	Transportation planner for Metroplan Orlando.
Guernsey, Joe	Board member of Orlando Junior College and member of Orlando's movers and shakers; he advocated building a private rather than a public university to train Martin Marietta engineers.
Guevera, Robert	Osceola County commissioner critical of the Osceola Parkway financing plan.
Guillet, Cliff	Executive director of the East Central Florida Regional Planning Council who worried about having to disapprove Epcot.
Haines, Webber	City attorney in Winter Park during the conflict over routing I-4 through that city.
Hames, Jane	Orlando public relations consultant who advised Disney officials on dealing with county government.
Hamilton, Finley	Owner of the Hilton franchise in Orlando when Disney arrived; he built the first hotel between Orlando and wdw with his partner Jack Zimmer and later started International Drive.
Hamrick, Carroll	Co-owner of a key land parcel that became part of the wdw land purchase.

Hamrick, Wilson — Co-owner of a key land parcel that became part of the wdw land purchase.

Hancock, Cyndy — First president of the psta (Parent Student Teacher Association) at Celebration School.

Hanson, Harlan — Director of tri-county planning commission when Disney came to Orlando.

Harris, Jim — Former Orange County administrator who became vice president of Busch Properties, owners of Sea World.

Hart, Donna — Osceola County school board member during planning and construction of the Celebration project.

Hastings, Tom — Orange County director of engineering; he helped Harry Stewart assess what Disney owed in lieu of transportation impact fees in 1989.

Hawkins, Roy — Miami real estate broker who advised the Disney site-selection team and assisted in wdw land purchase.

Haynie, Martha — Orange County comptroller in the 1990s.

Helliwell, Paul — Miami lawyer who helped orchestrate the wdw land purchase and advised the Disney Co. on their government charter.

Hoenstine, Clarence — Orange County commissioner in the 1990s.

Holland, Spessard — U.S. senator from Florida and occasional editorial target of Martin Andersen's *Orlando Sentinel*.

Hood, Glenda — Mayor of Orlando from 1992.

Hoops, Terry — Florida Highway Patrol trooper who testified in the Sipkema lawsuit regarding working relationships with Disney security.

Ioppolo, Frank — Disney corporate counsel and specialist in affordable housing.

Irvine, Dick — Long-time Disney "imagineer" who helped design both Disneyland and Disney World.

Jacobs, Irwin — Corporate raider who threatened a takeover of the Disney Co. in 1984.

Jarhaus, Gary

Consultant to Major Realty, which sought to develop Major Center, strategically located between Orlando and WDW.

Jenkins, Bill

Co-owner with Bill and Jack Demetree of a key land parcel that became part of the WDW land purchase.

Johns, Charley

President of the Florida Senate who became acting governor in 1952 after Governor Dan MacCarty suffered an incapacitating heart attack; he was defeated by LeRoy Collins in the 1954 governor's race.

Johnson, Lyndon

U.S. president who knew Martin Andersen casually through their common mentor, Charles Marsh; Johnson rewarded Andersen for his support by sending the Naval Training Center to Orlando.

Johnson, Mary

Orange County commissioner in the 1990s.

Johnson, Philip

Architect who designed Celebration's town hall.

Johnston, David

Urban planner for Orange County when Disney arrived; he was later elected mayor of Winter Park.

Jones, Wilbur

Chairman of the State Road Board when the through-Orlando routing of I-4 was approved.

Jovanovich, William

President of Harcourt-Brace and owner of SeaWorld in 1989 when the Mag-lev train was proposed.

Kelley, Darrell

Head of the Economic Development Commission of Mid-Florida in the late 1990s.

Kelley, Richard

U.S. representative from Orlando; he defended the revised Epcot concept.

Killoren, Donald

Disney Development Co. executive involved in planning Celebration.

Kincaid, Kenneth

Assistant operations chief at Reedy Creek Improvement District; he testified in the Sipkema case regarding Disney's handling of "911" calls.

Kirk, Claude — Florida governor in 1967 when the Disney legislative package was approved.

Kissinger, Henry — U.S. Secretary of State who received special Epcot preview in 1975.

Kloehn, Mike — Osceola County planning director who was involved in approving the Celebration project.

Kohler, Tom — Director of Orlando's Downtown Development Board.

Lackey, Danny — Osceola County property appraiser before Bob Day.

Lalchandani, Ajit — Orange County public works director involved in the Osceola Parkway/I-4 interchange project; he later became county administrator.

LaLiberte, Rick — Disney attorney involved in negotiations with Osceola County Property Appraiser Bob Day regarding Disney's agricultural land classification.

Land, Henry — Florida state representative who helped win approval for bending Florida's Turnpike to Orlando.

Langford, Carl — Mayor of Orlando when Disney came to town, negotiated a twenty-year lease of McCoy Air Force Base.

Lanier, Wade — Osceola County tax assessor during original Disney negotiations; agreed to tax their vacant land as agricultural so long as they grazed cattle there.

Lee, Gary — Osceola County ranch property manager who closely observed negotiations for the Osceola Parkway project.

Leu, Henry — Owner of a hardware store in Orlando and a member of the city's movers and shakers in the 1950s and '60s.

Levitt, William — Builder of Levittown on Long Island, as well as Williamsburg in Orlando.

Lewis, Tom — Vice president of Disney Development Co., responsible for transportation projects; formerly he was secretary of both the Department of

Transportation and Department of Community Affairs in Florida.

Lindquist, Jack
Disney Co. marketing vice president who defended the revised Epcot concept.

Lloyd, Saxton
Chairman of the Florida Development Commission under Governor Collins; he opposed routing Florida's Turnpike through Daytona Beach.

Lund, William
Financial analyst for Economic Research Associates who played key role in WDW land purchase; he later married Walt Disney's adopted daughter, Sharon.

Makiyama, Akio
Chairman of Mag-lev Transit, Inc., and one of Japan's largest developers.

Mansfield, Mike
U.S. Senate majority leader, present for 1975 Epcot preview.

Mansfield, Todd
Head of Disney Development Co.–Florida with overall responsibility for Celebration.

Manuel, Thomas
Florida's Turnpike Authority chairman who supported bending Florida's Turnpike to Orlando.

Marlowe, Dick
Orlando Sentinel business writer who criticized Disney for taking private activity bonds.

Marsh, Charles
Texan who mentored the young Lyndon Johnson; he purchased two newspapers in Orlando in 1931 and dispatched Martin Andersen to run them.

Martin, Doug
Osceola County auditor who recalculated the cost of the Osceola Parkway project.

Martinez, Mel
Orange County chairman, elected 1998; became Secretary of U.S. Department of Housing and Urban Development in 2001.

Maxwell, Ray
Director of finance and planning for the Reedy Creek Improvement District.

McCarty, Dan
Florida governor who suffered an incapacitating heart attack after winning election in 1952.

McClendon, Bruce	Orange County planning director in the 1990s.
McCree, Bill	Orlando Planning Board member and amateur local historian who supported the through-Orlando routing of I-4.
Melton, Mel	Disney Co. vice president and member of the Project Winter site-selection team.
Metz, Steve	Attorney at Messer & Vickers in Tallahassee; he lobbied for the Mag-lev special legislation.
Miller, Mickey	City of Orlando finance director who crafted the financing plan for Universal Studios' I-4 interchange.
Miller, Ron	Son-in-law of Walt Disney who became chairman of the Disney Co.
Morgan, Dianna	Senior vice president for government and community relations at wdw; she also was a personal friend of Orlando mayor Glenda Hood and former Orange County Chairman Linda Chapin.
Morgan, Jim	Florida Ranch Lands salesperson who helped acquire the outs for what became the wdw land purchase.
Morris, Bob	Activist resident of Celebration.
Morris, Max	Law partner of Tom DeWolf; he was involved in securing land options for the Mag-lev train project.
Morris, Pam	Activist resident of Celebration.
Morrow, Bob	Disney Co. vice president and member of the Project Winter site-selection team.
Moses, Robert	President of 1964 New York's World Fair and friend of Walt Disney, he encouraged Walt to build exhibits for the fair.
Moses, Tom	District manager of the Reedy Creek Improvement District; successor to Joe Potter, he originated their performance-based building code system.
Moye, Jim	Deputy comptroller of Orange County under Martha Haynie.

NeJame, Mark — Orlando nightclub owner and local defense attorney.

Newsom, John — Orlando city commissioner who opposed the city's participation in the federal urban renewal program in 1964.

Newton, Jeff — Orange County deputy county attorney involved in the Osceola Parkway/I-4 interchange project.

Nickerson, George — Bond counsel to Osceola County for the Osceola Parkway project.

Nunis, Richard — President of Disney World Attractions and long-time company employee.

Nusbickel, David — Florida Ranch Lands salesperson who helped acquire outs for what became the WDW land purchase.

O'Dell, Larry — Osceola County public works director who helped negotiate the Osceola Parkway deal; he later went to jail for accepting a bribe linked to the financing plan.

Ovitz, Michael — Briefly served as president of the Walt Disney Co. under Chairman Michael Eisner.

Paulucci, Jeno — Founder of the Chun King frozen food brand and developer of Heathrow, an upscale office and residential development along I-4, north of Orlando.

Peebles, Willard — Member of the State Road Board in 1967 when Disney's initial road needs were funded.

Peeper, Bill — President of the Orlando/Orange County Convention & Visitors Bureau.

Pelli, Cesar — Architect who designed the cinema at Celebration.

Perkins, Judd — Executive with Bombardier Co., which built WDW's monorail; he was involved in Disney's review of the Mag-lev project.

Perry, Belvin — Orange County Circuit Court judge who presided in the evidentiary hearing connected with the *Sipkema v. Disney* lawsuit.

Peterson, C. H. (Pete)   Project Manager for Florida's Turnpike in the 1950s.

Pflug, J. Lynn   Mayor of Winter Park in 1958; he opposed the original, easterly routing of I-4 through that city.

Phillips, Robert   Disney Security host who pursued Eric Faddis's vehicle after Faddis sought to take pictures of Disney Security van.

Pickett, Paul   Orange County commissioner in the 1970s; he opposed Disney and never visited the WDW theme park.

Pinellas, Anna   Osceola County housing grants administrator; she was responsible for affordable housing programs.

Plater-Zyberk, E.   Miami architect associated with New Urbanism whose design for Seaside influenced plans for Celebration.

Pope, Dick   Founding owner of Cypress Gardens, the largest Orlando-area attraction before WDW.

Pope, Verle   President of the Florida senate when the Disney legislative package was approved in 1967.

Potter, William (Joe)   Vice president of the 1964 New York World's Fair; he became a Disney Co. executive and, later, president of the Reedy Creek Improvement District, responsible for building WDW's public works.

Price, Harrison   President of Economic Research Associates, site consultant for WDW project.

Reader, Perry   Celebration general manager in late 1990s.

Rhodes, Bob   Attorney who lobbied for Disney and worked for Arvida when Disney owned the real-estate company.

Robertson, Jacqueline   Architect who, with Robert Stern, executed principal design for Celebration.

Robinson, James   Orange County Attorney in 1967; he negotiated with the Disney Co. regarding their government charter.

Rosen, Harris

Orlando's largest hotel owner after the Disney Co.; he worked for them in the late 1960s as administrator of hotel planning.

Rosen, Teresa

Celebration School parent who filed a lawsuit alleging that Disney reneged on a promise to homebuyers.

Ross, Jaime

Housing specialist for 1000 Friends of Florida; she was involved in affordable housing negotiations with Disney.

Rotival, Maurice

An internationally known city planner who prepared Winter Park's first city plan, in 1956, as part of effort to defeat the original, easterly routing of I-4 through that city.

Rouse, James

Urban planner and developer of "festival markets"; he described Disneyland as "the greatest piece of urban design in the United States."

Rummell, Peter

President of Disney Development Co., and later, Walt Disney Imagineering, under Michael Eisner.

Russ, David

Attorney with Department of Community Affairs; he was involved in review of Reedy Creek comprehensive plan.

Sayers, Jack

Disney Co. executive involved in site selection for what became WDW.

Segal, Martin

Orlando-area lawyer and dealmaker who advised Martin Andersen on acquiring the William Goldstein property for what became WDW.

Shands, William

Florida senator and former fraternity brother of Billy Dial; he helped Dial win legislative approval for the inland route of Florida's Turnpike.

Sheinberg, Sid

President of MCA, founder of Universal Studios in Orlando.

Shevin, Robert

Florida attorney general who ruled that Disney was exempt from the DRI requirement.

Sikes, Bob

U.S. representative from Pensacola and longtime chairman of the House Military Appropriations Subcommittee; he helped Orlando acquire the Naval Training Center in the mid-1960s.

Sipkema, Robert "Robb," III
Nineteen-year-old who was killed in an auto accident just outside Disney property.

Smart, Jim
Member of the Orange County planning staff when Disney came to town.

Smith, Phil
Disney Co. attorney who helped explain the Reedy Creek Improvement District charter to legislators in 1967.

Speer, Sim
Airline pilot and land speculator who inadvertently helped expose Bill Lund's role in the WDW land purchase.

Staly, Rick
Orange County undersheriff in 1998; he commented on his department's relationship with Disney Security in an interview with the author.

Starling, Alan
Osceola County auto dealer who opposed an increase in the county sales tax.

Steinberg, Saul
Corporate raider who prepared to make takeover bid for the Disney Co. in 1984.

Stern, Robert
Architect who, with Jacqueline Robertson, executed the principal plan for Celebration; also a member of the Disney corporate board.

Stewart, Harry
Orange County Attorney in the 1980s; he crafted the county's first impact fee ordinance and negotiated the 1989 interlocal agreement with Disney/Reedy Creek.

Stoddard, Todd
Attorney at Burke & Burke in New York who forwarded phone calls to Bill Lund in California following Lund's scouting trip to Orlando.

Straughn, J. Ed
State revenue director in 1967; he agreed to exempt 40 percent of the cost of WDW's attractions for tax purposes.

Stuart, Jacob
President of the Greater Orlando Chamber of Commerce; he runs Workforce 2020 program.

Surguine, F. B.
Orange County commissioner at time of Disney land purchase.

Swan, Jim

Osceola County commissioner who supported the Osceola Parkway project.

Swann, Richard

Attorney representing Universal Studios; he was involved in inserting "poison pill" in Mag-lev special legislation.

Tabuchi, Sam

Japanese citizen who worked in the Florida Department of Commerce before trying to put together the Mag-lev deal with support of Japenese investors.

Tatum, Donn

Disney Co. executive and member of the Project Winter site-selection team.

Thornall, Campbell

Attorney from Orlando who served on the State Road Board and, later, on the state Supreme Court.

Tiedtke, John

Winter Park investor who was a contemporary of Martin Andersen and Billy Dial.

Train, Russell

U.S. Environmental Protection Agency administrator; he attended the 1975 Epcot preview.

Treadway, Lou

Orange County commissioner who led effort to adopt impact fees and later proposed challenging Disney's charter.

Vermillion, Marshall

Central Florida president of First Union Bank.

Wadsworth, Charley

Orlando Sentinel columnist who vetted the latest rumors about the "mystery land buyer" in his "Hush Puppies" column.

Walker, Card

Top Disney executive who went to work at Disneyland right out of college as a messenger boy and eventually became part of the triumvirate that directed the company after Walt and Roy died.

Walter, Scott

Florida Highway Patrol trooper who investigated the auto crash in which Robb Sipkema, III, was killed.

Weaver, Jim

Disney security host involved in confrontation with attorney Eric Faddis.

Weidenbeck, Richard

Vice president for design and engineering at the Walt Disney Co.; he was involved in review of the Mag-lev proposal.

Notes

CHAPTER 1: SERENDIPITY

1. Memo from Donn Tatum to Walt Disney, 8 Jan. 1964, Disney Archives-Burbank.

2. Joe Fowler interviewed by Jay Horan, 12 March 1984; Joe Fowler interviewed by Bob Thomas, 20 March 1973; video interview with Joe Fowler, 13 Jan. 1988, Disney Archives-Burbank.

3. Walt Disney Productions, "Florida's Disney Decade," 12 Oct. 1981, Disney Archives-Burbank.

4. *Ibid.*

5. Sam Hodges, "Carl Langford in the Slow Lane," *Orlando Sentinel*, 30 July 1990.

6. Reedy Creek Improvement District, "Public Review Draft Comprehensive Plan," December 1990.

7. Gregg Zoroya, "Orlando Overload: How Much Is Too Much at Rapidly Expanding Theme Parks," *USA Today*, 7 May 1999.

8. "Disney Executive Outlines Legislative Proposals," press release, Walt Disney Productions, 2 Feb. 1967; Disney World Depository-Orlando Public Library.

9. Albert O. Hirschman, *Exit, Voice, and Loyalty: Responses to Decline in Firms, Organizations, and States* (Cambridge: Harvard Univ. Press, 1970).

10. Michael Storper, "Toward a Structural Theory of Industrial Location," in John Rees et al. (eds.), *Industrial Location and Regional Systems* (Brooklyn: J. F. Bergin, 1981), pp. 17–41.

11. Paul Peterson, *City Limits* (Chicago: University Chicago Press, 1981), esp. chap. 7.

12. See, for example, Clarence Stone, *Regime Politics* (Lawrence, Kansas: University of Kansas Press, 1989), esp. chap. 9; and Clarence Stone, "Summing Up: Urban Regimes, Development Policy, and Political Arrangements," in Clarence

Stone and Heywood Sanders (eds.), *The Politics of Urban Development* (Lawrence, Kansas: University of Kansas Press, 1987), pp. 269–298.

13. Nancy Burns, *The Formation of American Local Governments: Private Values and Public Institutions* (New York: Oxford Univ. Press, 1994), chap. 6.

14. John D. Donahue, *The Privatization Decision: Public Ends, Private Means* (New York: Basic Books, 1989), p. 7.

15. Dennis Judd and Susan Fainstein, "Global Forces, Local Strategies, and Urban Tourism," in Dennis Judd and Susan Fainstein (eds.), *Places to Play* (New Haven: Yale University Press, 1999), pp. 1–17.

16. Policom Corp., "Orange County, Florida: History, Comparative Economic Analysis," a study for the Economic Development Commission of Mid-Florida, 8 Aug. 1999, p. i.

17. Robert Putnam, *Making Democracy Work* (Princeton: Princeton University Press, 1993), p. 179; see also Douglass C. North, *Institutions, Institutional Change and Economic Performance* (Cambridge: Cambridge University Press, 1990).

CHAPTER 2: SEDUCTION

1. Interview of Adm. Joe Fowler, Vice President of Walt Disney Productions, by Richard Hubler, 23 July 1962, Disney Archives-Burbank.

2. Walt Disney press conference, Orlando, Florida, 15 Nov. 1965; Florida State Archives-Tallahassee.

3. Interview with Billy Dial, 6 July 1990.

4. Interview with Joe Guernsey, a contemporary of Dial's and, during this period, president of Florida Savings & Loan, 24 Oct. 1990.

5. Interview with Hartwell Conklin, former public relations director for the *Orlando Sentinel*, 2 July 1990.

6. Some names were added to this by Joe Guernsey; interview with Joe Guernsey, 24 Oct. 1990.

7. Remarks by Martin Andersen on his induction to the Central Florida Business Hall of Fame, November 1977; from the files of Junior Achievement of Central Florida, Orlando, Florida.

8. Ormund Powers, *Martin Andersen: Editor, Publisher, Galley Boy* (Chicago: Contemporary Books, 1996), p. 138.

9. Interview with Hartwell Conklin.

10. Interview with Robert Howard, former managing editor of the *Orlando Sentinel*, 30 June 1990.

11. *Ibid.*

12. Interview with Manning Pynn, former copy boy and now editorial page editor of the *Orlando Sentinel*, 26 June 1990.

13. Information from interview with Robert Howard.

14. Interview with Billy Dial.

15. *Ibid.*

16. Remarks by Martin Andersen, Junior Achievement of Central Florida.

17. "Roads the Key to Progress (editorial)," *Orlando Evening Star,* 11 Nov. 1965.

18. Jane Jacobs, *Cities and the Wealth of Nations: Principles of Economic Life* (New York: Random House, 1985), chap. 3.

19. Henry F. Swanson, *Countdown for Agriculture* (Orlando: Designers Press, 1975), pp. 4–5.

20. Ed Hayes, "Highway 50," *Orlando Sentinel-Star,* 18 Dec. 1977.

21. Charlie Jean, "US 441," *Orlando Sentinel-Star,* 18 Dec. 1977.

22. "Florida's Early Highways," appendices to Florida State Road Department, *Facts and Figures on Florida Highways,* February 1963.

23. "Two Groups Support Expressway," *Orlando Sentinel,* 23 April 1957.

24. Supplementary Report, *1955 Annual Report of the Florida Turnpike Authority,* Box 42, Florida State Archives-Tallahassee.

25. Memo from Thomas B. Manuel, chairman of the Florida Turnpike Authority, to Turnpike Authority Members, 23 Feb. 1955, Florida State Archives-Tallahassee.

26. Interview with Billy Dial.

27. *Ibid.*

28. Letter from Thomas B. Manuel, chairman of the Florida Turnpike Authority, to Governor LeRoy Collins, 3 Feb. 1955; Series 776A, Box 42, Florida State Archives-Tallahassee.

29. Interview with C. H. Peterson, project manager for Florida's Turnpike, 2 Nov. 1990.

30. E. H. Gore, *From Florida Sand to "The City Beautiful": A Historical Record of Orlando, Florida,* (Orlando, Florida: n.p., 1971), chap. 6.

31. Interview with Wilbur Jones, chairman of the Florida State Road Board from 1955 to 1958, 22 Oct. 1990.

32. Interview with Billy Dial.

33. Paul Peterson, *City Limits,* pp. 30–32.

34. Interview with Richard F. Trismen, former Winter Park City Attorney and lifelong resident, 18 Oct. 1990.

35. Interview with Webber Haines, 30 Oct. 1990.

36. Citizens Expressway Association, "Objections and Recommendations to the Proposed Routing of Interstate Highway 104 through Orlando, Florida," n.d. (c. 1957); Florida State Archives-Tallahassee.

37. *Orlando Sentinel,* 21 April and 25 April 1957.

38. Interview with W. A. McCree, Jr., 29 June 1990.

39. Frank Murphy, "Expressway Opponents Attack *Sentinel,*" *Orlando Sentinel,* 23 April 1957.

40. Interview with Billy Dial.

41. Interview with W. A. McCree, Jr.

42. Jim Halbe, "2,000 Attend Hearing on Expressway," *Orlando Sentinel,* 26 April 1957.

43. Billy Dial to Ralph Davis, executive director of the State Road Department, 23 July 1957.

44. Interview with John Tiedtke, 22 June 1990.

45. Interview with Harry Bertossa, senior partner in the firm of Howard, Needles, Tammen, and Bergendoff, 17 Oct. 1990.

46. Interview with Wilbur Jones.

47. "The Wrong Letter to the Wrong Person" (editorial), *Winter Park Herald,* 17 April 1958.

48. Peterson, *City Limits,* chap. 7.

CHAPTER 3: SECRECY

1. Deposition of Harrison Price, Florida Ranch Lands v. Walt Disney Productions and Economic Research Associates, U.S. District Court for the Middle District of Florida, Orlando Division, No. 67–162-ORL-CIVIL, commencing 1 Feb. 1968 [hereafter cited as FRL V. WDP].

2. Quoted in Bob Thomas, *Building a Company: Roy O. Disney and the Creation of an Entertainment Empire* (New York: Hyperion, 1998), p. 2.

3. Deposition of William S. Lund, FRL V. WDP.

4. Brad Kuhn, "The Beginning: Project X Conceived to Fund Walt's Moviemaking," *Orlando Business Journal,* 24 Aug. 1986, p. 1.

5. "New York World's Fair, 1964–65: A Disney Retrospective," Walt Disney Productions, 1984, Walt Disney Depository, Orlando Public Library.

6. Joe Potter interviewed by Bob Mervine, February 1980.

7. Jack Sayers memo to Walt Disney, 17 Oct. 1963; Disney Archives-Burbank.

8. Joe Potter interviewed by Bob Mervine.

9. Deposition of William S. Lund, FRL V. WDP.

10. Documents, FRL V. WDP.

11. Economics Research Associates, *Preliminary Investigation of Available Acreage for Project Winter,* prepared for Walt Disney Productions, 16 Jan. 1964.

12. "Disney Creates a Magic Kingdom in Orlando," *Florida Trend,* June 1983, p. 76.

13. Deposition of Roy Hawkins, FRL V. WDP.

14. Deposition of Paul Helliwell, FRL V. WDP.

15. Deposition of Roy Hawkins, FRL V. WDP.

16. Deposition of Jack Demetree, FRL V. WDP.

17. *Ibid.*

18. Deposition of William Demetree, FRL V. WDP.

19. Deposition of Roy Hawkins, FRL V. WDP.

20. Deposition of Nelson Boice, FRL V. WDP.

21. Interview with Nelson Boice, 26 Nov. 1991.

22. Deposition of Jack Demetree, FRL V. WDP.

23. Bruce Dudley, "Disney World Assembler Tracked 2 Tituses," *Orlando Sentinel,* 7 June 1966.

24. Bob Thomas, *Walt Disney: An American Original* (New York: Pocket Books, 1976), p. 360.

25. Interview with Tom DeWolf, 30 April 1998.

26. Robert Foster interviewed by Bob Mervine, 2 Feb. 1980; Disney Archives-Burbank.

27. Interview with Nelson Boice.

28. Thomas, *Walt Disney,* p. 360.

29. Robert Foster interviewed by Bob Mervine.

30. *Ibid.*

31. Deposition of Roy Hawkins, FRL V. WDP.

32. Interview with William Dial.

33. Interview with Martin Segal, 31 July 1991.

34. Interview with Dorothy Goldstein, 15 Aug. 1991.

35. Interview with Martin Segal.

36. Dial told me this story in an interview; Andersen told this story in an interview with Bob Mervine, February 1980; Disney Archives-Burbank.

37. "Mystery Buy Tops $5M," *Orlando Evening Star*, 28 May 1965.

38. Interview with Emily Bavar Kelly, 30 July 1991.

39. "Burns Makes Move Official," *Orlando Evening Star*, 25 Oct. 1965.

40. The story of the hurry-up announcement was told in a column "Good Evening!" in the *Evening Star* on 29 Oct. 1965; see Leonard E. Zehnder, *Florida's Disney World: Promises and Problems* (Tallahassee: Peninsular Publishing, 1975), pp. 30–31; see also Thomas, *Walt Disney*, pp. 361–62.

41. Interview with Charles Wadsworth, 15 July 1991.

42. William Dial interviewed by Bob Mervine, February 1980; Disney Archives-Burbank.

43. Martin Andersen interviewed by Bob Mervine, February 1980.

44. Zehnder, *Florida's Disney World*, p. 61.

45. "Disney Tells of $100 Million Project," *Orlando Sentinel*, 16 Nov. 1965.

46. Thomas, *Walt Disney*, pp. 363.

47. "It's D (for Disney) Day in Orlando," *Orlando Sentinel*, 15 Nov. 1965.

48. Interview with Nelson Boice.

49. Deposition of William Lund, FRL V. WDP.

50. Interview with Nelson Boice.

CHAPTER 4: MARRIAGE

1. "Walt Disney to Wave His Magic Wand Over Us," *Orlando Sentinel*, 24 Oct. 1965.

2. "Area Leaders See Solid Growth in Disney Industry," *Orlando Sentinel*, 29 Oct. 1965.

3. Elvis Lane, "Disney Tells of $100 Million Project," *Orlando Sentinel*, 16 Nov. 1965; and Don Rider, "Some Commissioners Feel County Slighted," *Orlando Sentinel*, 16 Nov. 1965.

4. Zehnder, *Florida's Disney World*, p. 44.

5. Bob Bobroff, "Osceola Officials Voice Varied View," *Orlando Sentinel*, 11 Nov. 1965.

6. Interview with Frank Stockton, former executive assistant to Governor Burns, 7 Aug. 1991.

7. Interview with C. W. Beaufort, member of the State Road Board under Governor Burns, 9 Aug. 1991.

8. Ed Hensley, "What About Disneyland?" *Orlando Sentinel*, 4 Nov. 1965.

9. "Effect of Road Loss Uncertain," *Orlando Sentinel*, 4 Nov. 1965.

10. "Disney Offered Tax Break," *Orlando Sentinel*, 27 Jan. 1967.

11. "Disney Envoy Happy—After Area Talks," *Orlando Sentinel*, 5 Nov. 1965.

12. "Disney Aid Pledged," *Orlando Sentinel,* 27 Oct. 1965.

13. Elvis Lane, "Disney Tells of $100 Million Project," *Orlando Sentinel,* 16 Nov. 1965.

14. Bob Thomas, *Walt Disney,* p. 364.

15. "Epcot film," Walt Disney Productions, 2 Feb. 1967.

16. Richard Foglesong, *Planning the Capitalist City* (Princeton: Princeton University Press, 1986), chap. 5.

17. Economic Research Associates, *Planning a New Community: Key to an Effective Approach,* prepared for Walt Disney Productions, 30 Sept. 1966, Disney Archives-Burbank.

18. Deposition of Jack Demetree.

19. Interview with John Tiedtke, 23 Oct. 1990; this story was told to Tiedtke by Irlo Bronson, now deceased, who was there.

20. Gee & Jensen Consulting Engineers, *Preliminary Report on Water Control: The Disney Properties, Orange and Osceola Counties, Florida,* December 1965; Disney Archives-Burbank.

21. Interview with Tom DeWolf.

22. Economic Research Associates, *Experimental Prototype City of Tomorrow: Outline of Presentation [to] Department of Housing and Urban Development,* prepared for Walt Disney Productions, 15 Aug. 1966; Disney Archives-Burbank.

23. *Ibid.,* p. 22.

24. *Ibid.,* p. 20.

25. Memorandum on the Establishment of Special Taxing Districts and Municipalities on the WDP Property, from Paul Helliwell to Walt Disney, 23 May 1966; Disney Archives-Burbank.

26. Interview with William Dial.

27. *Ibid.*

28. "Disney Proceeds on Schedule," *Orlando Evening Star,* 22 Dec. 1966.

29. Edward L. Prizer, "The Disney Decade," *Orlando-Land,* Oct. 1981, p. 38.

30. Norma Lee Browning, "Magic Cities for Young, Old Foreseen by Disney," *Chicago Tribune,* November 1966.

31. "City of Epcot, Orange County," *Orlando Sentinel,* 28 Oct. 1966.

32. Interview with Sarah Howden, aide to Sen. Beth Johnson, 23 Oct. 1990.

33. "Epcot film," Walt Disney Productions, 2 Feb. 1967.

34. "Disney World Amusement Center with Domed City Set for Florida," *New York Times,* 3 Feb. 1967.

35. Walt Disney Productions, "Disney Executive Outlines Legislative Proposals Relating to 'Disney World' Project," 2 Feb. 1967, Orlando Public Library-Disney Depository.

36. *Ibid.*

37. Walt Disney Productions, "Excerpts of Remarks by Governor Claude R. Kirk, Jr.," 2 Feb. 1967, Orlando Public Library-Disney Depository.

38. Interview with Harlan Hanson, then director of the Tri-County Planning Commission, 1 March 1991.

39. Interview with Sarah Howden.

40. *Ibid.*

41. Don Rider, "Disney Asks Creation of 2 New Cities," *Orlando Sentinel*, 5 Feb. 1967.

42. Don Rider, "Disney World Being Built on Political Foundation," *Orlando Sentinel*, 16 March 1967.

43. *Ibid.*

44. Interview with Orange County Attorney James Robinson by Bob Mervine, February 1980, Disney Archives-Burbank.

45. Interview with James Robinson, 17 March 1998.

46. "Disney World Confab Fails to Settle Issues," *Orlando Sentinel*, 22 April 1967.

47. "Legislation Outlined," *Orlando Sentinel*, 13 April 1967.

48. Interview with J. J. Griffin by Bob Mervine, February 1980, Walt Disney Archives-Burbank.

49. Don Rider, "General Accord Reached," *Orlando Evening Star*, 21 April 1967.

50. D. G. Lawrence, "Disney Objections Filed," *Orlando Sentinel*, 19 April 1967.

51. Don Rider, "General Accord Reached."

52. Interview with state Sen. Robert Elrod, 12 Feb. 1998.

53. Interview with state Rep. Henry Land, 19 Oct. 1990.

54. Interview with James Robinson.

55. Walt Disney Productions, "Excerpts of (Donn Tatum's) Remarks Regarding Disney World's Effect on Florida Traffic Patterns," 2 Feb. 1967, Orlando Public Library-Disney Depository.

56. Interview with Willard Peebles, 3 Aug. 1991.

57. Interview with Charlie Gray, 2 Aug. 1991.

58. *State of Florida v. Reedy Creek Improvement District*, Supreme Court of Florida, 27 Nov. 1968.

59. Interview with state Sen. John Ducker, 31 Oct. 1990.

60. Interview with James Robinson.

CHAPTER 5: GROWTH

1. David Brinkley, excerpt from NBC telecast, February 1972; Disney Archives-Burbank.

2. "Disney Site Rapidly Taking Shape," *Orlando Sentinel*, 8 Dec. 1968.

3. Charles Lindblom, *Politics and Markets* (New York: Basic Books, 1977), p. ix.

4. Interview with Don Greer, 27 April 1998.

5. Joe Potter interviewed by Jay Horan, 7 March 1984; Disney Archives-Burbank.

6. Walt Disney Productions, "The First Twenty Years . . . from Disneyland to Walt Disney World," 1976; Orlando Public Library-Disney Depository.

7. Joe Potter interviewed by Jay Horan, 7 March 1984; Disney Archives-Burbank.

8. Quoted in Edward L. Prizer, "The Disney Era in Florida," *Orlando-Land Magazine*, Oct. 1976, p. 38.

9. Joe Potter interviewed by Jay Horan, 7 March 1984; Disney Archives-Burbank.

10. *Ibid.*

11. *Ibid.*

12. Interview with Tom Moses, 30 April 1998.

13. *Ibid.*

14. *Ibid.*

15. Joe Potter interviewed by Jay Horan, 7 March 1984; Disney Archives-Burbank.

16. Interview with Harris Rosen, 20 May 1998.

17. Interview with Tom Moses.

18. Dick Irvine interviewed by Richard Hubler, 14 May 1968.

19. Peter Blake, "Mickey Mouse for Mayor?" *New York*, 7 Feb. 1972, p. 41.

20. Press release, "The First 20 Years . . . from Disneyland to Walt Disney World," Walt Disney Productions, 1976; Disney Depository-Orlando Public Library.

21. "Disney Dollars," *Forbes Magazine*, 1 May 1971.

22. Presentation by Elmer Sevor, SEIU Local 362, 31 March 1997.

23. "As Disney Celebrates 25th Birthday Unions Commemorate Strike of 1968," *Local 362 Union News*, March 1997.

24. Ormund Powers, *The Sun Bank Story, 1934–1984* (n.p.: Sun Bank, 1984), pp. 53–55.

25. Interview with Robert Howard.

26. Martin Andersen interviewed by Bob Mervine, February 1980; Disney Archives-Burbank.

27. Interview with Billy Dial.

28. Carl Langford, *Hizzoner the Mayor* (Orlando, Florida: Chateau Publishing Co., 1976), pp. 58–61.

29. Interview with James Robinson, 17 March 1998.

30. Interview with Tom Brownlee, June 1990.

31. Interview with Buell Duncan, president of Sun Bank, 27 Dec. 1990.

32. Orlando Area Chamber of Commerce, *News & Views*, 11 Nov. 1973.

33. *Orlando Sentinel*, 5 Feb. 1967.

34. Elizabeth Whitney, "Things Are Picking Up a Little Around Orlando," *The Floridian* (Sunday supplement of *The St. Petersburg Times)*, 2 Nov. 1969.

35. Interview with Harlan Hanson, 21 April 1998.

36. Carl Feiss, "Regional Design: A Report on the Region's Form and Appearance," East Central Florida Regional Planning Council, March 1965.

37. Interview with Harlan Hanson.

38. Interview with Don Greer.

39. *Ibid.*

40. Interview with David Johnston, 11 May 1998.

41. Interview with Don Greer.

42. Economic Research Associates, *Experimental Prototype City of Tomorrow*.

43. Interview with Finley Hamilton, 3 May 1998.

44. *Ibid.*

45. Interview with Jack Zimmer, 2 May 1998.

46. Interview with Jack Snyder, 11 May 1998.

47. Interview with David Winter, 13 May 1998.

48. Interview with Gary Jarhaus, 13 May 1998.

49. Interview with Harris Rosen.

50. Interview with Tom Moses.

51. Interview with Todd Mansfield, 19 April 1999.

52. Letter from Finley Hamilton to Donn Tatum, 29 Nov. 1971; given to the author by Hamilton.

53. Interview with Finley Hamilton.

54. "Disney World Wakes Sleepy Orlando," *Business Week,* 14 Nov. 1970.

55. Elizabeth Whitney, "Things Are Picking Up."

56. Quoted in "Disney Impact Greater Than Expected," *Florida Trend,* November 1972, p. 78.

57. Interview with David Johnston.

CHAPTER 6: CONFLICT

1. Dick Marlowe, "Epcot Gains Notice from D.C. to U.S.S.R.," *Orlando Sentinel,* 21 Sept. 1975.

2. Interview with Cliff Guillet, 30 June 1998.

3. Marlowe, "Epcot Gains Notice."

4. "Developments of Regional Impact, Applicability of Ch. 380 to Disney World," Annual Report of the Attorney General, (077–44) 16 May 1977.

5. Hirschman, *Exit, Voice and Loyalty.*

6. "Epcot film," Walt Disney Productions, 2 Feb. 1967.

7. Lynn Phillips, "Epcot's Future World Showcase Still in Future," *Orlando Sentinel-Star,* 5 June 1977.

8. Dick Marlowe, "Disney Asks World to Use 'Showcase': Epcot Could Be Started by 1977," *Orlando Sentinel,* 15 July 1975.

9. "Supercali." (editorial), *Sentinel Star,* 3 Oct. 1978.

10. *Ibid.*

11. Charlie Jean, "SupercalifragilisticEPCOTalidocious," *Orlando Sentinel,* 2 Oct. 1982.

12. Charlie Jean, "Bottom Line: Ease the Pain with the Gain," *Orlando Sentinel,* 26 Sept. 1983.

13. Vicki Vaughan, "Epcot Puts New Spark in Tourism," *Orlando Sentinel,* 25 Sept. 1983.

14. Vicki Vaughan, "Epcot Hits," *Orlando Sentinel,* 27 Sept. 1992.

15. Interview with Jim Harris, 7 July 1998.

16. Lynn Phillips, "Disney's Still Dreaming," *Orlando Sentinel,* 4 Oct. 1982.

17. Charlie Jean, "Bottom Line."

18. Bonnie Welch, "Orlando Is Outgrowing Its Mickey Mouse Image," Florida Trend Yearbook, 1985.

19. Interview with Bruce McClendon, 2 Aug. 1999.

20. Interview with Bill Frederick, 7 July 1998.

21. *City Limits,* chap. 7.

22. See, for example, Clarence Stone, *Regime Politics.*

23. Ron Grover, *The Disney Touch: How a Daring Management Team Revived an Entertainment Empire* (Homewood, Illinois: Business One Irwin, 1991), pp. 13–15.

24. *Ibid.,* pp. 23–24.

25. Interview with Vera Carter, 29 June 1998.

26. *Ibid.*

27. Interview with Jim Harris.

28. Quoted in Lynn Phillips, "The Disney Doubters," *Orlando Star*, 27 Sept. 1981.

29. Interview with Lou Treadway, 15 June 1998.

30. Interview with Harry Stewart, 12 June 1998.

31. Interview with Lou Treadway.

32. Interview with Harry Stewart.

33. Interview with Lou Treadway.

34. *Orlando Sentinel*, 10 July 1985.

35. Matt Walsh, "It's Not Easy Living with the Mouse," *Florida Trend*, Dec. 1986, pp. 70–75.

36. "Bring Disney into the Real World" (editorial), *St. Petersburg Times*, 13 Feb. 1988, p. 14A.

37. Gary Marx, "Treadway's Attitude Sparks Criticism," *Orlando Sentinel*, 16 Sept. 1985.

38. Michael Blumfield, "Treadway: Challenge Disney's Autonomy," *Orlando Sentinel*, 31 Jan. 1988.

39. Minutes, Orange County Board of County Commissioners, 1 Feb. 1988.

40. Letter to the author from Jeno F. Paulucci, 23 June 1998.

41. Interview with Lou Treadway.

42. Interview with Harry Stewart.

43. Highlights of the report were read to the author over the phone by a confidential informant. Jane Hames confirmed she was the author; interview with Jane Hames, 22 Sept. 1998.

44. *Ibid.*

45. Interview with Tom Dorman, 26 June 1998.

46. Interview with Vera Carter.

47. Interview with Lou Treadway.

48. Interview with Vera Carter.

49. Interview with Lou Treadway.

50. Michael Griffin and Laura Lafay, "Most Officials Take Disney's Freebies," *Orlando Sentinel*, 1 Oct. 1989, p. A1.

51. Michael Griffin and Laura Lafay, "Politicians Must Ask for Free Disney Tickets," *Orlando Sentinel*, 8 Feb. 1990, p. A1.

52. Interview with Harry Stewart.

53. *Ibid.*

54. Interview with Judge Robert Shevin, 25 Oct. 2000.

55. Minutes, Orange County Board of County Commissioners, 24 July 1998.

56. Interview with Vera Carter.

57. Interview with Harry Stewart.

58. *Ibid.*

CHAPTER 7: ABUSE

1. Interview with Jane Hames.

2. Interview with Sam Tabuchi, 23 Sept. 1998.

3. *Ibid.*

4. Interview with Jane Hames.

5. Dan Tracy, "Maglev Loses Out on Epcot Stop," *Orlando Sentinel,* 29 Sept. 1989.

6. Interview with Jane Hames.

7. Interview with Dave Grovdahl, 25 Sept. 1998.

8. Interview with Lou Treadway.

9. Interview with Bob Cox, 25 Sept. 1998.

10. Interview with Sam Tabuchi.

11. Interview with Bob Cox.

12. Interview with Sam Tabuchi.

13. Interview with Richard Crotty, 22 Sept. 1998.

14. Dan Tracy, "Plans for 300-mph Train Slow to Surface," *Orlando Sentinel,* 13 April 1988.

15. *Ibid.*

16. Interview with Jim Harris.

17. Interview with Bob Cox.

18. Interview with Richard Crotty, 22 Sept. 1998.

19. Interview with Dick Batchelor, 24 Sept. 1998.

20. "How to Derail a Good Idea" (editorial), *Orlando Sentinel,* 17 May 1989.

21. Interview with Sam Tabuchi.

22. Lawrence J. Lebowitz, "Bill Would Throw Curve at Fast Train," *Orlando Sentinel,* 28 March 1989.

23. Interview with Bob Cox.

24. Executive Summary, *Orange County Affordable Housing Task Force Final Report,* Sept. 1989, pp. 19, 24.

25. Interview with Glenn Hosken, attorney at Florida State Division of Bond Finance, 7 Oct. 1998.

26. Interview with Ray Maxwell, 7 Oct. 1998.

27. "Disney's Grab Angers Area Officials," *St. Petersburg Times,* 7 Jan. 1990.

28. Minutes, Orange County Housing Finance Authority, 21 March 1998.

29. *Ibid.*

30. Interview with Linda Chapin, 27 Oct. 1998.

31. Interview with Lisa Fisher, 20 Oct. 1998.

32. Interview with Tom Lang, 20 Oct. 1998.

33. Tape recording, meeting of the Orange County Board of County Commissioners, 8 Jan. 1990.

34. Dick Marlowe, "Bond Issue Raises Questions of Disney's Status, Public's Best Interest," *Orlando Sentinel,* 12 Jan. 1990.

35. Interview with Linda Chapin.

36. Interview with Harry Stewart.

37. Interview with Phil Brown, 20 Oct. 1998.

38. Interview with Ray Maxwell.

39. "Fairness on Bonds and No Private Deals" (editorial), *Orlando Sentinel,* 14 Jan. 1990.

40. Minutes, Orange County Board of County Commissioners, 19 March 1990.

41. Minutes, Orange County Housing Finance Authority, 21 March 1998.

42. *Ibid.*

43. Michael Griffin, "Housing Officials to Put the Heat on Disney," *Orlando Sentinel*, 22 March 1990.

44. Adam Yeomans, "Disney Offers a Compromise on Bonds," *Orlando Sentinel*, 5 April 1990.

45. Interview with Tim Deratany, 27 Oct. 1998.

46. Michael Griffin, "Disney May Help Orange Deal," *Orlando Sentinel*, 30 May 1990.

47. Interview with Lisa Fisher.

48. Interview with Linda Chapin.

49. "Disney Chief Raps Orlando's Officials, Then Apologizes," *Los Angeles Times*, 12 May 1990.

50. Testimony of Ron Davis, *Sipkema v. Walt Disney Co.*, evidentiary hearing, Case No. CI96–114 [hereafter *Sipkema v. WDW*], pp. 642–650.

51. *Ibid.*

52. Testimony of Robert Phillips, *Sipkema v. WDW*, pp. 183–215.

53. Testimony of Susan Buckland, *Sipkema v. WDW*, pp. 322ff.

54. Testimony of Trooper Scott Walker, *Sipkema v. WDW*, p. 223.

55. *Ibid.*, p. 226.

56. Deposition of Thomas M. Moses, *Sipkema v. WDW*, 15 Dec. 1995.

57. Testimony of Susan Buckland, *Sipkema v. WDW*, pp. 298.

58. Testimony of Capt. Robert Eugene Flemming, *Sipkema v. WDW*, pp. 362–68.

59. Testimony of Kenneth Kincaid, *Sipkema v. WDW*, pp. 827–34.

60. Interview with Rick Staly, 30 Oct. 1998.

61. Attorney Eric Faddis, "First Amended Complaint to Produce Public Records Under Chapter 119, Florida Statutes," *Sipkema v. WDW*, p. 10.

62. Testimony of Capt. Robert Eugene Flemming, *Sipkema v. WDW*, pp. 372–76.

63. Testimony of Trooper Randolph Bush, *Sipkema v. WDW*, pp. 392–93.

64. Testimony of Trooper Terry Hoops, *Sipkema v. WDW*, pp. 397–402.

65. Eric Faddis, *Sipkema v. WDW*, p. 223.

66. *Ibid.*, pp. 994–98.

67. Letter from Eric Faddis to Circuit Court Judge Belvin Perry, *Sipkema v. WDW*, 2 April 1996.

68. Judge Patricia Fawsett in *Pamela Lang et al. v. RCID and WDW*, No.94–693-CIV-ORL-19, 8 Nov. 1995.

69. Evidentiary hearing, *Sipkema v. WDW*, Exhibits 14 and 27.

CHAPTER 8: NEGOTIATION

1. Interview with Robert Day, 11 May 1999.

2. Interview with Larry Whaley, 15 Jan. 1999.

3. Interview with Robert Day.

4. Lawrence J. Lebowitz, "Appraiser Claims Politics Muddles Disney Tax Fight," *Orlando Sentinel*, 28 Sept. 1990.

5. "Settle Disney Tax Dispute (editorial)," *Osceola Sentinel*, 30 Sept. 1990.

6. Interview with Todd Mansfield.

7. Interview with Peter Rummell, 13 Jan. 1999.

8. Michael Eisner with Tony Schwartz, *Work in Progress* (New York: Random House, 1988), p. 407.

9. Robert Foster interviewed by Bob Mervine, 2 Feb. 1980, Disney Archives-Burbank.

10. Interview with John DeGrove, former DCA secretary, 31 March 1999.

11. Interview with George Stuart, former chairman of the Senate Natural Resources Committee, 1 April 1999; and interview with Jon Mills, former chairman of the House Natural Resources Committee, 2 April 1999.

12. Interview with Tom Moses, 19 April 1999.

13. Confirmed by Bob Rhodes via email, 7 April 1999.

14. Interview with Peter Rummell.

15. Interview with Carl Gosline, 31 July 1998.

16. Lawrence J. Lebowitz, "Disney Lends Hand to Tax Proponents," *Orlando Sentinel*, 1 June 1990.

17. Interview with Alan Starling, 26 April 1999.

18. Annie Tin, "Disney, County Agree on Road Financing Plan," *Osceola Sentinel*, 15 Dec. 1993.

19. Interview with Bob Day.

20. Interview with Mary Jane Arrington, 12 May 1999.

21. Interview with Gary Lee, 15 June 1999.

22. Lawrence J. Lebowitz, "Dart Deal Goes Public Monday," *Osceola Sentinel*, 15 March 1992.

23. "Parkway Deal Good for County (editorial)," *Osceola Sentinel*, 26 July 1992.

24. Chris Cobbs, "Auditor Is Determined to Refinance Parkway," *Osceola Sentinel*, 11 April 1998.

25. Chris Cobbs, "Parkway Payoff in Works," *Osceola Sentinel*, 28 Aug. 1998.

26. Interview with Gary Lee.

27. Interview with Robert Guevara, 12 May 1999.

28. Interview with Todd Mansfield.

29. Michael Pollan, "Mickey for Mayor?" *House & Garden*, Oct. 1966, p. 68.

30. "Affordable Housing Business Plan," attached to a memo from Jeff Drew to "Distribution," Disney Development Company, 9 Sept. 1992; *Heidrich v. DDC* case file.

31. Interview with Peter Rummell.

32. Fishkind & Associates, "Projected Distribution of Demand by Unit Cost and Positioning of Heidrich, n.d.; *Heidrich v. DDC* case file.

33. Interview with Susan Caswell, 9 March 1999.

34. Interview with David Russ, 4 April 1999.

35. Letter from Gregory Golgowski, Director of Project Review on the Celebration DRI, ECFRPC, to Brenda Eckmair, DDC, 28 Feb. 1994; files of ECFRPC.

36. Disney Development Co., *Celebration DRI Application for Development Approval*, June 1991, Table 20–8, p. 20–11.

37. Letter from Thomas Beck, Chief, DCA Bureau of State Planning, to Greg Golgowski, ECFRPC, 13 April 1992.

38. Interview with Anna Pinellas, 9 March 1999.

39. Interview with Mike Kloehn, 5 March 1999.

40. *Ibid.*

41. Interview with Judith Kovisars, 24 March 1999.

42. John Koenig, "Orlando Area Economy Best in State—But That Doesn't Mean Much," *Orlando Sentinel,* 14 June 1999.

43. Memo from Kris Wilhelm to Don Killoren, 4 Nov. 1993; *Heidrich v. DDC* case file.

44. Letter from Thomas Beck to Brenda Eckmair, 1 Feb. 1994.

45. *Ibid.,* p. 20.

46. Jack Snyder, "Who Governs Celebration," *Orlando Sentinel,* 23 June 1996.

47. Douglas Frantz and Catherine Collins, *Celebration U.S.A.: Living in Disney's Brave New Town* (New York: Henry Holt & Co., 1999), p. 167.

48. Evan McKenzie, *Privatopia: Homeowner Associations and the Rise of Residential Private Government* (New Haven: Yale Univ. Press, 1994), p. 183.

49. DeEtte Abeyta, *Disney@xone.net,* 4 June 1999, 13:59.

50. Douglas Frantz, "Living in a Disney Town, With Big Brother at Bay," *New York Times,* 4 Oct. 1998.

51. Frantz and Collins, *Celebration, U.S.A.;* and Andrew Ross, *The Celebration Chronicles: Life, Liberty, and the Pursuit of Property Values in Disney's New Town* (New York: Ballantine, 1999).

52. *Work in Progress,* p. 408.

53. *Ibid.*

54. Interview with Alan Starling.

55. Howard Schaffer, communications director of the Public Education Network in Washington, D.C.; quoted in Muriel Cohen, "Disney Aims for a Model School, *Boston Sunday Globe,* 20 April 1997.

56. Leslie Postal, "Disney's Experiment in Education Takes Off, *Orlando Sentinel,* 13 Aug. 1996.

57. Susan Jacobson, "Celebration Charter School? Parents Explore Education Options," *Osceola Sentinel,* 13 Nov. 1998.

58. Interview with Donna Hart, 8 July 1999.

59. Mike Harford, Osceola School Board meeting, 6 July 1999.

60. Parent press conference following Osceola School Board meeting, 6 July 1999.

61. Jackie Flannigan, Osceola County School Board meeting, 15 June 1999.

62. Excerpts from "Celebration Contract Document/Disclosure Statement Regarding: The Celebration School," 17 Nov. 1997.

63. Wendy Treat, *Disney@xone.net,* 16 June 1999, 23:56.

64. Interview with Pam Morris, Celebration School parent, 6 July 1999.

65. Diane Wilkins Production, "A Day in the Life of a Celebration Student," 3 July 1994.

66. Interview with Robert Morris, 15 June 1999; interview with DeEtte Abeyta, 29 July 1999.

67. "Still Concerned," posting to *Disney@xone.net,* 16 June 1999, 20:04.

68. Interview with DeEtte Abeyta.

69. Remarks by Richard Daly, Celebration School parent, Osceola County School Board meeting, 6 July 1999.

70. *Work in Progress*, pp. x–xi.

71. Pam Morris, *Disney@xone.net*, 19 June 1999.

72. Interview with Robert Morris.

73. E.g., Katherine Salant, "A New Town's Growing Pains," *Washington Post*, 26 July 1999.

CHAPTER 9: THERAPY

1. Tape of Orange County Board of County Commissioners meeting, 25 June 1996.

2. Interview with Alan Eberly, 19 Aug. 1999.

3. Videotape of Orlando City Commission meeting, 5 June 1995.

4. *Ibid.*

5. Interview with Jim Harris, 4 Aug. 1999.

6. Interview with Linda Chapin, 30 Aug. 1999.

7. Walt Disney Co., "Orange County/I-4 Interchange Q&A," n.d.

8. Interview with Jim Moye, 29 July 1999.

9. Interview with Mark Fostier, 18 Aug. 1999.

10. Memo from Howard Tipton, Jr., to Linda Chapin regarding the Orange County/Reedy Creek Improvement District Interchange Cost-Sharing Agreement, 17 June 1996.

11. Cory Lancaster, "Disney Seeks Deal on I-4 Interchange," *Orlando Sentinel*, 24 June 1996.

12. Interview with Clarence Hoenstine, 5 Aug. 1999.

13. Interview with Donald Lepsic, 11 May 2000.

14. Interview with Mary Johnson, 19 Aug. 1999.

15. Interview with Ajit Lalchandani, 18 Aug. 1999.

16. Interview with Jeff Newton, 18 Aug. 1999.

17. Memo from Joe Passiatore to Tom Wilkes, 30 May 1996.

18. Interview with Tom Wilkes, 27 Aug. 1999.

19. Interview with Linda Chapin, 30 Aug. 1999.

20. Interview with Jim Moye.

21. Tape of Orange County Board of County Commissioners meeting, 25 June 1996.

22. Interview with Clarence Hoenstine.

23. Interview with Linda Chapin, 30 Aug. 1999.

24. Interview with Tom Wilkes.

25. Interview with Harry Stewart.

26. Interview with Jim Moye.

27. Letter from Bill Warren, Director of Public Affairs, Walt Disney World Co., December 1999.

28. Interview with Mel Martinez, 24 Sept. 1999.

29. Interview with Jacob Stuart, 1 Sept. 1999.

30. Policom Corp., "Orange County, Florida: History, Comparative Economic Analysis," a study for the Economic Development Commission of Mid-Florida, 8 Aug. 1999, p. i.

31. Interview with Mike Duffy, 26 July 1999.

32. "Big 3 Can't Find Enough Workers, Ignore the Obvious: Raise Wages," *What the *#?!: A Newspaper for Central Florida's Tourism Workers*, SEIU Local 362, Oct/Nov 1998, p. 3.

33. Scott Kim, radio interview with Wendy Crudele, manager of casting services at Walt Disney World, WMFE-FM, 2 May 1999.

34. Cory Lancaster, "Orlando's 'Job Machine' Is Expected to Throttle Back," *Central Florida Business*, a supplement of the *Orlando Sentinel*, 4 Jan. 1999.

35. Quoted in Craig Dezern, "Disney Labor to Add Jobs, Curtail Costs," *Orlando Sentinel*, 13 Nov. 1994.

36. Interview with Mike Duffy.

37. Interview with William Peeper, President, Orlando/Orange County Convention & Visitors Bureau, 24 Oct. 1999.

38. Bill Peeper, "Update Briefing of the Orlando/Orange County Convention & Visitors Bureau," a presentation to the Orange County Board of County Commissioners, n.d. (1999), pp. 29–31.

39. Policom, "Orange County."

40. Orlando/Orange County Convention and Visitors Bureau, "A Report on Tourism's Economic Impact," n.d. [c. 1998], p. 6.

41. Interview with Bruce McClendon, 2 Aug. 1999.

42. Interview with Bob Windham, 27 Aug. 1999.

43. Interview with Tom Kohler.

44. Paul Peterson, *City Limits*, chap. 7.

45. Interview with Tom Wilkes.

46. Interview with Marshall Vermillion, 6 Oct. 1999,

47. Interview with Ted Edwards, 10 Sept. 1999.

48. Robert Reich, *The Work of Nations* (New York: Knopf), chap. 4.

49. See, for example, Clarence Stone, *Regime Politics*, esp. chap. 9; Clarence Stone, "Summing Up: Urban Regimes, Development Policy, and Political Arrangements," pp. 269–298; and Todd Swanstrom, *The Crisis of Growth Politics* (Philadelphia: Temple University Press, 1985).

50. Interview with Martha Haynie, 30 Aug. 1999.

51. Interview with Tom Wilkes.

52. I am indebted to Robyne Turner for this observation.

53. Interview with Todd Mansfield.

54. Joe Potter interviewed by Bob Mervine, February 1980; Disney Archives-Burbank.

55. Interview with Martha Haynie.

56. P. Clavel and N. Kleniewski, "Space for Progressive Local Policy; Examples from the United States and the United Kingdom," in John Logan and Todd Swanstrom (eds.), *Beyond City Limits: Urban Policy and Economic Restructuring in Comparative Perspective* (Philadelphia: Temple Univ. Press, 1990), p. 207.

57. Hirschman, *Exit, Voice and Loyalty*, p. 82.

58. *Regime Politics*, pp. 200–18, 242–44.

59. North, *Institutions, Institutional Change and Economic Performance*, chaps. 1, 11–12.

60. *Exit, Voice, and Loyalty*, pp. 94–95.

61. *Ibid.*

62. Interview with Mel Martinez.

63. *Ibid.*

64. McKenzie, *Privatopia*, p. 193.

65. Louis Uchitelle, "Minimum Wages, City by City," *New York Times*, 19 Nov. 1999.

66. Donahue, *Privatization Decision*, p. 12.

67. Burns, *Formation of American Local Governments*, pp. 116–17.

68. Daniel Yankelovich, *Coming to Public Judgment: Making Democracy Work in a Complex World* (Syracuse University Press, 1991), pp. 53–55, 186–88.

69. Amitai Etzioni, *The New Golden Rule: Community and Morality in a Democratic Society* (New York: Basic Books, 1996), pp. 106–10.

Index

5000 Shankland Dr